HOPE AND INSUFFICIENCY

HOPE AND INSUFFICIENCY

Capacity Building in Ethnographic Comparison

Edited by
Rachel Douglas-Jones and Justin Shaffner

berghahn
NEW YORK • OXFORD
www.berghahnbooks.com

Published in 2021 by
Berghahn Books
www.berghahnbooks.com

© 2021 Berghahn Books

Originally published as a special issue of *The Cambridge Journal of Anthropology*, Volume 35, issue 1 (2017).

All rights reserved. Except for the quotation of short passages for the purposes of criticism and review, no part of this book may be reproduced in any form or by any means, electronic or mechanical, including photocopying, recording, or any information storage and retrieval system now known or to be invented, without written permission of the publisher.

Library of Congress Cataloging-in-Publication Data

Names: Douglas-Jones, Rachel, editor. | Shaffner, Justin, editor.
Title: Hope and insufficiency : capacity building in ethnographic comparison / edited by Rachel Douglas-Jones and Justin Shaffner.
Other titles: Cambridge anthropology.
Description: New York : Berghahn Books, 2021. | "Originally published as a special issue of The Cambridge Journal of Anthropology, Volume 35, issue 1 (2017)"—Title page verso | Includes bibliographical references and index.
Identifiers: LCCN 2021034163 | ISBN 9781800730991 (hardback) | ISBN 9781800731004 (paperback) | ISBN 9781800731011 (ebook)
Subjects: LCSH: Organizational change—Social aspects. | Organizational sociology. | Community development.
Classification: LCC HN49.C6 H659 2021 | DDC 306.3/4—dc23
LC record available at https://lccn.loc.gov/2021034163

British Library Cataloguing in Publication Data

A catalogue record for this book is available from the British Library

ISBN 978-1-80073-099-1 hardback
ISBN 978-1-80073-100-4 paperback
ISBN 978-1-80073-101-1 ebook

Contents

List of illustrations   vii

Preface   ix
   Verbal Sophisms and Problems with Capacity Building
     Martha Macintyre

Introduction   1
   Capacity Building in Ethnographic Comparison
     Rachel Douglas-Jones and Justin Shaffner

Chapter 1   19
   Professionalizing Persons and Foretelling Futures: Capacity Building in
     Post-Earthquake Haiti
     Kristin LaHatte

Chapter 2   33
   Capacity as Aggregation: Promises, Water and a Form of Collective Care in
     Northeast Brazil
     Andrea Ballestero

Chapter 3   51
   Building Capacity in Ethical Review: Compliance and Transformation in the
     Asia-Pacific Region
     Rachel Douglas-Jones

Chapter 4   69
   Corrective Capacities: From Unruly Politics to Democratic *Capacitación*
     Susan Ellison

Chapter 5   86
   Capacity Building as Instrument and Empowerment: Training
     HealthWorkers for Community-Based Roles in Ghana
     Harriet Boulding

Chapter 6 101
Personal and Professional Encompassment in Organizational Capacity Building: SOS Children's Villages and Supportive Housing
Viktoryia Kalesnikava

Chapter 7 116
Community Capacity Building: Transforming Amerindian Sociality in Peruvian Amazonia
Christopher Hewlett

Chapter 8 133
'Integrating Human to Quality': Capacity Building across Cambodian Worlds
Casper Bruun Jensen

Afterword 148
Measurable Subjectivities and Discoverable Worlds
George Mentore

Index 153

Illustrations

2.1:	Exhibiting promises on index cards during one of the Pact workshops.	40
2.2:	Detail of Leviathan's illustration.	45
2.3:	Andy Lomas, Aggregation series. http://www.andylomas.com/.	46
8.1:	'Integrating Human to Quality', Street 63, Phnom Penh.	134

Preface

Verbal Sophisms and Problems with Capacity Building

Martha Macintyre

In their 2015 article, Moretti and Pestre analyse 'Bankspeak' – the shift in language use by the World Bank over the past 50 years. Among the many changes they observe is the use of increasingly vague, nominal forms and the decline of finite verbs. Whereas agencies used to 'build roads', 'improve farming methods', 'lend money' etc. now all their activities are expressed in the language of Management. Reports are replete with statements such as: "IDA has been moving toward supporting these strategies through programme lending." It has not actually done anything – it has been moving towards doing something that will be 'supporting'. In their conclusion they note the constant use of gerunds indicating unspecific activity: 'Institutional strengthening', 'Boosting growth'; 'Sharing knowledge'; 'Bridging the social gap'. "All extremely uplifting–and just as unfocused: because the function of gerunds consists in leaving an action's completion undefined, thus depriving it of any definite contour. An infinitely expanding present emerges, where policies are always in progress, but also *only* in progress" (2015: 99). Capacity building is such a process.

Capacity building, the term addressed in this collected volume is, like many terms in policy documents dealing with development projects, euphemistic. It is both a policy and a practice that is offered as a solution to a problem that has been externally identified by the donor agency as an inadequacy or incapacity. It is often at odds with local understandings of capacity and almost invariably geared towards introducing practices that can be audited, so that the intervention can be monitored. While it originally drew on radical left-wing ideals of communities as agents of change *for themselves*, it has become a term that is inextricably linked to neoliberal policies of aid provision that stress reductions in government spending, privatisation of former state services and the political embrace of market forces. It is verbal sophistry.

There is a fundamental contradiction generated by aid policies that on the one hand stress participation – insisting on consultation with recipient governments and communities – and on the other hand construct elaborate forms of evaluation and auditing that demonstrate 'accountability' to the donor agency.

In Australia, the idea of capacity building as a core development strategy arose during the 1990s, the same period that managerialism began to dominate government agencies and non-government organizations. This followed fast on the heels of aid agencies being referred to (without irony) as the 'Development Industry'. The magic word 'accountability' was introduced into reports and assessments. Government aid agencies were required to demonstrate that their aid projects had clearly defined goals that could be measured; that taxpayers' money was being used responsibly and that staff could not only account for all expenditure, but also provide evidence that 'capacity' had been 'built'. Privatisation of service provision, a cornerstone of Australian neoliberal policies aimed at reducing government spending, ensured that aid programs were contracted to commercial companies that 'delivered' aid in the form of projects. They had strict budgets; were designed to be audited and monitored; their objectives had to be clearly stated; their outcomes outlined and 'key performance indicators' specified. While the design of the project would incorporate consultations with selected beneficiaries of the project, once the project was designed its implementation was inflexibly tied to the budget, reporting requirements and regular auditing. By the time any project begins, its parameters have been rigidly defined and the contractor knows precisely what the 'deliverables' are, how the progress of the project will be measured and the criteria by which it will be judged successful. These are defined in the contract.

The idea of capacity building is central to the work of foreign aid agencies, non-government organizations working in the field of development and increasingly, commercial enterprises operating in developing nations. It is central to the rhetoric of development, conceptualized as economic advancement and the improvement of state administration. It is also discursive ploy that attempts to obscure the power relationship between donors and recipients of aid. As the objectives of the project are subject to a contract between the donor government and the agency that has been selected (usually by winning a competitive tender), the recipients of a capacity building enterprise are presumed to accept the project as it is defined in the agreement. Most of these processes require that the in-country acceptance of a project is done by a senior bureaucrat rather than those whose capacities have been judged insufficient and in need of improvement.

I began with a brief analysis of the linguistic mode of capacity building precisely to stress its rhetorical implications and the power dynamics that are implied. The shift to vague managerialist terminology expresses also the move from practical material aid to the purveyance of an ideology of neoliberalism and Western styles of corporate management that are ill-suited to projects with governments of developing countries. This is especially the case in Pacific countries where the state is weak, corrupt and decidedly lacking in state resources that can be subjected to commercialisation or 'market forces'.

My experience working on the design and implementation of a project aimed at building the capacity of the police force to establish close cooperative relations with communities (usually called Community Policing) in Papua New Guinea, between 1998 and 2001, illustrates some of the problems that managerial models drawn from advanced industrial nations present in nations where state institutions are poor and the assumed forms of civil society barely exist. Even in towns, the organisations that draw together people from disparate backgrounds are limited (consisting mainly of churches, a few business and sporting associations); but in the rural areas they are absent. Local level government is often ineffective and churches are reluctant to involve themselves with policing strategies, for obvious and justifiable reasons. The organisations that exist – such as the Rotary Club, The National Council of Women, the Chamber of Commerce – draw membership mainly from the educated middle class. They were rarely people who have experienced police raids on their villages. They were more likely to have been victims rather than perpetrators of theft and their encounters with police were thus less likely to have proven difficult. But these were the selected representatives of 'civil society' who were consulted in the design of a project. Their views of 'law and order' prevailed over those villagers whose relations with police needed to change in the interests of lowering crime rates and increasing trust in law enforcement. Such people are also less likely to criticize the assumptions of the donor's project, as they are in many respects complicit in the preconceptions about their power to effect change beyond their own social worlds. In this way the consultation process that precedes the design of aid is often compromised from the outset.

The world envisaged in managerialist discourse is not populated by people with conflicting interests. But the world in which a project is implemented is. The verbiage and 'buzzwords' of plans, agreements and log-frames do not necessarily convince the aid recipients that donors have their interests in mind. The use of terms such as 'partners' and 'counterparts' does not disguise the hierarchy between the aid worker and those whose 'capacity' is being built. In some instances a project is accepted because it will bring with it items that allow local people to work effectively, such as fax machines, computers, vehicles and other equipment. The participants do not necessarily require training; often the only reason they attend workshops is to get the 'sitting fee' or free lunch. They lack the material means to provide services, not the skills, knowledge or capacity to do so effectively. Where the state is weak (as is the case in Papua New Guinea) the absence of equipment, or a budget for maintenance, or a safe, congenial working environment are far greater hindrances to service delivery than any shortcomings of those who are meant to do so.

Yet, as Moretti and Pestre observe, the shift in language signals a shift in the nature of aid from material goods to ideologies and vacuous promises of improvement. I recall one of my fellow aid workers, a former senior police officer from Australia, whose task was to improve the ways that police understood and implemented responses to a range of criminal activities. After a few training workshops he remarked that the participants were possibly the best trained police officers he had encountered. But morale was abysmally low – their housing was dilapidated; the stations that they worked in were old and poorly maintained; there were too few vehicles and sometimes no fuel for those that existed; the telephones did not function because bills had not been paid. In short, most of the inefficiencies were because of inadequate facilities that were meant to be state-funded. In such an environment low morale and frustration was often expressed in antagonism and hostility towards communities and criminals.

As the papers in this collection amply demonstrate, Capacity Building as a discourse is constructed around imagined agreements as well as assumed insufficiencies and needs. As Ellison shows, the ideas of capacity that the recipients of aid hold are frequently at odds with those of the donor (this volume). There are gaps in the preconceptions, as Kalesnikava shows us. Across the chapters we see spaces for improvisation that open in the pragmatics of implementation of a project. In these spaces and gaps participants can adapt, subvert or refuse elements of the design and its objectives. The power dynamics inherent in the discourse can be confounded by the actions of participants. While theoretical critiques of the discourses of development are crucial – ethnographic analysis of the course of a project can reveal how participants' agency can confound the intentions of bureaucratic policy and expose the verbal sophistry that permeates them.

Martha Macintyre is an Honorary Principal Fellow at the University of Melbourne, and Honorary Professor at the University of Queensland, Australia. She has undertaken research in Milne Bay and New Ireland Provinces in Papua New Guinea over a thirty year period, and combines anthropological and historical scholarship with practical and policy concerns. Her most recent books are *Transformations of Gender in Melanesia* (co-edited with Ceridwen Spark) and *Emergent Masculinities in the Pacific* (co-edited with Aletta Biersack).

Reference

Moretti, F. & D. Pestre. 2015. 'Bankspeak: the language of World Bank Reports'. *New Left Review*, 92, March/April: 75–99.

Introduction

Hope and Insufficiency
Capacity Building in Ethnographic Comparison

Rachel Douglas Jones & Justin Shaffner

Introduction

On June 11th, 2019, three very different events took place around the world under the heading of capacity building.[1] The Chinese Embassy in Ethiopia celebrated forty-five graduates, returned after an eight-month stint in Zhengzhou, China on a competitive capacity building training for train drivers, to begin their jobs traversing the new line between Addis Ababa and Djibouti's Port of Doraleh (FOCAC 2019). Across the Atlantic, the Global Climate Change Alliance of Suriname sat down in Paramaribo at their WaterForum to address concerns about the country's water management infrastructure they felt best addressed by a new capacity building program (GCCA 2019: 7). And on the same day, participants gathered at a capacity building workshop at the Centre de Recherche Forestière in Rabat, Morocco to discuss how to bring about large-scale forest and landscape restoration, echoing conversations occurring in Burkina Faso, Cambodia, Fiji and more (Silva Mediterranea 2019, UNFAO 2019). From skills to physical infrastructure, conversation to networking, capacity building is a concept full of hope and potential. Yet, as we aim to show in this collection, across its instantiations, it operates from perceptions of insufficiency or absence, summoned because the future it works towards is seen as more desirable than the present.

In this edited collection, we bring capacity building into ethnographic focus. We use the tension between hope and insufficiency at work in capacity building to explore its intended and unintended effects. Since neither the term nor the practices it engenders have been systematically examined or theorised within the social sciences, we ethnographically interrogate how and where the concept is put to work. Central to many projects under anthropological scrutiny, from institution building and national development projects to individual and community initiatives, capacity building is 'presented as the core solution for solving global problems' (Bueger and Tholens 2021: 22). Reaching across ethnographies from different sectors and continents, the contributions to this collection question capacity building's ubiquity and self-evident character. Along the way, the chapters open up what *capacities*, human or otherwise, are thought to be. By not taking capacity building's promises for granted, these ethnographic accounts both advance our understanding of capacity building's ubiquity and develop anthropological purchase on its persuasive power.

To lay the ground for the ethnographies to follow, we outline the history of capacity building within development, before showing its transition to a rich life of its own in the lexicons of government, religious organisations, environmental campaigns, biomedical trainings and more. We offer a thematic framing of the contributions, which are based on ethnographic fieldwork in from Bolivia, Brazil, Cambodia, Ghana, Haiti, Peru, the Philippines, Russia, and the United States. Each chapter is ethnographically specific, yet the effect of reading them alongside one another captures capacity building's mobile character, and points to the political consequences of the malleability evidenced in the opening news stories. A comparative approach provides an opportunity to theorise the concept's emergence and ubiquity at this particular historical moment, where what we might call 'conceptual borrowing' or 'templating' (Simpson 2012: 157) is happening rapidly, and on a global scale (Ong and Collier 2005). Terms from one sector arise in another: collaborations and agreements, for example, push the repeated use of 'partnership' (Jensen and Winthereik 2013; Brown 2015; Herrick and Brooks 2018; Gimbel et al. 2018), and capacity building travels easily. We use this broader observation as an entry point to a theoretical discussion that highlights the challenges the widespread use of 'capacity building' poses for analysis. If audit receives attention as a pervasive governing technology (Shore and Wright 2015), should not capacity building also be examined as 'a mode of thinking and analysis that makes particular political actions seem reasonable and justified' (Merry 2015: 435)? If missionizing Christianity's overt and implicit efforts at salvation have, as some have argued, been difficult for anthropologists to see for the way they share values and teloi, what can we learn from attempts to uncover this 'theoretical repressed' from the within anthropology itself? (Cannell 2005, 2006; Robbins and Engelke 2010; McDougall 2013)? We emphasise three questions for current and future anthropological engagement. First, how do we theorise capacity building as a concept and practice constrained neither by cultural or geopolitical region, nor by classical thematic divisions within anthropology? Second, who gets to define capacities – as present, lacking, or needing to be built? How do these claims gain legitimacy? Finally, what strategies are available to us as anthropologists to analytically address the way those who use capacity building conceptualise and enact change? Let us begin by first providing a brief genealogy of capacity building.

Approaching Capacity

Though the term capacity building is now colloquially familiar, it entered development terminology in the late 1980s and early 1990s (Eade 1997) when 'capacity' became tied to terms of improvement like 'strengthening', 'enhancement' and 'development' itself (Fuduka-Parr et al. 2002; UNDP 1995, 1998, 2003; OECD 2006). At the outset, the new term appeared to leave some commentators almost breathless with a sense of possibility. Take this description of the 'spiral' model of capacity building from the late 1990s, which

> assumes that behind every new latrine, weaving room, or irrigation canal in a village, for example, there are less visible but equally important changes in individual and group knowledge, attitudes and skills (Robinson and Cox 1998: 127)

In this un-sited description of 'village life', we encounter a capacity building which locates measurable efficacy in material artefacts – latrines and weaving rooms – yet extends into less visible capacities such as 'knowledge'. Capacity building can be put to work as both an approach and objective, as a set of methodologies towards a goal and itself a measurable outcome (Bolger 2000: 1). As mode and goal, what capacity building targets may be anything from 'abilities' to 'understandings, attitudes, values, relationships, behaviours, motivations, resources and conditions' (Bolger 2000: 2). Given such an all-encompassing mandate, it is little wonder that capacity building has been critiqued within development discourse for its vagueness: it is 'elusive' (Kaplan 2000: 517), 'ambiguous' (Black 2003: 116), 'elastic' (Lusthaus et al. 1999: 3) or worse, a 'sloppy piece of aid jargon' (Eade 2010: 204). Given its generic character, commentators wonder: which capacities are desired? Where should efforts be targeted?

These questions are asked by many practitioners. Capacity building emerged during a time when top-down development strategies were being dismantled, with 'partnership' and 'dialogue' promoted as a shift away from hierarchical language (Linnell 2003). Thus questions it elicited – of which capacities, and whose – were imagined as part of an open conversation between those who sought to intervene and those who stood as partners or participants in such projects. Capacity building was, and still is,[2] seen to take into account paradigm shifts towards 'local ownership' of initiatives (OECD 1996) as well as a growing recognition of the role 'external factors in the broader environment' have on the 'capacity of an individual, team, organisation or system' (Milèn 2001: 2). Attending to a broader environment, in turn, involved the dismantling of a further dominant association of capacity with what were termed 'technical competences' (Cherlet 2014). By 1996, critiques of a 'technical' mindset had taken hold, with increasing acknowledgement that capacity meant more than mere technical competence. 'The international development community was mistaken', Lusthaus et al. remarked cuttingly, 'when it thought that the technologies required to build a bridge were the same as those required to build a society – civil or otherwise'

(1999: 19). Amidst these changes, however, calls for capacity building continued to grow. Towards the end of the 1990s, Deborah Eade, a prominent commentator on capacity building noted that 'no UN Summit goes by without ritual calls for capacity building programmes for NGOs' (Eade 1997: 1). Two decades on, her observation has remained apposite: From the Accra Agenda for Action (OECD 2008) to the UN's Millennium Development Goals (UNMDG 2013), the SAMOA Pathway (United Nations 2014) and the Sustainable Development Goals (United Nations 2015), capacity building is centrally placed as a key instrument of change.

Even in this thumbnail sketch, it is evident that the rhetoric of capacity building has been caught between – and captured the imagination of – different movements in policy and become enrolled into quite different forms of political service. As structural adjustment policies shrank the state and downplayed institutions capacity building became a tool to attend to individuals, and their capacities. Through these shifting eras, definitional clarity remained elusive. As a result, those using the term go to some lengths to pin it down and organise its conceptual landscape – in rapidly proliferating new configurations. We find capacities arranged by 'levels' and 'types', separated into 'functional and technical' (UNDP 2009), 'soft' elements (motivational and process) and 'hard' elements (technical) (Land 1999). Some took issue with the idea of building at all: In 2006, the OECD sought to replace 'building' with 'development' in a document aimed at good practice, arguing '[t]he "building" metaphor suggests a process starting with a plain surface and involving the step-by-step erection of a new structure, based on a preconceived design. Experience suggests that capacity is not successfully enhanced in this way' (OECD 2006: 9). Yet between defining capacities to building them, practitioner authors offer key steps to success, from initial stakeholder engagement to end of project evaluation. For this reason, Chris Roche of Oxfam sets up capacity building as a concept to be *tested* (Roche 1997: v), measured against a *goal*, marking an alignment with policy orientations wherein capacities are 'most usefully assessed in relation to their development purpose' (Malik 2002: 27). The question of 'which capacities' is transformed into a concern about 'which ends', opening new sets of disagreements of what capacity building might ultimately be 'for'.

Amidst this disagreement, change is given central importance. 'Whether they are aware of it or not', write Lusthaus, et al., 'those involved in the field of capacity development are engaged in trying to understand and predict change' (1999: 10). They are also trying to bring it about. Commentators emphasise the importance of a 'baseline' from which change can be measured, anxieties arising about 'pejorative' assumption of deficits entailed (Linnell 2003). Yet once insufficiencies have been defined and a plan drawn up, implementation is key: the express aim being as explicit as 'chang[ing] a society's rules, situations and standards of behaviour' (Morgan and Qualman 1996: no pagination). A focus on change places capacity building alongside ideas that aid its smooth passage within managerial worlds, such as monitoring and evaluation, results based management, and good practice (Milèn 2001; OECD 2005). Is it working? Is capacity actually being built? *What has changed?* As Gimbel et al. observe for global health, the 'data expectations' of donors place heavy demands, with reporting indicators requiring further disaggregated data: 'by 2017', they tell us, 'more than 350 additional data points were required' (2018: 87), the data collection on health outcomes also being seen as building local capacity in monitoring and evaluation. Measurement brings the problem of definitional clarity to the fore: how to measure, evaluate or enhance something that is poorly defined from the outset? Monitoring and evaluation intensify the hopeful promises of capacity building – transformation becomes the new 'essential ingredient', what capacity building is 'fundamentally about' (Bolger 2000: 2). Scrutinised within a reflexive community of practitioners, then, the latest advice is that there are no recipes, and 'the particulars of [mistakes and successes] must be scrutinised carefully to determine what can be replicated, what can't and why' (UNDP 2009: 35).

If this is how capacity building appears in development and government literatures, what might an anthropological approach to this arena entail? Yarrow and Venkatesen's *Differentiating Development* (2012) provides a starting point oriented away from antagonistic positions, with a call that anthropologists relinquish 'the belief that anthropologists *see* more than various development workers because they *know* more' (2012: 6). They push us instead to attend to what development comes to mean in particular social contexts (Venkatesan 2009) and for reading development issues 'more squarely in relation to mainstream anthropological concerns' (Yarrow and Venkatesan 2012: 23). Yet despite the differentiation of development that ensues in Yarrow and Venkatesen's broad collection, the concept of capacity building is arguably even *more* expansive, an easy 'actionable' generic, ready for uptake in any social field. As West notes, capacity development schemes are 'thought to be appropriate for all scales: individuals, organizations, and whole societies' (2016: 71). As such, '*how* exactly it is manifested in projects' remains obscured (Mayville 2020: 1).

In the first two decades of the twenty-first century, capacity building[3] has noticeably decoupled from development agendas and is now valued as a tool of governance, administration, future building, and 'progress' in its own right. A bewildering range of sites today present themselves: it can be found in the lexicons of government (Hughes et al. 2010), third sector (Linnel 2003; O'Reilly 2011), heritage (Bortolotto et al. 2020), religious (McDougall 2013), medical (Kelly 2011; Geissler et al. 2014), transport (Heslop and Jeffery 2020), maritime security and piracy (Bueger et al. 2020), environmental (Watanabe 2019; UNEP 2002), conservation (West et al. 2006) and even familiar academic agendas (Danaher et al. 2012; Pfotenhauer et al. 2013; Pfotenhuaer et al. 2016). One of the questions we seek to explore in this edited collection is thus how 'capacity building' has been made to 'work' in such diverse settings? What in it carries such broad ranging appeal?

The concept of capacity has a rich history both in Euro-American philosophy and science as well as in anthropological thinking. Invoking 'capacity' means mobilising a concept borrowed into English from fifteenth-century French's Latinate *capacité*, meaning the ability to hold. Capacity retains its early definition: we still speak of a reservoir's capacity to hold water, or – for a contemporary reference – the capacity of the internet's material infrastructure to transport data as light, down optic cables (Starosielski 2015). This sense of 'holding' transfers in the familiar usage of capacity as a role one might take – to write in my capacity (a position or role I *hold*) as chairperson, or friend. Yet we also speak of our personal capacities, often to refer to the ability to learn: 'the mind in ignorance is like a sleeping giant', wrote the English essayist Usher early in the nineteenth century, 'it has immense capacities without the power of using them'

(Usher 1824: 465). It is this 'capacity view' of the person – certainly not confined to the 1800s – which opens towards intervention, development, and potential. It provides a moment in which we might consider the relationship between a capacity that is held (*in potentia*) and a capacity that is expressed (*in actualitas*), being brought forth in action.

The history of anthropology is bound up in the conceptualisation of capacities, human and otherwise. Readings have wavered between capacities being human universals, and specific capacities being thought absent, not observed or demonstrated by encountered 'others'. A full account of these shifting tides would take us through the significance of how, since the beginning of the discipline, capacities were attributed explicitly or otherwise, or entire peoples seen to be 'lacking' in one measure or another – belief systems, kinship systems, the presence of 'law' (Nader 2002, Falk Moore 2004, Foblets et al. 2020). Such attribution took place against the backdrop of evolutionary and colonial frames informed by moral judgments both of emerging nineteenth century empirical sciences (Tylor [1871] 2010; Spencer [1855] 1999; Squadrito 2002) and of who and what they studied (Moore 1994). Indeed, Paige West shows how capacity building's ideology smuggles back in the assumptions that there is 'an inherent lack in non-European persons, institutions and social systems' as the driver for technical solutions such as training, structures and audit cultures (West 2016: 72). Similarly, in her trenchant critique of the vernacular of development in West Africa, Jemima Pierre identifies 'capacity building' as a companion to discourses of 'corruption' and 'resource curse' in 'construct[ing] Africans as peculiar types of beings" (Pierre 2019: 87). Though a full historical review of the guises taken by the concept of capacity is beyond the scope of this introduction, an historical frame is nonetheless significant for how anthropological accounts position themselves relative to capacities today. For some, capacity continues to hold validity as a route for discussions that would 'bring the nature of the human again to the centre of anthropological deliberation' (Rapport 2005: 2). However, the resonance we find for capacity building with contemporary work lies not in pursuing it against ideas of 'human nature', but in the common ground between capacity and 'potential'.

In their overview of *potentiality* as an anthropological keyword, Taussig et al. (2013) turned to the Oxford English Dictionary (OED):

> 1.a A capacity, a possibility; an instance of the latent capacity for development of a person, thing, etc., in which the quality of having potential is embodied.

Here, potential *is* itself a capacity, latent or otherwise. Though their article deals with the suffusion of potentiality in the 'contemporary life sciences and medical practice' (Taussig et al. 2013:S3), their breadth of discussion bears upon our interest in capacity. Clear parallels emerge: potential shares with capacity the trait of having been both 'explicit and tacit in the history of anthropology' (2013: S3); it is (unequally) allocated and attributed (2013: S11), giving rise to what the 'right' potentials or capacities might be (2013: S10); and, in what could be a critical reading of capacity building within development discourse, it is concerned with identifying the absences that are preventing the realisation of more promising futures, 'even as promises and expectations continually recede on the horizon' (2013: S10). As Taussig et al. note, '[t]o study potentiality as an empirical object [….] can provide a route to renewed reflexivity along with a better understanding of the implications of how people think about human capacities and where they are located' (2013: S7).

The chapters in this edited collection take off from the following proposal: where in potentiality Taussig et al. find capacities, in capacities we find potentials. Yet if employing potentiality analytically requires an 'anthropological awareness that things could be other than they are' (Taussig et al. 2013: S6), the combination of 'capacity' with 'building' means we must attend to how (and which) capacities can become sites of cultivation or intervention. For the intention of capacity building is precisely to make things other than they are: to transform. And with this transformational intent come a broad range of empirical sites. A critical anthropological insight thus obtains: it cannot be known in advance how much of their 'originary' contexts concepts carry within themselves (Wagner 1986) when they are put to use in new settings. We also cannot assume that the 'understandings that produced them' (Strathern 1995: 154) – the priorities, intentions, frameworks – will be borrowed along with the terms themselves.

Exemplary of this analytical caution are two recent explorations of capacity building practices in Myanmar and the Maldives. When Watanabe explores a Japanese NGO's concurrent use of *hitozukuri* alongside 'capacity development' it is to understand how the practice of the Japanese concept of *hitozukuri* – 'cultivation of people's holistic character as well as skills' (Watanabe 2019: 17) – continue even as vocabularies shift (2019: 48); when Heslop and Jeffery attend to the Sinhala word *dharanaya* (capacity) and Divehi phrases that approximate it in their work on road construction in the Maldives it is to show how capacity is made multi-scalar: from personal skills to the financing of roadbuilding, '[a] lack of capacity is at the heart of subcontracting' (2020: 289). As many are coming to realise, the 'object of capacity building […] is developed in the conduct of performing the practice of capacity building' (Bueger and Tholens 2021: 24). In this way, capacity building's current ubiquity presents a broader challenge for an anthropology that seeks to both describe and interrogate it, for as it moves, it carries its promises of hope and creation of insufficiency in uneven and unequal measure.

Overview of themes and arrangement of the collection

The stimulus for the present collection follows from our discomfort with how capacity building frequently goes unquestioned in ethnographic accounts. Each chapter addresses a distinct encounter with capacity building, and each presents a variation on what ethnographic attention does for critical analysis. The first set of overarching questions in the collection are ethnographic. What does capacity building look like in practice? Who is involved? How does it gain traction and translate into activities, events and policies? Through this attention, a second set of questions appear: where is capacity thought to inhere? In what or in whom? The third set of questions take up the themes which give this collection its title: the interplay of hope and insufficiency which – we suggest – makes the idea of capacity building persuasive. Following the lead of Miyazaki, whose work on Fijian knowledge practices links philosophical literature on hope with questions of ethnographic method (2004), many scholars have taken up the concept of hope in diverse settings (Mattingly 2010; Pedersen 2012). Our interest in the hope of 'capacity building' lies in its ties to promised futures, and the transformations that will ferry participants there. This requires attending to how possibilities and potentials are invoked and mobilised in the pursuit of other ways of doing or being. Where hope may be 'held' and sustained by a range of supporting infrastructures – people, documents, devices – it is rarely measured, and attempts to quantify it sit uneasily with both its intangible expansiveness and its often-private character.

Capacity building, in contrast, is increasingly implicated in mechanisms of measurement, enmeshed in the politics of governing futures. Conceptualising capacity through the *absences* it uses as its starting points, which it identifies in order to 'fill,' the chapters attend to *what it is* that capacity building projects intend to remedy. We argue that capacity building 'works' through comparative transformation. It must generate (preferably measurable) insufficiencies which need to be made appear – an absence that becomes a potential. How, then, is this absence or 'lack' identified, codified and made available, given the potential, for intervention? What is defined as insufficient, and crucially, by whom? The position and power to make claims specifying absences gives shape to the global currency of capacity building. Critical questions our authors ask include: what becomes of other ways of doing and being, or unwelcome new capacities? What and whose are the standards against which a present is deemed insufficient? What of the capacity to rework projects, to refuse engagement or intervention (Benjamin n.d.: 2016)?

These questions result in tensions across the chapters in how the authors read capacity building: is it a neo-colonialist imposition, or a site for creative re-working on the part of partners or other participants? Are we speaking of the coercive reproduction of familiar power structures, or rather of arenas of re-descriptive hijacking, where projects are re-purposed towards new ends by those who are its targets? Furthermore, if we attribute flexible interpretation to those who would build capacity, can those it targets not receive the same credit? The opening chapter by Kristin LaHatte takes us to the heart of this question. As she shows, in post-earthquake Haiti, 'capacity building' has been naturalised as part of both societal and infrastructural reconstruction. But what is being (re)built? LaHatte shows us projects for the rebuilding of homes, yes, but in her careful analysis of the ways in which capacity building projects intervene with a valuation of certain relationships over others, we find competing notions of capacity building's purpose and potential mapped amongst those engaged in it. LaHatte introduces us to the Haitian phrase *moun pa'm se dra* ('My people are my sheets') which becomes an entry point for her reading of a Haitian 'blanket' of relationships, a sociality understood by local capacity builders to persist through time, into a future when NGO 'projects' will inevitably dry up. Working with Haitian NGO staff, who both carry out capacity building and remain subjects of it, we see through LaHatte's ethnography how staff select which capacities to cultivate relative to anticipated futures. Such futures do not always match those of their funders, who, in their implicit critique of Haitian social worlds, would see changed persons and a more 'morally appropriate' sociality. Andrea Ballestero takes up this theme of capacities which secure futures in her ethnography of a political device called the 'Water Pact' in North-eastern Brazil, an experimental intervention in problems of water scarcity designed to increase a community's 'capacity' to care for water. Ballestero takes us from low reservoirs to public meetings and the index cards of promises through which the pact to manage water is built. It is in these ethnographic moments where conceptual puzzles arise: what is the pact if there is nothing to 'belong' to? Ballestero's analysis takes us into new readings of the capacities of the aggregate, highlighting in contrast with the part-whole dynamics of Hobbesian collectives the importance of criteria – *selectivity* – as a device which allows, in this form of aggregation, for a collective capacity based on moral commitments, not holistic identification.

Similar questions of moral commitment arise in Rachel Douglas-Jones's chapter, which examines the capacity building work taking place amongst ethics review committees in the Asian region. Explicitly named, capacity building in this setting involves implementing standards formulated in international documents, and crucially, learning how to demonstrate and evidence adherence to those standards. Having capacity in this setting is fulfilling a pre-defined role. Yet Douglas-Jones goes on to introduce a contrast between ethics as a capacity to be displayed by committees and a capacity for ethics, where trainers focus instead on the qualities of the person. Doing ethics and being ethical are mutually targeted capacities, with capacity building exercises targeting both institutional and personal transformations. Susan Ellison's chapter also encounters individualised capacity building within initiatives that target specific forms of social relationships in the Bolivian Andes. We learn through her ethnography about a place and people long targeted by international capacity building interventions heavily oriented at statecraft, bureaucracy and institutions. As capacity building is newly captured by shifting policy modes, recent projects have begun instead to foreground interpersonal habits of speech, deportment, and techniques of deliberation seen as necessary for a national, democratic future. Ellison shows that select modes of interacting – regarded by capacity builders as conflictual, militant, resistant – are the target of interventions by so-called *conversatorios*. In these spaces, the democracy-ready skills of speaking respectfully and listening can be rehearsed, and displace an unwanted, excess 'capacity': the 'unreasonableness' and 'irrationality' which is dangerously present in the union trained citizenry. Ellison formulates the tension precisely: *conversatorios* 'unmask competing political stakes and expectations of state-citizen relations as skeptical participants revalorize demonized capacities' (Ellison, this collection).

The disjunction in Ellison and Douglas-Jones's chapters between the value of new capacities and those they replace is also taken up by Harriet Boulding, drawing on fieldwork with health workers in the Shai-Osudoku district of Ghana. Boulding's approach traces how the *definition* of capacity building within Ghana's Community-Based Health Planning and Services Program implicates health workers' home visits with communities. From the 'blueprints' for improved interaction provided at trainings – laudably oriented at supporting and growing trusting relationships between rural communities and their health workers – we find contact time coded into 'regular visits' and pre-set questions. As Boulding's ethnography shows, these time slots find no place in the practices of health workers or their communities, resulting in missed sessions or worse, endangerment of employees. The required questions leave health workers struggling to handle the sociality of home visits, and the politics of talking about reproductive health publicly in close-knit communities. In the equation of capacity building with training activities, then, other 'capacities' are overlooked, with capacity building's definitional *rigidity* itself becoming the object of the analysis. Viktoryia Kalesnikava's chapter similarly stays with these definitional problems, pushing us to consider the capacities of categories to sustain the work of different institutions of social care, SOS Children's Villages and Supportive Housing, aimed at ensuring respectively that children are linked up with families, and the homeless are provided with affordable housing. Her core interest lies in showing ethnographically the capacity of concepts to organise, muddle, order and even break institutions. Drawing on ethnographic and document work in Australia, Russia and the US, she selects moments where divisions between capacities associated with personal and professional domains collapse, or re-shape institutional life. Tracing her own biographical transition from trainee anthropologist to trainee social worker, Kalesnikava is in the unique position of being able to draw on her own shifting positions as she takes the reader between fieldwork sites, herself moving between roles.

The transformation of persons is central to Hewlett's chapter, which is focused on decades long 'capacitation' in the Peruvian Amazon. Hewlett examines a Summer Institute of Linguistics (SIL) project originating in the1950s which had the intention of bringing isolated groups, such as the Amahuaca with whom he worked, into the 'modern world' so they would participate as productive members of Peruvian society. The main mechanism for this was bringing Amahuaca people to 'live together'. The sixty year timespan of this work produced a wealth of historical documents, earlier ethnographies, life histories and present day ethnography, which Hewlett channels to show the changing readings of what needs to be transformed, and how the SIL's 'living together' articulates with Amahuaca understandings of bodily transformations and becoming kin. By the time we arrive at Casper Bruun Jensen's chapter, we are also reaching the limits of the concept of capacity building itself, simply by troubling *which* capacities are being targeted. Jensen's question is whether capacity building, in spite of its apparently comprehensive mandate, is *sufficiently* encompassing. His question seems simple: Are there capacities which would not fall under capacity building's gaze? How might they appear? He asks in order to perform a 'lateral' comparison (Gad and Jensen 2016): that is, one intended to test capacity building's conceptual capacities against other contexts. In this case the capacities within the working lives of bureaucrats and sex workers in the Cambodian capital of Phnom Penh. Here, we see different orders of 'growing one's capacity' evidenced, but – as Jensen shows – when laterally compared, they do not fit within 'expected' orders of capacity building's personal, collective, or institutional improvement. Thus, by holding up unexpected descriptions of capacity building, we start to see the edges of where capacity building might, despite its breadth, find limits.

The challenge of capacity: intervention, transformation and social change

This collection brings ethnographic depth to studies of capacity building. It also identifies the wide variety of things that are targeted as 'capacities'. Where Kalesnikava pushes for closer attention to how capacities for care are attributed, Ballestero ponders how a collective capacity can be conceptualised. Where capacities for living together take on double meanings in Hewlett's piece – as both the capacitated bodies of Amazonians and their political participation in national projects – Ellison's *conversatorios* rapidly become *contestatorios*, rejecting the naivety of 'new', training sanctioned capacities. Each chapter gives nuance to the ways capacity building is used, demonstrating that the identification of 'capacity', as well as its absence, is a political project, whether these identifications occur in the empirical cases or in our ethnographic descriptions. It therefore remains for us to lay out some of the challenges that exploring capacity building poses for anthropology, and put forward possible strategies for readers who bring it to their ethnographic attention.

We return first to the problem posed at the opening: how do we develop an anthropological approach to concepts that operate across quite distinct settings? The issue is one of shifting conceptual meanings in an era of mobile policy and practice. In this sense, capacity building keeps company with a growing repertoire of concept-practices such as audit (Strathern 2000; Shore and Wright 2015), ethics (Simpson 2012, Douglas-Jones 2015), collaboration (Konrad 2012; Sariola and Simpson 2019) and partnership (Jensen and Winthereik 2013), which act upon accepted and desired form(at)s of knowledge and practice. This edited collection employs comparison across ethnographic settings as a key technique for drawing contrasts in how capacity building is put to use. The capacity building used by Boulding's community health officers is simply not the same thing as that used by Haitian capacity builders in LaHatte's account, a connection produced through differentiation rather than similitude (Viveiros de Castro 2004). In its ubiquity, capacity building provides an ideal vehicle for experimental cross-regional conversations about the lives of contemporary concepts (Koselleck 2002). As the papers in this collection demonstrate, the purchase of capacity building is not everywhere the same. Therefore, while comparison between settings is generative, so too is comparison within: if a concept seems to proliferate, where, when pushed to its 'limits', does it break down in relation to itself? Described in Jensen's closing chapter as 'lateral comparison', this move opens new questions at the edges of a conceptual arena. Where capacities might be imagined as infinite, when they are tied to the everyday work of building, as Jensen shows, the term paradoxically has limits. Asking what capacity cannot contain makes visible what will count as the 'right' capacities.

A second challenge lies in how capacity building re-describes the world in its own terms – defining people and situations as having potential, while also constituting them in the present as insufficient, relative to an envisaged future. In Ellison's chapter, for example, the 'capacity' view of NGO trainers makes it possible to cast existing modes of political interaction as 'unwelcome' capacities, and to replace them with 'good' ones, grown in 'corrective' training sessions. Re-described as an insufficiency, combative debate is made – and made useful – as a justification for imposing other capacities. Yet re-description is also a capacity itself, cultivated particularly within anthropology (Strathern 2005: xiv, Corsín Jiménez 2015). The lesson Ellison's Bolivian interlocutors teach us – through their reactions to capacity building's dismissive re-description of their capacities for debate – is that doing re-description is political work. The opportunity arises, therefore, to turn the lens back – as Hewlett's chapter does – on accounts of these descriptions and attributions, with a view to critiquing the identification and valuation of some capacities over others. Laura Mentore has demonstrated that it is not only capacity builders who work conceptually with capacity building (2017, see also Arthur 2021). Presenting the 'workshop space' of sustainable development and conservation projects taking place in Erefoiomo and Surama villages in Guyana, Mentore shows how those who stand to be 'capacitated' rework the intentions of capacity building projects. Mentore argues that willingness to 'go along' with the exercises is rooted not in compliance but 'in-the-hope-of-transformation' of their *guests* (2017: 304),[4] demonstrating how clearly workshop participants recognise the political work that concepts like capacity building do, and the ways they seek to redeploy this power.

The final, and possibly most significant, challenge for analysis is the way the generic form of capacity building appears self-evident to development experts, policy-makers and some enrolled in its projects. Such self-evidence generates a sense that the forms of change, progress, and transformation that it heralds are unremarkable. The chapters collected here illustrate that while capacity building does carry generic principles and assumptions, we cannot know in advance how these will be put to work in practice. It important to examine how the targets of capacity building shape its enactment. In Ballestero's analysis, for example, focusing on capacity allows for novel theorization around images: the selective aggregate versus holistic membership, a water Pact open to multiplicity versus one predicated on commonality. Ethnographies should explore *how* these models for change are put into practice. Capacity building not only tries to bring about change, it *necessarily* carries models of how that change can happen and what it will mean with it, and ethnographic attention is needed at moments of action and inaction alike. Exemplary of this approach are Tess Lea's accounts of Australian state bureaucracy (2008, 2020). Lea shows ethnographers how to keep in view the worlds of those who would enact change, seeing how, in swings between 'futility and optimism [...] the compulsion to act flourishes at the very point where the ability to act seems annihilated' (Lea 2008: 12). By studying policy makers, she makes an extended case for studying how '[p]olicies infect psyches, making some relationships and forms of well-being feel natural or deserved, cutting into and lacerating others' (2020: 167). Capacity building, we suggest, is one such policy in need of close ethnographic attention.

Engaging with models of change analytically requires that we also engage reflexively with the models of change and transformation we bring into anthropological description (Viveiros de Castro 2012, see also Hewlett this collection). If those within the field of capacity building are asking 'who, actually, is building whose capacity?' (Eade 2010: 203), then so too, must anthropologists suspend assumptions about the direction and character of change in encounters between those who intend to capacitate, and those who stand to be capacitated.

Conclusion

Capacity building was intended to be transformative (UNDP 2009), yet it is now also itself transformed. In this introduction we have traced a brief genealogy of its emergence, and its expansion into many new arenas. To date, we argue, it has been analytically and empirically overlooked in anthropological accounts. The approaches outlined above extend and support existing anthropological sensitivities which routinely highlight the capacities of others: whether in the form of imaginations, practices or concepts. To bring this sensitivity to encounters with capacity building activities is to retain a non-determinate view of capacities, one which prepares the analyst for the contestations, struggles and ambitions embedded in such projects (Crook 2007) the potential within a given capacity building exercise for its terms to be redrawn (MacIntyre, this collection; Mentore 2017) and the importance of attending the capacity to refuse (Benjamin 2016). The chapters in this collection all point to disagreements about what will count as a desirable capacity (Lahatte, Douglas-Jones, Ellison) what capacities themselves might be (Hewlett, Ballestero, Boulding) or what will trouble the concept of capacity building itself (Kalesnikava, Jensen). By opening up capacity building activities to analysis in these varied ways, we hope to stimulate further empirical engagement with its practices and policies, its hopes and insufficiencies, and also spark discussion of the descriptive and transformational capacities of anthropology itself.

Acknowledgements

We thank the Interest Group for the Anthropology of Policy for their role in this collection, as well as Alberto Corsín Jiménez and Sue Wright. This volume was developed with the support of the Wenner-Gren Foundation during a 2015 workshop in Copenhagen. Our thanks to Ruha Benjamin, Martha Macintyre, Laura Mentore, George Mentore, Morten Nielsen, Sebastian Pfotenhauer, Bob Simpson, Paige West and Brit Ross Winthereik for their generous comments and suggestions.

Rachel Douglas-Jones is Associate Professor at the IT University of Copenhagen, where she is Head of the Technologies in Practice research group and co-directs the ETHOS Lab. She conducts research on questions of ethics and the governance of science and technology, and is currently the PI of *Moving Data, Moving People*, a study of emergent social credit systems in China through the lens of trust. Her recent publications include 'Committee as Witness' (The Cambridge Journal of Anthropology, 2021) and 'Bodies of Data' (JRAI 2021). She is the editor (with Antonia Walford and Nick Seaver) of *Towards an Anthropology of Data* (JRAI, 2021).

Justin Shaffner is a Research Associate at the Center for Social Solutions at the University of Michigan where he focuses on issues related to the "future of work" and global commodity chains. His doctoral research at the University of Cambridge, based in Papua New Guinea with Anim speakers, focused on the experiences of community leaders as they attempted to elicit and maintain productive relations across various global alliances, from regional ritual networks to relations with transnational corporations, NGOs and the state. He is editor (with Huon Wardle) of *Cosmopolitics: The Collective Papers of the Open Anthropology Cooperative, Volume 1* (OAC Press, 2017); and co-founder of *Hau: Journal of Ethnographic Theory*.

Notes

1. These examples update the original set dating from 2015 (Douglas-Jones and Shaffner 2017), illustrating that any given day could be chosen. A good classroom exercise would be to pick a week of the given year and search international newspapers. Capacity Building, or Capacity Development will show up.
2. The United Nations Framework Convention on Climate Change (UNFCCC) established a new series of talks in November 2020, the second of which focused on fostering ownership and thereby facilitating more effective and sustainable capacity-building (UNFCCC 2021)
3. Mayville covers the distinction between capacity building and capacity development in her analysis of institutional framework definitions (2017: 47–49).
4. For further analyses of mutual entanglements of Indigenous and non-Indigenous worlds, see de la Cadena 2015.

References

Arthur, J. L. 2021. 'The Impact of Capacity Building on Community Leadership for Bui Communities Impacted by Dam Construction'. *African Geographical Review* [Online First] doi: 10.1080/19376812.2020.1866044

Benjamin, R. n.d. 'Informed Refusal: Salvaging the Capacity to Talk Back'. Paper presented at Hope and Insufficiency: Capacity Building in Ethnographic Comparison, Copenhagen, 20–22 May 2015.

Benjamin, R. 2016. 'Informed Refusal: Toward a Justice-based Bioethics'. *Science, Technology and Human Values* 41 (6): 967–990. doi: 10.1177/0162243916656059

Black, L. 2003. 'Critical Review of the Capacity Building Literature and Discourse.' *Development in Practice* 13 (1): 116–120.

Bolger, J. 2000. 'Capacity Development: Why, What and How'. *Canadian International Development Agency (CIDA)* Policy Branch Capacity Development Occasional Series. Volume 1 (1): 1–8.

Bortolotto, C., P. Demgenski, P. Karampampas, and S. Toji. 2020. 'Proving Participation: Vocational Bureaucrats and Bureaucratic Creativity in the Implementation of the UNESCO Convention for the Safeguarding of the Intangible Cultural Heritage'. *Social Anthropology* 28 (1): 66–82.

Brown, H. 2015. 'Global Health Partnerships, Governance and Sovereign Responsibility in Western Kenya'. *American Ethnologist* 42 (2): 340–355.

Bueger, C. and S. Tholens. 2021. 'Theorising Capacity Building'. In C. Bueger, T. Edmunds and R. McCabe (eds), *Capacity Building for Maritime Security: The Western Indian Ocean Experience*. New York: Palgrave Macmillan, 21–48.

Bueger, C., T. Edmunds, and R. McCabe. 2020. 'Into the Sea: Capacity Building Innovations and the Maritime Security Challenge'. *Third World Quarterly* 41 (2): 228–246.

Cannell, F. (ed.). 2006. *The Anthropology of Christianity*. Durham, NC: Duke University Press.

Corsín Jiménez, A. 2015. 'The Capacity for Redescription', In T. Yarrow, M. Candea, C. Trundle and J. Cook (eds), *Detachment: Essays on the Limits of Relational Thinking*. Manchester: Manchester University Press, 179–197.

Cherlet, Jan. 2014. 'Epistemic and Technological Determinism in Development Aid'. *Science, Technology and Human Values* 39 (6): 773–794.

Crook, T. 2007. '"If You Don't Believe Our Story, At Least Give Us Half of the Money": Claiming Ownership of the Ok Tedi Mine, PNG'. *Le Journal de la Société des Océanistes* 125: 221–228.

Danaher, P., L. De George-Walker, R. Henderson, K. J. Matthews, W. Midgely, K. Noble, M. A. Tyles and C. H. Arden (eds). 2012. *Constructing Capacities: Building Capabilities through Learning and Engagement*. Newcastle upon Tyne: Cambridge Scholars Publishing.

De la Cadena, M. 2015. *Earth Beings: Ecologies of Practice Across Andean Worlds*. Durham, NC: Duke University Press.

Douglas-Jones, R. 2015. 'A "Good" Ethical Review: Audit and Professionalism in Research Ethics.' *Social Anthropology* 23 (1): 53–67.

Eade, D. 1997. *Capacity Building: An Approach to People-Centered Development*. London: Oxfam.

Eade, D. 2010. 'Capacity Building: Who Builds Whose Capacity?' In A. Cornwall and D. Eade (eds), *Deconstructing Development Discourse: Buzzwords and Fuzzwords*. Rugby, England: Practical Action, 203–215.

FOCAC (Forum on China-Africa Cooperation). 2019. 'China helps Ethiopia Drive Modern Railway Tech Aspiration', https://www.fmprc.gov.cn/zfhzlt2018/eng/zfgx_4/jmhz/t1713607.htm. Accessed June 15, 2021.

Foblets, M-C., M. Goodale, M. Sapignoli, and O. Zenker (eds). 2020. *The Oxford Handbook of Law and Anthropology*. Oxford: Oxford University Press.

Fuduka-Parr, S., C. Lopes and K. Malik. 2002. *Capacity for Development: New Solutions to Old Problems*. London: Earthscan.

Gad, C., and C. B. Jensen. 2016. 'Lateral Comparisons'. In J. Deville, M. Guggenheim and Z. Hrdličková (eds), *Practicing Comparison: Logics, Relations, Collaborations*. Mattering Press: Manchester, 189–220.

GCCA (Global Climate Change Alliance). 2019. 'Capacity Building for Integrated Water Resource Management'. Paramaribo: WaterForum Suriname. https://sr.undp.org/content/dam/suriname/docs/Fenvironment/GCCA/IWRM_SR.pdf

Geissler, P. W., H. Moore, B. Poleykett, R. J. Prince and N. Tousignant. 2014. Convenors of *Making Scientific Capacity in Africa: An Interdisciplinary Conversation*. 13–14 June 2014. Centre for Research in the Arts, Social Sciences and Humanities, Cambridge.

Gimbel, S., B. Chilundo, N. Kenworthy, C. Inguane, D. Citrin, R. Chapman, K. Sherr, J. Pfeiffer. 2018. 'Donor Data Vacuuming: Audit Culture and the Use of Data in Global Health Partnerships'. *Medicine Anthropology Theory* 5 (2): 79–99.

Herrick, C. and A. Brooks. 2018. 'The Binds of Global Health Partnership: Working out Working Together in Sierra Leone'. *Medical Anthropology Quarterly* 32 (4): 520–538.

Heslop, L and L. Jeffries. 2020. 'Roadwork: Expertise at Work Building Roads in the Maldives'. *Journal of the Royal Anthropological Institute* 26 (2): 284–301.

Hughes, B., C. Hunt and B. Kondoch. 2010. *Making Sense of Peace and Capacity-Building Operations: Rethinking Policing and Beyond*. Leiden: Martinus Nijhoff Publishers.

Jensen, C. B. and B. R. Winthereik. 2013. *Monitoring Movements in Development Aid: Recursive Partnerships and Infrastructures*. Cambridge, MA: MIT Press.

Kaplan, A. 2000. 'Capacity Building: Shifting the Paradigms of Practice'. *Development in Practice* 10 (3–4): 517–526.

Kelly, J. 2011. *State Healthcare and Yanomami Transformations: A Symmetrical Ethnography*. Tucson: The University of Arizona Press.

Konrad, M. (ed). 2012. *Collaborators Collaborating: Counterparts in Anthropological Knowledge and International Research Relations*. New York: Berghahn Books.

Koselleck, R. 2002. *The Practice of Conceptual History: Timing History, Spacing Concepts*. Stanford: Stanford University Press.

Land, T. 1999. 'Conceptual and Operational Issues Arising: Overview Paper'. Paper prepared for the Joint DAC Informal Network/ACBF Workshop on Institutional and Capacity Development, Harare, October.

Lea, T. 2008. *Bureaucrats and Bleeding Hearts: Indigenous Health in Northern Australia*. Sydney: University of New South Wales Press.

Lea, T. 2020. *Wild Policy: Indigeneity and the Unruly Logics of Intervention*. Stanford, CA: Stanford University Press.

Linnell, D. (ed.) 2003. *Evaluation of Capacity Building: Lessons from the Field*. New York: Alliance for Non-profit Management.

Lusthaus, C., M.-H. Adrien, and M. Perstinger. 1999. 'Capacity Development: Definitions, Issues and Implications for Planning, Monitoring and Evaluation.' *Universalia Occaional Paper* 35, September.

Malik, K. 2002. 'Towards a Normative Framework: Technical Cooperation, Capacities and Development'. In S. Fukuda-Parr, C. Lopes and K. Malik (eds), *Capacity for Development: New Solutions to Old Problems*. London: Earthscan Publications, no pagination.

Mattingly, C. 2010. *The Paradox of Hope: Journeys through a Clinical Borderland*. Berkeley: University of California Press.

Mayville, A. K. 2020. *The Transformation of Capacity in International Development: Afghanistan and Pakistan (1977–2017)*. London: Anthem Press.

McDougall, D. 2013. 'Spiritual capacity? Overseas religious missions in RAMSI-era Solomon Islands.' SSGM Discussion Paper 2013/3. Canberra, ACT: ANU Research School of Pacific and Asian Studies, State, Society and Governance in Melanesia Program.

Mentore, L. 2017. 'The Virtualism of "Capacity Building" Workshops in Indigenous Amazona: Ethnography in the New Middle Grounds. *HAU: Journal of Ethnographic Theory* 7 (2): 279–307.

Merry, S. E. 2015. 'Comment on C. Shore and S. Wright, "Audit Culture Revisited: Rankings, Ratings and the Reassembling of Society"' *Current Anthropology* 56 (3): 421–444.

Milèn, A. 2001. 'What Do We Know About Capacity Building? An Overview of Existing Knowledge and Good Practice'. Geneva: Department of Health Service Provision, World Health Organization (WHO).

Miyazaki, H. 2004. *The Method of Hope: Anthropology, Philosophy and Fijian Knowledge*. Stanford: Stanford University Press.

Morgan, P. and A. Qualman. 1996. 'Institutional and Capacity Development: Results-Based Management and Organizational Performance'. Paper prepared for the Canadian International Development Agency.

Moore, H. L. 1994. *A Passion for Difference: Essays in Anthropology and Gender* Indiana: Indiana University Press

Moore, S. F (ed). 2004. *Law and Anthropology: A Reader*. Hoboken, NJ: Wiley Publishing.

Nader, L. 2002. *The Life of the Law: Anthropological Projects*. Berkeley: University of California Press.

Robinson, S. A. and P. Cox. 1998. 'Participatory Evaluation in Human Resource Development: A Case Study for Southeast Asia'. In E. T. Jackson and Y. Kassam (eds). *Knowledge Shared: Participatory Evaluation in Development Cooperation*. West Hartford, CT: Kumarian Press, 122–150.

Roche, C. 1997. 'Preface'. Pp v–vi in *Capacity Building: An approach to people-centered development*. Ed. D. Eade. London: Oxfam.

Robbins, J. and M. Engelke 2010. 'Global Christianity, Global Critique'. Special Issue of *South Atlantic Quarterly* 109 (4).

O'Reilly, K. 2011. 'Building capacity, extracting Labour: The Management of Emotion in NGOs'. Paper presented at 'Traces, Tidemarks and Legacies', 110th annual meeting of the American Anthropological Association, Montreal, 16–20 November.

OECD (Organisation for Economic Co-operation and Development).1996. 'Shaping the 21st Century: The Contribution of Development Cooperation'. Paris: OECD.

OECD (Organisation for Economic Co-operation and Development). 2005. 'Living up to the Capacity Development Challenge: Lessons and Good Practice'. Draft. Paris: Learning Network on Capacity Development, Development Assistance Committee Network on Governance.
OECD (Organisation for Economic Co-operation and Development). 2008. 'The Accra Agenda for Action'. Paris: OECD.
Ong, A. and S. Collier (eds). 2005. *Global Assemblages: Technology, Politics and Ethics as Anthropological Problems*. Oxford: Blackwell Publishing.
Pedersen, M. A. 2012. 'A Day in the Cadillac: The Work of Hope in Urban Mongolia.' *Social Analysis* 56 (2): 1–16.
Pfotenhauer, S., D. Roos and D. Newman. 2013. 'Collaborative Strategies for Innovation Capacity-Building: A study of MIT's International Partnerships'. In P. Teirlinck, F. de Beule and S. Kelchtermans (eds), *Proceedings of the 8th European Conference on Innovation and Entrepreneurship*. Brussels: Belgium, 498–506.
Pfotenhuaer, S., D. Wood, D. Roos and D. Newman. 2016. 'Architecting Complex International Science, Technology and Innovation Partnerships (CISTIPs): A Study of Four Global MIT Collaborationsø. *Technological Forecasting and Social Change* 104: 38–56. doi 0.1016/j.techfore.2015.12.006.
Pierre, J. 2019. 'The Racial Vernaculars of Development: A View from West Africa'. *American Anthropologist* 122 (1): 86–98.
Rapport, N. (ed). 2005. *Human Nature as Capacity: Transcending Discourse and Classification*. Oxford: Berghahn Books.
Sariola, S. and B. Simpson. 2019. *Research as Development: Biomedical Research, Ethics and Collaboration in Sri Lanka*. Ithaca, NY: Cornell University Press.
Spencer, H. [1855] 1999.*The Principles of Psychology*. Bloomsbury USA Academic: London.
Starosielski, N. 2015. *The Undersea Network*. Durham, NC: Duke University Press.
Shore, C. and S. Wright. 2015. 'Audit Culture Revisited: Rankings, Ratings and the Reassembling of Society'. *Current Anthropology* 56 (3): 421–444.
Silva Mediterranea. 2019. Aetelier de Planification Opérationelle des Activités de la Composante Marocaine du Project "The Paris Agreement in Action: Upscaling Forest and Landscape Restoration to Achieve Nationally Determined Conditons" http://foris.fao.org/meetings/download/_2019/atelier_de_planification_op_rationnelle_des_activi/misc_documents/tdr_v2.pdf.
Simpson, B. 2012. 'Building Capacity: A Sri Lankan Perspective on Research, Ethics and Accountability.' In M. Konrad (ed.), *Collaborators Collaborating*. New York: Berghahn Books, 147–164.
Strathern, M. 1995. 'The Nice Thing About Culture is Everyone Has It.' In M. Strathern (ed.), *Shifting Contexts: Transformations in Anthropological Knowledge* London: Routledge, 153–170.
Strathern, M. (ed.) 2000. *Audit Culture: Anthropological studies in Accountability, Ethics and the Academy*. London: Routledge.
Strathern, M. 2005. 'Prologue.' In M. S. Mosko and F. H. Damon (eds), *On the Order of Chaos: Social Anthropology and the Science of Chaos*. New York: Berghahn Books, xii–xv.
Squadrito, K. 2002. 'Locke and the Dispossession of the American Indian.' In J. K. Ward and T. L. Lott (eds), *Philosophers on Race: Critical Essays*, Oxford: Blackwell Publishing, 101–125.
Taussig, K.-S., K. Hoeyer and S. Helmreich. 2013. 'The Anthropology of Potentiality in Biomedicine: An Introduction to Supplement 7', *Current Anthropology* 54 (S7): S3–S14.
Tylor, E. B. [1871] 2010. *Primitive Culture: Researches Into the Development of Mythology, Philosophy, Religion, Art, and Custom*. Cambridge: Cambridge University Press.

UNDP (United Nations Development Programme). 1995. 'Capacity Development for Sustainable Human Development'. New York: United Nations Development Programme.

UNDP (United Nations Development Programme). 1998. 'Capacity Assessment and Development in a Systems and Strategic Management Context'. MDGB Technical Advisory Paper 3.

UNDP (United Nations Development Programme). 2003. 'Ownership, Leadership and Transformation: Can We Do Better for Capacity Development?' London: Earthscan Publications.

UNDP (United Nations Development Programme). 2009. 'Capacity Development: A UNDP Primer'. New York: United Nations Development Programme.

UNEP (United Nations Environment Programme). 2002. 'Capacity Building for Sustainable Development: An Overview of UNEP Environmental Capacity Development Activities'. New York: United Nations Environmental Programme.

UNFAO. 2019. The forest and Landscape Restoration Mechanism. http://www.fao.org/in-action/forest-landscape-restoration-mechanism/our-work/countries/en/

UNMDG (United Nations Millennium Development Goals.) 2013.'United Nations Millennium Development Goals'. http://www.un.org/millenniumgoals/.

United Nations. 2014. SIDS Accelerated Modalities of Action (SAMOA) Pathway. A/RES/69/15. https://www.un.org/ga/search/view_doc.asp?symbol=A/RES/69/15&Lang=E Last accessed May 21, 2021.

United Nations. 2015. 'Transforming our world: the 2030 Agenda for Sustainable Development' https://sdgs.un.org/goals Accessed May 21 2021.

UNFCC (United Nations Framework Convention on Climate Change). 2021. 'Capacity-building Talks', https://unfccc.int/Capacity-building%20Talks Accessed June 20, 2021.

Usher, G. 1824. 'Thoughts on Human Capacity'. In V. Knox (ed.) *Elegant Extracts: Or Useful and Entertaining Passages in Prose* London: JG Barnard, 328.

Venkatesan, S. 2009. *Craft Matters: Artisans, Development and the Indian Nation*. Hyderabad: Orient Blackswan.

Viveiros de Castro, Eduardo. 2004. 'Perspectival anthropology and the method of controlled equivocation.' *Tipiti* 2: 3–22.

Viveiros de Castro, E. 2012. '"Transformação" na antropologia, transformação da "antropologia" [Tranformation in anthropology, transformation of anthropology.]' *Mana*, 18 (1): 151–171.

Wagner, R. 1986. *Symbols That Stand for Themselves*. Chicago: University of Chicago Press.

Watanabe, C. 2019. *Becoming One: Religion, Development and Environmentalism in a Japanese NGO in Myanmar*. Honolulu: University of Hawai'i Press

West, P., J. Igoe and D. Brockington. 2006. Parks and Peoples: The Social Impact of Protected Areas. *Annual Review of Anthropology* 35: 251–277.

West, P. 2016. *Dispossession and the Environment: Rhetoric and Inequality in Papua New Guinea*. New York: Columbia University Press.

Yarrow, T. and S. Venkatesan. 2012. 'Anthropology and Development: Critical Framings'. In T. Yarrow and S. Venkatesan (eds), *Differentiating Development: Beyond an Anthropology of Critique* Oxford: Berghahn Books, 1–20.

Chapter 1

Professionalizing Persons and Foretelling Futures
Capacity Building in Post-Earthquake Haiti

Kristin LaHatte

'*Moun pa'm se dra*', Raoul said to me with an affirmative nod of his head, pouring more Haitian rum into our small mismatched glasses as another hot and muggy summer evening descended in Port-au-Prince.[1] We were sitting on his veranda in Haitian-made rocking chairs, which tilted precipitously backwards beyond my comfort level, watching the sun descend over the hazy city. A university-educated agronomist, Raoul had spent the past twenty-plus years working for several of the major international non-governmental organizations (INGOs) in Haiti and was willing to indulge me in a discussion on the idea of capacity building in the country. '*Moun pa'm se dra*', I repeated back to him, thinking through the meaning of this phrase. It translates literally as 'my people are sheets', but a more accurate meaning would be to say that 'my people' [*moun pa'm*], a notion encompassing a wide range of personal social relationships in Haiti, create a security blanket in life. Forming along both hierarchical and lateral social axes in Haiti, the relationships woven within this blanket are reciprocal, obligatory and lasting, and thus can be called upon in moments of need and relied upon in the future. While this idea of the security blanket is easily understandable, what made this reference particularly interesting was that Raoul was employing it to offer me a definition of what capacity building means in Haiti. 'Yes', he said in English in response to my curious repetition of the phrase, '*Moun pa'm se dra*, that's how we [Haitians] build capacity'.

Whether deemed a 'buzzword' (Eade 2007) or a 'fetish' (Clarke 2010), capacity building is firmly entrenched in the development encounter. An ambiguous and ubiquitous term in development aid, attempts to define capacity building at the different levels at which it is implemented – societal, institutional or individual – continue to be an ongoing source of debate. Despite this definitional ambiguity, and like its compatriots 'participation', 'partnership' and 'empowerment', capacity building has become a 'spiritual duty' and 'moral obligation' (Cooke and Kothari 2001) in the project of 'doing good' (Fisher 1997). Capacity building, positioned as a technical, apolitical solution to development's intractable failures, is part of the broader neoliberal development agenda that has come to dominate development practice. Within this agenda, capacity building occurs through education, training and human resource development, all aimed at instilling 'good governance' and increasing development effectiveness through measurable, transferable and auditable outcomes.

Development practitioners actualize capacity building efforts through the sanctioning of certain kinds of relationality. According to the development aid idea of capacity building, practitioners should seek to engage with beneficiaries, as well as other practitioners, as individuals unencumbered by the social ties that create dependency, which is seen to thwart efforts towards building capacity. Such relational 'lightness' (Redfield 2012) ostensibly allows practitioners to be fair, impartial and independent, all professional attributes deemed necessary for a modern society to arise. Development organizations thus embody neoliberal development values and position themselves as both *models of* and *models for* the ways in which capacity is built. These assertions, however, rely on the presupposition that it is precisely by 'changing hearts and minds' that the promises of the development narrative will come to fruition. And yet, as Ferguson (2006) has compellingly demonstrated, the narrative of modernization, progress and temporality has begun to 'decompose'. The future this narrative avows 'appears as a broken promise' not only among those who ardently critique aid from the upper echelons (e.g. Moyo 2009) but also for many of those who are on the ground, 'doing' development (Ferguson 2006: 186–187).

As the 'Republic of NGOs', Haiti provides an apt lens to consider these tensions. Though raised to the international stage after the 2010 earthquake killed more than 200,000 people and resulted in one of the largest humanitarian responses ever seen, Haiti has long been an epicentre of the aid world (O'Connor et al. 2014). Prior to 2010, it was estimated that upwards of 10,000 NGOs were operating in the country (Edmonds 2012). A constitutive site for the formation of the development aid industry, the 'parade of acronyms' began in 1946 and has never ceased (Trouillot 1990: 140). Beginning in the late 1980s and extending to the present day, this proliferation of NGOs is part of a global trend in which international financial institutions required governments in the Global South to 'liberalize' their economies in order to receive loans and continued aid support. Such policies created a 'gap' for NGOs to fill as public and social services were privatized (Schuller 2009). In the context of Haiti, the acceptance of these structural adjustment policies was even a conditional piece of former President Aristide's US-backed return to power after his overthrow in 1991 (Dupuy 2005). In Haiti, NGOs provide upwards of 80 per cent of the country's public services and 70 per cent of the country's health care (Edmonds 2012; Zanotti 2010). Though legally recognized as non-state actors, Hallward (2007) proposes that NGOs in Haiti should be labelled 'other governmental organizations', echoing many scholars' assertion that NGOs constitute a 'shadow' or 'parallel' government, detrimentally bypassing and undermining the Haitian state (see Farmer 2011; Schuller 2009; Smith 2001). While the humanitarian response after the earthquake was 'one of the largest ever mounted' (O'Connor et al. 2014), this circumvention continued; according to Fisch and Mendoza (2010), the government of Haiti received approximately one penny of every US dollar sent for disaster relief. Despite decades of intervention from NGOs and bilateral and multilateral aid sources, as well as the presence of an international peacekeeping mission for more than a decade, a household survey conducted in 2012 by the Haitian Institute of Statistics and Informatics (IHSI) indicated that approximately 50 per cent of Haitians continue to live below the poverty line and 25 per cent live in extreme poverty (World Bank and L'Observatoire National de la Pauvreté et de l'Exclusion Sociale 2014).

Within this landscape of international development aid, this chapter examines the conflicts generated by the inherent promises imbued in capacity building from the perspective of Haitian nationals who work for INGOs in Port-au-Prince, referred to in this chapter as local aid practitioners. First, it considers the relational values and kinds of sociality that neoliberal development aid attempts to inhibit and reform in order to build capacity. Second, it examines how such values at times contradict and elide those that Haitians consider socially and morally appropriate. Through the frames of obligation, reciprocity and dependence, it explores capacity building in the context of the relationships of '*moun pa'm*' [my people]; lastly, it considers how these relations inform understandings of what will 'hold' [*kenbe*] and 'let go' [*lage*] as practitioners grapple with what and who can be relied upon in the future. In this framing, Haitian aid practitioners' understanding of capacity building looks to the future, but it is a future that remains uncertain. For those who are both the purveyors of capacity building and the targets of such efforts, *moun pa'm se dra* [my people are sheets] represents a distinct understanding of the future promises of development aid and what capacity building hopes to achieve.

Building what or building whom?

Given its broad scope and the numerous kinds of capacities that development may seek to build – 'intellectual, organizational, social, political, cultural, representational, material, technical, practical, or financial – and most likely a shifting combination of all of these' (Eade 2007: 633) – it is easy to lose sight of the fact that within all these kinds, and at all levels of their implementation, capacity building efforts actually occur through persons. In this way, we can see capacity building as ultimately a process of transformation, specifically the transformation of persons. Inherent to and implied within this transformation, as Hewlett (this issue) notes, is a deficiency of ability (or capacity) that once corrected will allow persons, institutions and societies to advance, quite literally, towards becoming 'developed'.

This conceptual framing of capacity building as the transformation of persons is made particularly evident in the definition employed by the Food and Agricultural Organization of the United Nations, which states, '… capacity building encompasses … actions directed at helping participants in the development process to increase their knowledge, skills and understandings and to develop the attitudes needed to bring about the desired developmental change' (Ku and Yuen-Tsang 2011: 470). In this framing, capacity building engenders appropriate 'attitudes' through which both aid recipients and development practitioners 'are being empowered to be elements in the great project of the modern' (Stirrat and Henkel 2001: 182).

For aid practitioners, efforts to change 'attitudes' are rooted in the standardization of processes and the cultivation of professionalism, which became a cornerstone of the neoliberal development agenda during the mid-1990s. Development projects, and most significantly those who work within them, are increasingly oriented towards evidence-based results, which can be written into donor reports to demonstrate project effectiveness, and adherence to the pervasive culture of audit (Kusek and Rist 2004; Strathern 2000). These transformations are seen as capacity building efforts that work towards producing 'responsible populations' (Phillips and Ilcan 2004: 397) through governance aimed at decentralization, privatization and individualism. By building such productive capacities, development practitioners render visible their compliance in implementing projects in a transparent, accountable and equitable manner, all part of the practices of good governance. These practices of good governance are positioned as diminishing the opportunities for nepotism and corruption, hallmarks of 'premodern' societies (McKinnon 2013), and thus 'attitudes' to be corrected.

Consequently, a central aspect of the relational values that capacity building efforts seek to engender in local aid practitioners is the importance of keeping one's relations with aid recipients as well as other practitioners on a 'professional' level. Foregrounding the importance of individual agency, this relational ethics of professionalism compels practitioners to treat everyone as equal individuals. As a result of this need to 'treat everyone the same', development practitioners are to behave as independent actors uncompromised by the dependent networks of patronage, nepotism and hierarchy through which recipients are seen to operate (Cox 2009). Becoming involved in personal relationships with aid recipients, whether through the exchange of material help, favours, gifts or long-term commitments, is to be avoided (Mosse 2005; Stirrat and Henkel 2001). Such personal relationships are seen to violate core values of the professional ethics of the development aid industry, which include impartiality, transparency and accountability, and lead instead to the cultivation of dependence. Even in the case of 'community-based' projects in which practitioners are expected to form 'personal' relations with community members, relations are often circumscribed so that they fail to allow practitioners to form locally meaningful relationships with beneficiaries (see Boulding this issue). In this way, development aid practice does sometimes call for relationality, but it does so without allowing for certain forms of sociality for fear that they could result in the failure to practise good governance.

Thus, local practitioners are encouraged to emulate their 'materially heavy but socially light' ex-patriot co-workers who successfully avoid the messy entanglements of 'the local' (Redfield 2012). Or as the adage goes, development practitioners should 'teach' beneficiaries to fish rather than 'give' them a fish, but not because it would allow them to only eat for today, but because giving the fish would show favouritism and require the exchange of gifts and the personal sharing of food – all actions that should exist outside the domain of professional practice and are therefore viewed as undermining the values that are central to the neoliberal development agenda.

The ties that bind

In the context of Haiti, the kinds of personal social relationships thought to diminish capacity building and impede development are the kinds of relationships people believe nourish and protect life itself. The ethnographic and historical literature compellingly demonstrate the centrality of personal social relationships to everyday life, where being situated in webs of dependence rather than independence is highly valued (Alvarez and Murray 1981; Richman 2005; Stevens 1995). Initiated at the household level and extending outward, individuals are personally and collectively drawn into these webs of dependence through which they conceptualize, perform and negotiate a world of positively valued relations. These relations, constituted through shared substance, acts of food sharing, the exchange of material help, favours, gifts and long-term commitments, form along both hierarchical and lateral axes in Haiti. Such relationships of mutual obligation and reciprocity influence how people access land, find work, acquire food, sell commodities, secure labour assistance and afford education in an increasingly insecure economy. Glick-Schiller and Fouron liken these relationships to a tree 'with underground roots not always visible yet capable of giving sustenance and support to the various branches extending in different directions' (2001: 60). Indeed, following the earthquake in 2010, as tens of thousands of people fled Port-au-Prince for the countryside, it was precisely these networks that were activated. In the Central Plateau, the initial joy of seeing family members alive and the shared sorrow over the loss of many others soon gave way to the question of how to care for these kin, particularly given that the rural households who came to shelter them were often barely sustaining themselves and, in many cases, had been relying on their urban kin for support. This sudden presence in the countryside necessitated a renegotiation of daily material concerns but, significantly, and despite the additional pressure on scarce resources, help was given.

These relationships extend beyond such pragmatic purposes and also serve as a medium through which personhood is constituted (Brown 2001; Metraux [1959] 1972; Perez 2001; Richman 2005). Indeed, failing to be properly situated in these webs of personal relationships marks one as a 'stranger' [*etranje*] rather than a 'person' [*moun*], a category that according to Haitian cultural logic is inherently suspect and threatening (Lowenthal 1987; Metraux [1959] 1972). Or as put by anthropologist Karen McCarthy Brown, 'In Haiti, human connection is the assumption; it is separation that requires both effort and explanation' (2001: 13). The aid to 'one's people', as demonstrated by the countryside residents above, is not merely the return of a material exchange but rather a morally prescribed act in which they situated both themselves and those on the receiving end as 'persons', deeply embedded in a system of care, trust and respect.

Previous ethnographic accounts have often portrayed the relationship of *moun pa'm* negatively. Such relations have been examined in terms of their role in the acquisition of political power (Fatton 2002) or as corrupt practices of favouritism within Haitian 'bureaucraft' (James 2010). I do not argue against the assertion that such relations can be and are used maliciously at times, but I propose that these depictions have overshadowed the ways in which these relationships are also situated within a broader moral framework of being and belonging in Haiti. *Moun pa'm* relations are at once both material and moral, and failure to fulfil one's part in these relations is not taken lightly. Local aid practitioners thus find themselves in the position of having to negotiate two incommensurable systems of value as they decide what kind of capacity they seek to build.

Practitioners in practice

Development practitioners in Haiti are commonly referred to as the 'Klas ONG' or the 'NGO class' (Schuller 2009). This class is composed predominantly of middle-income Haitian nationals who typically possess a university degree or certificate and speak French. It should be noted, however, that given the hierarchy of positions that fall under the umbrella of non-governmental organizations, from drivers and security guards to programme managers and directors, it is fair to say that the reach of NGO employment extends both below and above this middle class. Mark Schuller's (2009, 2012) extensive research on NGOs in Port-au-Prince demonstrates how donors not only influence development project priorities but also shape organizational structure, governing practitioners' interactions both among themselves and with project beneficiaries. Acting as intermediaries in a system of 'trickle-down imperialism', NGOs are required to continually demonstrate compliance and positive outcomes, as 'the moment an NGO director steps out of the sphere of allowable actions, the organisation can be disciplined' (2012: 184). And yet, despite this firm entrenchment in the neoliberal world of development, my ethnographic research suggests that some members of this 'NGO class' have not abandoned the Haitian idea of *moun pa'm*, as incommensurable as it may seem with their professional lives. Reimaging capacity building through understandings of obligation, reciprocity and dependence, capacity building, as Raoul stated in the opening vignette, is not something that can be acquired through education or training but is about working within a system of personal social relationships – the security blanket.

Julienne had spent the past year working for an INGO in Port-au-Prince that was engaged in the construction of t-shelters, the 't' standing for transitional. Following the earthquake, numerous organizations began to work on moving persons out of tents and into more semi-permanent housing, all being technically facilitated under the auspices of the humanitarian 'Shelter Cluster'.[2] T-shelters were intended to last for two to three years until more permanent housing could be constructed, although the quality of such shelters differed widely depending on the implementing organization (Klarreich and Polman 2012). Julienne often spoke of the difficulty of her position as many of 'her people' knew of her job and were asking to be given one of the t-shelters. One such person was Aunt Claudette, with whom Julienne had spent much of her childhood. Though not a biological relative, Aunt Claudette had been like a mother to Julienne for years. One night as we sat together on the street eating '*fritay*' [fried food], she lamented her predicament to me:

> You know I'm obligated to her [Aunt Claudette], I have no choice; I can't let her go. Her house has nearly fallen down and they've marked it red, she won't even go inside anymore. But if I get her the *ti-kay* [little house] everyone will come asking for one, you know problems are never ending (*pwoblèm pap janm fini*).

In the statement above, Julienne initially frames her understanding of Claudette's request as one of obligation, a reciprocal obligation she feels the need to return given all that Claudette did for her as a child. Immediately following this declaration, however, she recontextualizes Aunt Claudette as someone worthy of a t-shelter from her 'professional' perspective by noting the condition of her current home. Following the earthquake, the structural conditions of houses were assessed and subsequently marked using green, yellow or red spray paint depending on the damage sustained during the earthquake. Aunt Claudette's 'red' house indicated that it was no longer structurally sound. Invoking these two different frames, Julienne attempts to negotiate between the relational values and obligations of *moun pa'm* and development aid.

Julienne and I had frequently discussed the criteria being used by her organization to determine who was to receive a t-shelter. She often spoke of this specifically regarding the data she was collecting through household surveys in the neighbourhood where I was living, which included a large tent camp; data that were then used to determine who was eligible to receive a t-shelter. The survey she was implementing consisted of questions regarding household size, level of damage to the previous home, and intentions for the future, with each question having a fixed number of responses that were recorded for every household. Julienne was thus engaged in one of the central goals of capacity building. Within her position, she was producing certain kinds of documentation for her direct and indirect superiors to review. Her surveys provided quantifiable and standardized information about project recipients, demonstrating the project's overall effectiveness as well as compliance with externally imposed criteria of *fairness* and *impartiality* in selecting shelter recipients. Despite the condition of her house, Aunt Claudette failed to meet all the criteria of a worthy recipient; later, however, when I asked Julienne if she would still try to get her a t-shelter, she repeated to me again slowly with exasperation, 'I'm obliged', as though I had missed the point entirely.

Many times when I asked why people did certain things to help others, whether it was giving someone a ride, navigating the bureaucracy of the Haitian government or even, as in the case above, providing a transitional shelter, their reply was simply '*m'oblije*' [I'm obliged]. Such statements do not imply that people are cold or heartless but rather that their understanding of these moments and actions is rooted in a notion of reciprocity that comes with being nested in relations of care and respect. It is precisely within these reciprocal relations and the obligations that they carry that persons know they will not be 'let go' [*lage*]. The obligation to give, however, is not the same for everyone but determined in deference to a hierarchy that marks all of Haitian society; ultimately, one's obligations increase the 'better' one does. As Julienne states above, her assistance to Aunt Claudette will come at a substantial personal cost as it will result in more requests for help from others. This deep-rooted sense of reciprocity is often framed in terms of debt: debt to those who cared for you when you were young (Richman 2005), debt to those who helped you get to the city or even abroad (Glick-Schiller and Fouron 2001), or debt to your ancestors who have come before (Brown 2001). Debt in these contexts is not a tit-for-tat process, where you give me this and I give you that, but rather one in which persons should be nested in long-term reciprocal relationships of dependence structured by both giving and taking.

Another practitioner, Carlo, worked for an organization that sought to foster civic engagement and responsibility with young people through the use of sport, specifically football. Born and raised in Port-au-Prince, he moved through the city leisurely and seemed to know people everywhere he went. Carlo was described as someone who had 'many pistons' [*anpil piston*]; that is, he was someone who could move things forward and get things done through his relationships. It was precisely through such relationships that he was able to have the rubbish picked up from the football field, secure transportation for one of the youth teams to play a match in another part of the city, and ensure electricity for an evening event at the field.

When I asked him why the rubbish truck driver agreed to come by the field, however, it was not only the pragmatic nature of such relationships that Carlo referenced but also their moral implications:

> We know each other from a long time ago when I worked doing transportation logistics with the government. We reconnected when I started working in the neighbourhood ... he lived here and was in charge of picking up rubbish in the neighbourhood. Mostly he was picking up rubbish for the powerful people in the neighbourhood when he was told to, but then afterwards he would come by to get the rubbish from the field for me too. Our relationship is about respect for each other; we care about each other. If I don't see him, I call him and ask if he's okay, if his family is okay. Every time we see each other we greet each other, he is part of me, and I'm part of him. There's no money or contracts. I'm not a politician or bourgeoisie; I can't force people to do things or pay them to do things. People have to really know you, they have to trust you and respect you. You can't buy these kinds of relationships, it's about standing by each other's side. You can count on them.

This passage makes evident that relationships with 'one's people' are as much about doing for others as they are about having others do for you. Built on trust, respect and, as Julienne demonstrates, obligation, these reciprocal relationships weave people together in mutual dependence. For Carlo, these relationships were his 'sheets', which he actively relied upon in times of need. He was taking part in the 'dance of reciprocity' (Brown 2001: 177), where 'leading' and 'following', or giving and taking, are what it means to be a moral actor. However, when I asked Carlo if he discussed these relationships and their significance in his work with his American boss, he laughingly answered, 'I don't really talk about it, you know Americans', playfully darting his eyes back and forth to ensure that no one could overhear. 'They have their way of doing things, and that never changes.'

Carlo understood the role of reciprocity in his professional life to be a problematic one, and yet it was by relying on others that he accomplished his work. Continuing the conversation about his boss, he explained:

> It's hard to make Americans understand. They have this perception that we are all corrupt, that you shouldn't trust us. You know the things they say about Haiti. And okay, sometimes those things are true but that's not the whole story. But they [Americans] stay closed off and when they want something done and you say, 'no problem, I know someone who can help with that', they think *O!* he's corrupt.

Aware of the negative external narratives about Haiti, Carlo understood how the help he received and the relationships that he held would be perceived. And yet for Carlo such relations were not only morally prescribed; they were necessary. Carlo was an efficient and effective employee not in spite of his relationships but because of them. In fact, Carlo's boss and the organization's governing board considered the programme Carlo ran a great success. In light of such sentiments, if the goal of capacity building was truly to make development more effective, Carlo should be considered a success story. And yet his capacity, the relationships he built through long-term commitments of care, manifested materially in doing for others and having others do for him, is unacceptable in his professional world. Such relations and the values they necessitate are considered 'attitudes' to be corrected for development to succeed.

For both Julienne and Carlo, building their capacities as international development professionals requires them to work as autonomous individuals, disembedded from the relationships of *moun pa'm* [my people]. As Julienne shows, local aid practitioners are asked to relinquish such obligations and aid only those deemed worthy beneficiaries; to be a professional, they are expected to choose strangers over kin (Redfield 2012). For Carlo, such choices raise not only moral questions but material ones, including what the consequences will be for the programme's success if he decides to 'let go'. For both, adhering to such professional practices requires them to look to the future and consider what in the end will 'hold'.

Holding on and letting go

Inherent within capacity building efforts to transform persons is the promise that adhering to the ideas of relationality and sociality stipulated in the framework of good governance will, in fact, bring about a better future. That is, underlying such relational values is a particular orientation towards the future in which capacity building or 'helping others to help themselves' (Kenny and Clarke 2010) is what will bring about development. By correcting certain deficiencies and instilling in both aid recipients and local practitioners the correct attitudes towards autonomy and self-reliance, capacity building will allow them to be agents in their own future (Watkins and Swidler 2009). Development, therefore, promises a future in which its intervention will no longer be necessary as countries, and those persons within them, will finally achieve 'being developed'. Ironically, development works in the present to arrive at a midrange future in which it will no longer be needed (Ferguson 2006; Scherz 2013); it is an industry that declares it exists to put itself out of business.

While the development narrative proposes a steady march forward, in practice, development occurs in fits and starts, in an endless cycle of organizations and projects coming and going. In Haiti, the ephemeral nature of aid is evidenced by the numerous signs of previous development projects that stand along roadways, constituting what has been called an 'aid graveyard' (Minn 2011). The development narrative has consequently lost salience for people where 'the promise of modernization increasingly appears as a broken promise' (Ferguson 2006: 181). While the 'failure' of aid to deliver on its promises is not new, what is interesting is to consider the meaning of this failure for local aid practitioners who are both the purveyors and subjects of capacity building endeavours. As Hindman has noted, 'development workers are often depicted as mere conduits for modernising projects, but they are targets of the process of accountability and progress as well…' (2011: 172).

For local aid practitioners in Haiti, there is an acute sense of insecurity that results from the short-term nature of aid project funding and the shifting priorities of development donors. For example, in a survey of forty projects funded by the W. K. Kellogg Foundation in Haiti since 1 July 2015, the average awarded grant lasted approximately two years.[3] Local aid practitioners thus embody the structural vulnerabilities of development aid. As donor funding determines development project duration, local aid practitioners who are not full-time staff subsist on what I term, in development aid parlance, a project-based livelihood strategy, which leaves their future in doubt. It was this sense of insecurity that Julienne referenced later when I asked her specifically about her thoughts on capacity building in Haiti:

> They [facilitators] are always having trainings, telling us [staff] that we are building capacity so we can continue to grow toward the future, but we know that none of this will last, they're here now but then they leave, the project is over, and then what?

Julienne's positioning of herself vis-à-vis the workshop facilitators demonstrates precisely how the development narrative has begun to 'decompose' (Ferguson 2006). Though firmly entrenched in the work of the neoliberal development agenda, Julienne demonstrates the ways in which many of those situated within the work of development and who have themselves acquired 'status' and a better 'standard of living' still find the promise of development to be a broken one.

At the time that we sat together and talked about the idea of capacity building, Raoul, whose words opened this chapter, was coming to the end of his career and nearing retirement from the aid world of Haiti. He had watched the explosion of NGOs in Haiti, personally experienced how funds come and go in response to donor priorities and humanitarian crisis and, finally, survived the earthquake and the humanitarian deluge that followed. In being asked about the future, he spoke with a particular authority and gravitas as he articulated his thoughts on capacity building and the future in Haiti:

> Yes, yes, the future, the future. You [foreigners] are always talking about the future. But what you don't understand is that we are planning for the future too but you won't be here. The only thing you can be certain of in development is that none of it will last. NGOs come and go, projects come and go, the international staff come and go, but we are still here. They 'let us go' [*lage nou*]. You come in and tell us, 'do this for the future' and

we nod and say 'oh yes', and we go to your trainings and we do our reports but we know better. Development is the new *kolon* [colonist], it's not working for us, it has another master. So we plan for the future too, we build our capacity, but we do it with the thing that holds.

Used here by Raoul, and also by Julienne above, the term *lage* in *Kreyòl* means to let go, dismiss, undo or abandon (Valdman et al. 2007: 400–401). While it can be used in a playful manner, '… being *lage* is also an emotional or psychological state, as well as a material one – of hopelessness, powerlessness' (Wagner 2014: 160), in the phrase above, *lage* connotes a broader commentary on the power dynamics in a relation where only one side truly has the ability to let go. In opposition, *kenbe* is defined as to hold, support or sustain (Valdman et al. 2007: 340). After the earthquake, a common phrase one heard was *kenbe fè'm, pa lage*, meaning 'hold on tight, don't let go'. Long ago, President Bill Clinton had even uttered this phrase upon his visit to Haiti with the return of President Aristide in 1994 (Katz 2014: 46). Using these terms to represent the opposition between development and *moun pa'm*, letting go [*lage*] and holding on [*kenbe*], respectively, Raoul reveals the ways in which development is understood to abandon its role of care while your personal network of relationships will sustain and assist you.

For Raoul, the strengthening and broadening of one's ties was its own form of 'human resource development'; for him this was at the heart of *moun pa'm se dra* [my people are sheets]. In a future where you can be certain that development will 'let you go', it appears that capacity building as a method to 'help one's self' or 'fish for a lifetime' fails on its promise of change and is itself deemed insufficient. Development projects operate in the short term but aim to achieve long-term solutions, requiring that both those who work with them and those whom they work for trust in their promises for the future. While capacity building is part of the broader aim to one day arrive at a future where development interventions are no longer needed, Raoul's use of the term to 'let go' does not insinuate a moment of progress in which the state of being 'developed' has been reached. Rather, it is the recognition of the ways in which the development narrative has failed to live up to its promises and the implication that it will continue to do so in the future.

Consequently, local aid practitioners must strategically decide what kind of capacities they seek to build, decisions that, in the context of Haiti, are at once both material and moral. Choosing to help and be helped by 'one's people' positions one as a moral actor on the one hand and an unethical actor on the other, and vice versa. Negotiating this double bind has long-term consequences for those who remain 'on the ground' after development projects and their implementing organizations have gone. These choices make evident that capacity building efforts at this individual level are neither apolitical nor merely technical but a process of transformation, specifically the transformation of persons. Local aid practitioners must decide for themselves what personal and professional transformations their future will bring as they consider not only who they will hold or let go of, but who will hold or let go of them. Some, however, have already come to their own conclusions; as Raoul said to me later on that hot and muggy evening in Port-au-Prince, 'none of it lasts, but your people, that's what lasts'.

Acknowledgements

This research was generously supported by a Wenner-Gren Foundation Dissertation Fieldwork Grant. I thank the guest editors and two anonymous reviewers for their helpful suggestions and comments. I am also appreciative to those who participated in the 2011 AAA panel 'Legacies of the Past, Promises of the Future' and for those who continued and came into the conversation at the 2015 Wenner-Gren workshop, 'Hope and Insufficiency: Capacity Building in Ethnographic Comparison'. Most deeply, I give my thanks to those in Haiti who generously shared their insights and time with me during my fieldwork.

Kristin LaHatte is a Senior Associate Director for the Child Health and Mortality Prevention Surveillance program at Emory University. Since 2009, Kristin has conducted research on international development aid in Haiti, with a focus on relationality and morality. After years of working in public health in Haiti, she returned to the United States to focus on child health and well-being globally. Kristin is fluent in Haitian Kreyòl and a connoisseur of pikliz. She holds an MA in Anthropology from the University of Virginia.

Notes

1. All people in the text are referred to with pseudonyms.
2. Following the 2010 earthquake, the United Nations established twelve cluster groups, each focused on a different humanitarian sector, which were intended to promote coordination and integration among organizations.
3. https://www.wkkf.org/grants#pp=100&p=1&q=haiti. 'Grants, Haiti' (accessed 15 December 2016).

References

Alvarez, M. and G. Murray. 1981. *Socialization for Scarcity: Child Feeding Practices and Beliefs in a Haitian Village*. Report to United States Agency for International Development, Port-au-Prince.

Brown, K. M. 2001. *Mama Lola: A Vodou Priestess in Brooklyn*. Berkley, CA: University of California Press.

Clarke, M. 2010. 'Reimagining Capacity Building When Participation is Constrained: Illegal Burmese Migrants in Thailand'. In S. Kenny and M. Clarke (eds), *Challenging Capacity Building: Comparative Perspectives*. New York: Palgrave, 112–132.

Cooke, B. and U. Kothari. 2001. *Participation: The New Tyranny?* London: Zed Books.

Cox, J. 2009. 'Active Citizenship or Passive Clientelism? Accountability and Development in Solomon Islands'. *Development in Practice* 19 (8): 964–980.

Dupuy, A. 2005. 'Globalization, World Bank, and the Haitian Economy'. In F. Knight and T. Martinez-Vergne (eds), *Contemporary Caribbean Culture and Societies in a Global Context*. Kingston: UWI Press, 43–70.

Eade, D. 2007. 'Capacity Building: Who Builds Whose Capacity?' *Development in Practice* 17 (4): 630–639.

Edmonds, K. 2012. 'Beyond Good Intentions: The Structural Limitations of NGOs in Haiti'. *Critical Sociology* 39 (3): 439–452.

Farmer, P. 2011. *Haiti after the Earthquake*. New York: Public Affairs.
Fatton, R. 2002. *Haiti's Predatory Republic: The Unending Transition to Democracy*. Boulder, CO: Lynne Rienner Publishers.
Ferguson, J. 2006. *Global Shadows: Africa in the Neoliberal World Order*. Durham, NC: Duke University Press.
Fisch, Y. and M. Mendoza. 2010. 'Haiti Government Gets 1 Penny of US Quake Aid Dollar'. Boston.com, 27 January. http://archive.boston.com/business/articles/2010/01/27/haiti_govt_gets_only_1_cent_of_every_us_aid_dollar.
Fisher, W. F. 1997. 'Doing Good? The Politics and Anti-Politics of NGO Practice'. *Annual Review of Anthropology* 26 (1): 439–464.
Glick-Schiller, N. and G. Fouron. 2001. *Georges Woke Up Laughing: Long-Distance Nationalism and the Apparent State*. Durham, NC: Duke University.
Hallward, P. 2007. *Damning the Flood: Haiti, Aristide, and the Politics of Containment*. London: Verso.
Hindman, Heather. 2011. 'The Hollowing Out of Aidland: Subcontracting and the New Development Family in Nepal'. In A.-M. Fechter and H. Hindman (eds), *Inside the Everyday Lives of Development Workers: The Challenges and Futures of Aidland*. London: Lynne Rienner Publishers, Inc, 169–191.
James, E. 2010. *Democratic Insecurities: Violence, Trauma, and Intervention in Haiti*. Oakland, CA: University of California Press.
Katz, J. M. 2014. *The Big Truck That Went By: How the World Came to Save Haiti and Left Behind a Disaster*. New York: St. Martin's Griffin.
Kenny, S. and M. Clarke. 2010. *Challenging Capacity Building: Comparative Perspectives*. New York: Palgrave Macmillan.
Klarreich, K. and L. Polman. 2012. 'The NGO Republic of Haiti'. *The Nation*, 31 October.
Ku, H. B. and A. W. K. Yuen-Tsang. 2011. 'Capacity Building'. In M. Bevir (ed.), *The SAGE Handbook of Governance*. London: SAGE Publications, Ltd., 469–483.
Kusek, J. Z. and R. Rist. 2004. *A Handbook for Development Practitioners: Ten Steps to a Results-Based Monitoring and Evaluation System*. Washington, DC: World Bank.
Lowenthal, I. 1987. 'Marriage Is 20, Children Are 21': The Cultural Construction of Conjugality and the Family in Rural Haiti'. Ph.D. diss., Johns Hopkins University.
McKinnon, S. 2013. 'Kinship within and beyond the Movement of Progressive Societies'. In S. McKinnon and F. Cannell (eds), *Vital Relations: Modernity and the Persistent Life of Kinship*. Santa Fe, NM: SAR Press, 39–62.
Metraux, A. [1959] 1972. *Voodoo in Haiti*, trans. Hugo Charteris. New York: Schocken Books.
Minn, P. 2011. 'Where They Need Me: The Moral Economy of International Medical Aid in Haiti'. Ph.D. diss., McGill University.
Mosse, D. 2005. *Cultivating Development: An Ethnography of Aid Policy and Practice*. Ann Arbor, MI: Pluto Press.
Moyo, D. 2009. *Dead Aid: Why Aid Is Not Working and How There Is a Better Way for Africa*. New York: Farrar, Straus and Giroux.
O'Connor, D., K. Brisson-Boivin and S. Ilcan. 2014. 'Governing Failure: Development, Aid, and Audit in Haiti'. *Conflict, Security, and Development* 14 (3): 309–330.
Perez, M. P. 2001. 'Reciprocity and a Sense of Place: A Phenomenological Map of Haitian Space'. Ph.D. diss., The University of Texas at Austin.
Phillips, L. and S. Ilcan. 2004. 'Capacity Building: The Neoliberal Governance of Development'. *Canadian Journal of Development Studies* XXV (3): 393–409.
Redfield, P. 2012. 'The Unbearable Lightness of Ex-Pats: Double Binds of Humanitarian Mobility'. *Cultural Anthropology* 27 (2): 358–382.
Richman, K. 2005. *Migration and Vodou*. Gainesville, FL: University of Florida Press.

Scherz, C. 2013. 'Let Us Make God Our Banker: Ethics, Temporality, and Agency in a Ugandan Charity Home'. *American Ethnologist* 40 (4): 624–636.

Schuller, M. 2009. 'Gluing Globalization: NGOS as Intermediaries in Haiti'. *PoLAR: Political and Legal Anthropology Review* 32 (1): 84–104.

Schuller, M. 2012. *Killing with Kindness: Haiti, International Aid, and NGOs*. New Brunswick, NJ: Rutgers University Press.

Smith, J. 2001. *When the Hands Are Many: Community Organization and Social Change in Rural Haiti*. Ithaca: Cornell University Press.

Stevens, A. M. 1995. 'Manje in Haitian Creole: The Symbolic Significance of Manje in Haitian Creole'. *Haitian Studies Association* 1 (1): 75–88.

Stirrat, R. L. and H. Henkel. 2001. 'Participation as Spiritual Duty; Empowerment as Secular Subjection'. In B. Cooke and U. Kothari (eds), *Participation: The New Tyranny?* London: Zed Books, 168–182.

Strathern, M. 2000. *Audit Cultures: Anthropological Studies in Accountability, Ethics, and the Academy*. New York: Routledge.

Trouillot, M.-R. 1990. *Haiti, State against Nation: The Origins and Legacy of Duvalierism*. New York: Monthly Review Press.

Valdman, A., I. Iskrova, J. Pierre, and N. André. 2007. *Haitian Creole-English Bilingual Dictionary*. Bloomington, IN: Creole Institute.

Wagner, L. 2014. 'Haiti is a Sliding Land: Displacement, Humanitarianism, and Community in Post-Earthquake Haiti'. Ph.D. diss., University of North Carolina.

Watkins, S. C. and A. Swidler. 2009. 'Teach a Man to Fish: The Sustainability Doctrine and Its Social Consequences'. *World Development* 37 (7): 1182–1196.

World Bank and L'Observatoire National de la Pauvreté et de l'Exclusion Sociale. 2014. 'Investing in People to Fight Poverty in Haiti'. Reflections for Evidence-based Policy Making. http://documents.worldbank.org/curated/en/222901468029372321/pdf/944300v10REPLA0sment0EN0web0version.pdf.

Zanotti, L. 2010. 'Cacophonies of Aid, Failed State Building and NGOs in Haiti'. *Third World Quarterly* 31 (5): 755–771.

Chapter 2

Capacity as Aggregation
Promises, Water and a Form of Collective Care in Northeast Brazil

Andrea Ballestero

A significant tradition in political and environmental anthropology has documented the structural inequalities and transnational networks through which 'nature' is produced (Bakker 2010; Hayden 2003; Mosse 2003; West 2006). In the case of water, scholars have documented the fraught and unequal implications of material scarcity and excess, and of its commodification or recognition as a right (Aiyer 2007; Anand 2011; Ballestero 2015; Barnes 2014; Carse 2012; Morita 2016). Antina von Schnitzler (2016), for instance, calls attention to how the administrative governance of water infrastructures and service delivery are the grounds on which rights and obligations are adjudicated and the techno-politics of citizenship are negotiated. A large part of these negotiations happens in what she terms an 'administrative interface', the material space where citizens and public officials encounter each other. This chapter is located in that interface in the state of Ceará, Northeast Brazil. It examines the attempts of a set of public officials, civil servants and non-governmental organizations (NGOs) to refigure the ways in which water is collectively managed and organized. It traces an experiment that relies upon personal commitments to care for water as the means to create a collective interface that is different from the state. That formation is imagined as an aggregate, a type of flexible gathering whose existence does not depend on membership or identification. The aggregate is a peculiar construction that is scalable, while remaining context- and scale-specific. The rest of this chapter examines how that collective was produced, what its constituent units were and how the logic of aggregation allowed for its coalescence. My purpose is to re-examine the aggregate as a quantitative form that demands a qualitative reconsideration.

Ceará's Water Pact (WP) began with the commitment of a group of technical personnel with strong ties to the public sector to break with history. That history was characterized by the ambition of solving water scarcity problems by 'modernizing' infrastructure, institutions and the legal architecture of water. When these technical personnel envisioned the WP in 2008, they imagined that it would not follow the most recent set of reforms conducted in the 1990s. At that time, the state increased its capacity to store, move and charge for water. Technocrats also put in place a series of mechanisms to generate more technical knowledge and clearly define new water use rights.

While historically clientelist practices, large infrastructures and new regulations had become sedimented as unavoidable means to deal with water scarcity, after the 1990s reforms the organizers of the Pact amassed enough support for a new strategy. They hoped to tap into a different resource: people's capacity to care. They wanted to change Ceará's water landscape by resorting to an everyday sense of ethical action that would increase the State's capacity to care for water. Such capacity implied that every member of society would meet their ethical obligation to conserve and use water rationally and according to her own context. If living with scarcity, a person would help raise awareness of the need to save water. If facing pollution issues, a person would promote more environmentally healthy technologies. If wasting water due to inefficient technologies, a person would seek more appropriate techniques. The Pact organizers believed that moving away from the law and infrastructure as starting points would foster people's intimate and universal capacity to care, allowing them to articulate resources and knowledge in novel ways.

Three principles guided the Pact organizers' work. First, the Pact began from the idea that Ceará already had knowledge and solutions in its midst. What was missing was articulating knowledge, technical resources and personnel around a clear purpose. Second, organizers envisioned the Pact as a way of bringing 'society' together around water issues. Rather than putting responsibility for water on a small number of organizations, the Pact would make water a 'transversal' concern. This implied that ordinary citizens would be at the core of the Pact. But this principle proved elusive. Throughout the Pact's implementation, the more events the organizers conducted, the clearer it became that the Pact was mainly able to find the 'state' rather than the citizens who would represent 'society'. In an unexpected turn, the Pact's search for society led them to the state in the shape of its local, regional and state-wide representatives. Third, the Pact organizers conducted a series of public promise-making rituals whereby participants would commit to act ethically and do what was necessary to work with and through water in a more responsible way. These public meetings held throughout Ceará yielded large numbers of promises, first verbally uttered, then written on slips of paper, and finally entered into electronic documents. At the centre of the aggregate were their promises, a new type of interface this time between public actors and water itself.

Anthropologists and other social commentators have produced a number of concepts to help describe collectives and their capacity to act. The idea of a network, for example, has been used to explain the associations, connections and disconnects that lead to particular scientific and political capacities (Latour 2005; Strathern 1996). 'Assemblages' is used to highlight fleeting globalized formations with the power to redefine and redistribute political and economic capacities (Collier and Ong 2005). The concept of the multitude signals an unformed yet powerful collective with a revolutionary potential that is always at the verge of being actualized (Hardt and Negri 2005). And, of course, more classic notions such as nation-state (B. Anderson 1991; Bhabha 1994), community (Hayden 2003) and tribe (Malinowski [1926] 1966) have been used to describe collective capacities to intervene, actively or passively, in the world.

As a social form, the Pact contradicts much of what has been attractive about these notions, namely the different degrees of belonging they imply. In the Pact there is nothing to belong to. Instead, collectivity is built through a flexible and transient form of gathering that does not require participants to subscribe to any larger entity (for another articulation of political form, see Ballestero 2012). The Pact does not demand affiliation or membership. Rather than creating a whole, the Pact works by way of aggregation, gathering elements not seen as naturally belonging together into loose formations that are easy to assemble and disassemble.

In anthropology, 'aggregates' have historically had a negative resonance. They are often taken as constructions that dismiss social ties, erasing and homogenizing difference. During the heyday of structuralist thought, anthropologists used aggregates to map the shared cultural traits of collectives grouped under a 'single' culture or ethnicity. But this use of aggregation soon came to an end. Fredrik Barth, for instance, challenged the idea that ethnic groups were 'aggregates of people who essentially share a common culture' (Barth 1998: 9). Barth questioned the utility of defining cultural groups through lists of cultural characteristics and traits. On the contrary, he argued, the existence of an 'ethnic group' is better understood by tracing the changing boundaries between one group and another. Those boundaries allowed anthropologists to see cultural groups as entities that changed over time, as opposed to static accumulations of traits. Barth's challenge to aggregation as a static concept was methodological. He argued for studying processes rather than lists. Barth's thinking facilitated the transition of anthropology towards new theoretical approaches, and aggregation was soon abandoned as both empirical fact and analytic concept (Turner 1995; Gennep 1960; Guyer 1999).

Yet, in the twenty-first century, aggregation has regained relevance as a native concept (Anderson 2011; Coddington 2015) and as a political form (Juris 2012).

Today, rather than constituting stable wholes, aggregates are means to let unstable differences proliferate. Aggregates allow people to sidestep the problem of fixed and contradictory allegiances. The creation of collectives through aggregation does not limit the formations that people can potentially be a part of. On the contrary, aggregates allow people to participate in loose and temporary formations that can be done and undone according to different political, affective or epistemic affinities. If aggregate lists of traits were dismissed as ways to describe collectives because of their lack of attention to dynamic change, people's self-awareness of the speed and proliferation of change now makes aggregates helpful for tracking accelerated shifts in social organization.

Consider one type of aggregate that does not necessarily depend on intention: the database. Through endless databases built on dimensions (traits) of our social experience, those of us who are digitally tracked have become always already aggregated entities, regardless of our intention. Evelyn Ruppert (2012) calls attention to this phenomenon. She argues that rather than thinking in terms of how databases are surveillance of pre-defined categories and identities, we need to think of these technocratic infrastructures as topological aggregates of people's 'interactions, transactions, performance, activity and movements in relation to government' (Ruppert 2012: 119). Rather than given, aggregates are done and undone according to particular methods and questions. Commonalities are plucked and counted selectively for a specific purpose. The results they generate can be easily formed and dissolved. Not surprisingly, private corporations, especially those working across geographical boundaries, also actively use aggregation as a business strategy. For example, a prominent business magazine exhorts its readers, 'instead of treating geographically separate markets as distinct revenue pools, companies can aggregate these sales across time zones, nationalities, cultures, social networks and interests to serve truly global customer segments' (Borchardt et al. 2011: 21). Thus, as a preferred social form in the contemporary (Rabinow 2009), the aggregate becomes a generative strategy for producing novel capitalist, affective and political possibilities.[1] It is not surprising, then, that in Northeast Brazil the aggregate is also used to try to shape the future for water.

By tracing the making of this aggregate, I want to argue for a qualitative reconsideration of aggregation as a social form, particularly as a way to generate capacity.[2] The concept of aggregation helps us see the productivity of the Pact as a collective of commitments that does not claim any form of wholeness; as a plural construction that combines the multiplicity of its units without any aspiration to their amalgamation. The Pact is an aggregate that gathers without claiming to achieve unity. It selectively enrols the participants' willingness to make a promise to care for water, nothing more and nothing less. The remainder of this chapter traces the making of such a gathering, emphasizing the ideas that go into its construction. I focus on the assumptions that make state officials and consultants working at the administrative interface of water commit to this social form to increase the state's capacity to care for water in a place like Ceará.

My argument begins with an examination of the historical context from which the Pact emerges: its environmental and political conditions of possibility. I then focus on the methods necessary to generate promises and offer a few examples of how they are made and how their contents are distilled depending on whether they travel across scales or stay tied to one location. This analysis of the promise, the fundamental unit being accumulated in the Pact, takes us to the analysis of form and description as ways to intervene in collective affairs. I end with an illustration that compares two visualizations of aggregates: on the one hand Hobbes' Leviathan, and on the other a digital image produced by Andy Lomas, an artist who uses mathematics and philosophy to generate aggregates.

A pact in a dry landscape

As part of the semi-arid drought triangle of Northeast Brazil, Ceará is seen in Brazil as a land of stark poverty. The region has the second-worst well-being indicators in the country – second only to Amazonia. Historically vulnerable to the politics of water scarcity (Nelson and Finan 2009), residents of Ceará have seen a parade of ideas and projects, from rain harvesting to household water tanks, march through their neighbourhoods announcing definitive solutions to their historic exclusion from basic water infrastructures (Lemos 2003; Arons 2004). But despite its failure to provide universal access to water and its reputation as a 'backward' state, Ceará is also regarded as exemplary by specialized water institutions (do Amaral Filho 2003). During the 1990s, a reform, partially funded by the World Bank, modernized the state's 'outdated' water sector, with results often praised as exemplary disruptions of the dramatic water future that awaited the state (Simpson 2003). In fact, that reform, which was prior to similar institutional overhauls in the south and south-eastern industrial poles of Brazil, led water experts across the country to think of Ceará's professional circles as pioneers of water innovation. These innovations, according to many in the public sector, are the reason why the extreme multiyear drought the state has been experiencing since 2012 has not had the brutal social and environmental consequences characteristic of the Northeast's past.

But the success of the previous reforms could not turn around the legacy of inequalities and water scarcities that characterizes Ceará. A large proportion of the urban population continues to buy water in bulk from 'horse-drawn carts, motorized tanks, or from people who walk around the streets with large cans of water' (Caprara et al. 2009: S128). In the rural areas, droughts continue to hit vulnerable populations despite public and private experiments in securing continuous access in times of scarcity. Notwithstanding the inauguration in 2002 of the state's largest reservoir, the Açude Castanhão, water scarcity continues to lurk in people's memories and everyday experiences. By 2016, the state's water infrastructure had been pushed to the limit, with reservoirs at their lowest levels in thirty years.

Back in the 2000s, congressional representatives saw the state as being in something of a stalemate, unable to resolve its water access gaps and losing its innovative edge on water issues. After much discussion about new water laws and new institutional reforms, Congress decided to adopt a more fluid governance technology. In 2007 they officially inaugurated the Council for Advanced Studies and Strategic Issues with the mission of reducing the distance that separated citizens from their congressional representatives. The Council was charged with identifying strategic state-wide challenges and producing recommendations on how to confront those challenges. The Council's first responsibility was to promote an inclusive, state-wide dialogue to analyse the region's persistent water problems and determine future actions.

Against this background and over approximately four years (2007–2011), the Council worked to construct the Water Pact (WP). Although formally led by Congress, in practice the Council's executive director, Ernesto, developed the Pact process along with a group of consultants with long histories of water-related technical activism, combining diverse knowledge coming from academia, NGOs and public institutions. The team hoped to differentiate the Pact from other 'technical fixes' where authorities retained planning and decision-making powers. Practically, the Pact would ask for people's commitment to solve the imminent problems that water scarcity, pollution and climate change posed. Methodologically, the Pact consisted of a series of public rituals where participants would publicly make pledges to care for water. Materially, the Pact assembled prodigious quantities of written records, later exhibited as published documents and PowerPoint presentations, to openly display people's commitments. Although the organizers held sophisticated views on water issues, they refrained from actively imprinting those views on the Pact's contents to avoid imposing what they saw as extraneous concerns on promises that had to be context-specific. In their view, the methodology of the Pact could be pre-designed. Its contents, however, could not; this had to be determined locally.

By 2009, with almost eight thousand participants and eighty-six institutions involved, the Pact-making phase was brought to an end (Assembleia Legislativa do Estado do Ceará and Conselho de Altos Estudos e Assuntos Estratégicos 2009: 17). More than two hundred participatory events, an unimaginable number of intimate interactions, and rituals of political prestige gave shape to the aggregate that would multiply the state's capacity to care for water in ways that conventional state-centred and technical interventions could not. The Pact team put their faith in associating large numbers of people, mostly public servants but including some citizens as well, tapping into their sentiments and extracting promises for quotidian care for water, as a way to redraw the limits of the possible. All of this took place against the disbelief of many water managers in the public sector, who saw the Pact as an unnecessary waste of resources and a duplication of the work that water agencies were already doing through watershed planning efforts.

Methods of possibility

When I asked Rebecca, a sociologist in the organizing team, what exactly the Pact was, she answered by noting the difficulty in articulating a definition. 'The Pact', she said, 'is not a thing or a government plan, but a framework that will survive governmental changes and effect more perennial commitments'. It will 'go beyond political preferences to determine paths to be followed regardless of who comes to power'. Rebecca's invocation of a path is not accidental. In a state where lasting commitments are embodied in concrete structures, such as canals, reservoirs and irrigation districts, her projection of the Pact into the future required infrastructural analogies. During our conversation, Rebecca explained how a shared definition of this path not only did not exist but was somewhat irrelevant. In fact, she emphasized it was not important to ask *what* the Pact was, but to figure out *how* to pact; if the Pact was going to leave a lasting mark, it would be because of the method of its construction (see also Miyazaki 2004).

Stressing how important it was that I understood the methodology they had invented, Rebecca asked for my memory stick and saved 'Ernesto's document'. That document was a purified model full of text boxes, arrows and coloured letters that outlined the Pact's methodological phases. It had been put together by Ernesto, the congressionally appointed leader of the Council.

The first phase involved a broad base of participants from universities, water and sanitation companies, research centres and official water, health, education and agricultural agencies who produced a report on the situation of water resources in the state. The report aimed to be the go-to source of information on water issues. When Ernesto presented the document at a public event in 2008, he described it as a technical document unlike any other because 'ninety-seven institutions and more than five hundred hands, from two hundred and fifty-six *técnicos* [technical personnel]' helped to write it. Towards the end of a captivating speech, Ernesto proudly quoted Paulo Freire, a Brazilian education philosopher: 'this document is not a *mirar* but an *admirar*, which is to look inside with a critical perspective'. The Pact was taking a critical perspective on water issues while collecting all the available information.

The second phase of the Pact consisted of presenting the results of the report and disseminating the methodology that people were expected to use when they conducted their local, regional and state-wide promise-making events. The consultants facilitating the process travelled to the interior of the state to run explanatory meetings where they presented the technical findings of the report – including things like the gap between the demand and availability of water, the quantity of water used in agriculture, the climatological predictions for the next decade, the number of households lacking clean water and so on. They also introduced the methodology people were expected to use once they organized Pact events in their communities. These coordination meetings had between 80 and 150 participants and were all opened by Ernesto and the congressional representative of the area.

The Pact's third phase entailed the actual promise-making events at a variety of scales, beginning with municipal meetings and then at regional and state-wide events. At these events participants sat together to enunciate and write down their promises. The result was a large set of pledges first uttered in small groups, then written on coloured slips of paper or large sheets posted on walls, and finally turned into electronic documents. These promise-making events were temporally ordered in such a way that some promises could be scaled up. First, 156 municipal meetings were held, then representatives from each municipality came together in a series of regional events facilitated again by a Pact team member to establish inter-municipal and regional pacts. At this level, institutions could combine resources to fulfil each other's promises and address larger initiatives such as the construction of water treatment plants or solid waste management systems. Finally, representatives from each municipality

Illustration 2.1. Exhibiting promises on index cards during one of the Pact workshops.

and regional Pact attended a state-wide meeting where macro-pacts were produced, following the same promise-making methods.

The results of these meetings were all systematized into documents that were also called Pacts. The longest document was the state-wide Pact with 408 pages and a 25-page annex that recorded the names of participants, their institutions and the events they attended. By the end of the four-year process, each municipality, alliance of municipalities, watershed and the state as a whole would have their own Pact while being embedded in the Pact of the next scale up.

The purpose of this nested structure was to affirm the moral import of each scale and appreciate its complexity in its own terms, and not from the perspective of a centralized observer. The Pact was not organized to provide a God's eye view from nowhere (Haraway 2004) to oversee the complexity of all water issues across the state, and neither was it susceptible to the surveillance of a panopticon (Foucault 1975) that might police people's fidelity to their promises. The Pact's aggregate structure was, instead, capable of encompassing contradictory flows because it did not presume the need for cohesiveness across scales. This rationale allowed Pact participants to retain their connection to their context, to exist in their own specificity and complexity, without having to fold themselves under an all-encompassing banner as they would if the Pact had been about membership and participation in a more clearly defined entity – a committee, an association, a public institution, a governmental agency. Instead of visualizing a single techno-political future, the Pact relied on each pledge, the handshakes that sealed each promise and the personal care people put into them, to unleash people's apparently inherent capacity to care for water.

Distilling promises into words

Promises, while always touching upon intimate fibres, can take multiple forms. Angela Garcia (2014), for instance, has shown how promises express 'a much larger fabric of moral engagement, including the conflicting responsibilities and punishing demands' that being available to others can impinge upon us. At a less intimate level, and thinking about the future-oriented task of planning as a public activity, Simone Abram and Gisa Weszkalnys argue that governmental planning and policy plans are promises that seem to always be 'slightly out of reach, the ideal outcome always slightly elusive' (2011: 3).

The promises at the core of the Pact were somewhere between these two forms. They were elusive because their future-oriented effects are impossible to fully verify either in the present or at every scale at once. But, at the same time, they were intimate since originally they were all embodied utterances. Each promise emerged as a person-specific pledge, putting the emphasis on the body of the public servant rather than on the state as an abstract entity. But that intimate dimension disappeared as the promises were written down and documented. They changed form as they moved across scales in the Pact-making process.

The Pact methodology was designed to ask participants at the municipal, regional, watershed and state levels to make their own promises. Most participants, however, were involved at only one, or at most two of these scales. A few participants, given their political and technical standing, participated in Pact-making rituals across multiple scales. The promises also had diverse lives. In some cases, a particular promise travelled throughout different meetings at different scales. For the most part, however, the promises had uni-scalar lives; that is, if made at the municipal level or the watershed level, the promises stayed there. But in either case, whether a promise travelled across scales or stayed tied to a particular scale, the Pact-making methodology entailed at its very core a process of distillation. As the utterance of a promise was transformed into an exhibitable, movable unit (in the form of a coloured slip of paper) and ultimately transcribed into an electronic document, the wording of a pledge changed, its form converted.

At all Pact meetings, regardless of their scale, group work was fundamental. Once personal introductions were over and general instructions had been provided, subgroups of people sat together to speak about promises, aspirations, desires. These subgroups were mini-cosmologies where status, class, gender and history played out with all of their historical overdetermining power. Large landowners or municipal leaders spoke authoritatively; lower-level public servants and NGOs offered more tempered statements. A few strong women were able to become main characters; younger ones were relegated to secretarial tasks. In a few cases, subversions took place whereby farmers became outspoken and church NGOs challenged the reasons municipal workers provided for not offering to do much. In all cases, however, after some discussion people wrote down their commitments, making them fit onto the slips of paper they were instructed to use. The material limits of the slips, their size, combined with the instruction that only one promise could be inscribed in each slip, resulted in short, declarative statements such as the following:

- I can make sure that we include environmental education programmes in our Municipality.
- I will fight to get the resources to expand the water channel the municipality has been planning to build for three years.
- I will lobby my fellow health workers at the regional health directorate to start talking about water conservation with patients.
- I will hurry up the training programme we have on the books to share information about more efficient irrigation technologies with farmers.

This first moment of inscription was a qualitative distillation of the content of the promises. The richness of the group discussion was concentrated into a short statement. The slips of paper holding the statements were immediately exhibited on the wall, or laid out on the table if the group was small enough. In many cases, the promises ended their procedural life there. They were directly transcribed and remained as part of the local Pact-making exercise.

If the promises entailed actions that touched upon larger scales (watershed, or even the state as a whole), they continued their life. In order to make the particular promises from the group travel forward in the process, the statements had to be 'systematized'. Systematization consisted of entering each promise into a Word document that the consultants had previously populated with tables asking what scale the promise belonged to (municipal, regional, state-wide), who the promise maker was, and what other institutions could be invited to support its implementation. That task entailed another distillation of the promises into a new format. Throughout those conversions, what originally were textured, place- and person-specific commitments became generic statements in policy language, invoking ongoing public programmes and policies, and highlighting the institutions and organizations people worked for. Thus, what were highly specific statements became general declarations that looked like this:

- Attend the meetings at Solonópole, Potiretama and Iracema [names of small cities], along with representatives of EMATERCE [another governmental agency], and provide the necessary water-related information to allow them to make informed decisions. By: Almeida (Head of the Water Management Company).
- Conduct pedagogical workshops in public schools and the broader education community about the adequate use of water, 21 events, led by pedagogical coordinator of each school. By: Municipal Education Secretariat.
- Train agricultural engineers, foresters, agricultural technicians and rural training managers on organic agriculture, alternative plague management, 184 events, one per municipality. By: Agriculture Secretariat.

In this documentation process, the evidence of the intimacy of the promise, the 'I' in the statement, was gradually shaved off. The promise was distilled so that it could easily travel across policy-making and administrative scales and institutions. The promises were not necessarily made more abstract. If you only took into consideration the published Pact documents, it could seem that way – but bear in mind that each municipality and watershed had its own Pact, with its own documentation, that sometimes included only the collection of the slips of paper, or a binder where a print-out of individual pledges was kept.

The Pact organizers, the consulting team, did not have any way to follow up, monitor or evaluate these promises. And that was precisely what they hoped for. The idea of the Pact was that each scale would have promises made and documented in the form that seemed appropriate to each scale. State-wide documents would have policy-friendly language and would look like formal publications; municipal pacts would keep a more specific language and would have a more flexible publication form.

Capacity to intervene: describing the aggregate

Marilyn Strathern (2014: 23–24) has noted that, in welfare bureaucracies, 'interventions in the world of affairs rest on describing what is happening … description itself is an intervention'. Inspired by the legacies of welfare democracies, the Pact's capacity to intervene also depends on its descriptions of itself. Because of its aggregate form, the Pact describes itself through the promises of which it is made, rather than through a unified narrative of a future vision or a policy prescription. First uttered, then documented on slips of paper, then in Microsoft Word tables, and finally printed in documents, its descriptive form is not narrative but the form of the list. The final Pact documents are, in a way, nothing more than rolling lists associating aspirations with responsibilities. They are 'distillations of the maps of activity, accumulation, sociability, enterprise [and] aspiration that motivate action in the widest sense' (Philips 2012: 96). The lists of promises in the Pact condense thick histories and imaginaries of futurity – while mediating both through the promise, as a special form of description.

The Pact's reliance on lists as a form of description is due, in part, to the quality of the promiseas an utterance that is unquestionable across scales. The promise made at the municipal level is presumed appropriate to its context, and hence not subject to evaluation from the point of view of another scale (e.g. the watershed or the state), so an expanded narrative to explain its adequacy is unnecessary. The promise is a descriptive intervention that can only be evaluated at the scale of its production: only those who made it can assess it. Presumably, promise makers need no narrative description of something they already know. For that reason, each listed promise is valued, and shielded, by way of its context specificity. The effect of this valuation of context is that the documentation of the Pact is taken as intrinsically legitimate and, in a sense, keeps each promise sealed from critique unless that critique comes from the same people making the promise, or others with similar links to a particular context. This is a form of contextual legitimacy that Pact-makers believe builds capacity to care in a way that other political forms cannot. The commitment to that legitimacy requires organizers to work through flexible aggregation and not through narrative unity. To be sure, this makes the Pact precarious, dependent on the intimacy of the utterance for any enforceability. And yet that precariousness is also its potential strength. A promise kept, as anthropologists have shown, has the power to enliven and deepen social relations and forms of collective dependence (Mauss 1967). This contradictory potential, which resides very much in its form, is what characterizes the Pact as a different kind of intervention.

A visual form of aggregation

One of the claims to power of the Pact is that it brought together more than eight thousand participants. Yet its potential rests less on quantity than on how the promises of those eight thousand participants were aggregated. What makes the Pact interesting is that its form has the capacity to make a promise scalable and, at the same time, allow it to remain faithful to its particular scale and context specificities. If there is any potential in the Pact, it is tied to the rich and multi-scalar lives the promises can have. These promises are neither intimate ethical obligations to care for one another of the sort that Angela Garcia describes, nor completely elusive promises that fly away from any personal sense of responsibility as Abram and Weszkalnys note. The Pact promises are more than empty statements, but less than deep affective pledges to surrender to others. Their social significance is in their collectivity, their coming together as a gathering made up of place- and scale-specific social relations: a construction that is enacted as people follow a set of instructions, make verbal promises, write them on pieces of paper, come together to see them exhibited on walls, receive electronic documents with their transcription, come together again for more meetings at different scales, remind each other of the coffee they had together at the only local pact meeting they attended, or of the memorable joke that somebody told that day.

If the methodological logic that guides the Pact relies on the identification of promises that can be grouped and selectively gathered, it is not a logic of coarse accumulation that aims to add parts until they can complete a whole. The aggregate of the Pact is not an aggregate of individuals, it is a gathering of water-related promises. But, as we saw, each promise goes through a process of distillation, even transformation. These two logics – the logic of aggregation as a summation of individual entities, and the logic of aggregation as a gathering following a particular set of instructions – can be visualized when comparing two images. One is a classic in political theory, the other is closer to algorithmic and mathematic forms of aggregation.

This first image relies on images of addition to achieve unity. This peculiar sense is illustrated in the work of Thomas Hobbes, specifically his *Leviathan, or The Matter, Forme, and Power of a Commonwealth Ecclesiasticall and Civill* ([1651] 1991). In this image, we can see how the political aggregate is an all-encompassing whole where the liberal individual is subsumed under the state as a single, unified entity. In the illustration (Illustration 2.2), Leviathan is composed of the sum of whole units, the whole bodies of its subjects. For Leviathan, its constitutive elements are self-evident. The body of the subject is a familiar singularity that suggests her submission, in all of her facets, under the larger body of the ruler. Leviathan is also a clear bounded entity recognizable as a singularity. Yet this political imaginary of the aggregate as encompassing the whole subject is just one of its many possible renderings.

Another image that does not presume the need to incorporate whole and self-evident units has been visualized by Andy Lomas, a digital artist working on images of mathematical and philosophical aggregation (see Illustration 3.3). Unlike Leviathan's image, the details of Lomas's images do not offer their constitutive forms easily. The form of the aggregate is not readily available for recognition; its overall traits are not self-evident. In this photograph, it is difficult to see any uniformity, forcing us to take

Illustration 2.2. Detail of Leviathan's illustration.

one step back and ask, at a more abstract level, what quality might be shared among the units in the image so that they can be aggregated. Aggregation necessitates the identification of a shared parameter that makes it methodologically possible rather than operating as a smooth summation into singularity.

In Lomas's work, the property selected as the criterion for aggregation grants a set of elements their temporary gathering. The aggregate is only possible if we know what criteria are used to bring elements together, despite our uncertainty about what those elements are. Even if the methodological steps are predetermined, its ultimate contents are not. Even if we know slips of paper are the first form the promises take, their specific intentions – hurrying up a programme, convincing others to teach environmental education, lobbying for a water treatment plant – are not self-evident. This type of aggregate is solid and precarious at once; it is a gathering of many, yet not quite a stable single collectivity. The grouping is only possible because of the constant reaffirmation of the selection parameters that make it possible. The moment our attention shifts from those selection criteria, the possibility of perceiving the aggregate disappears in front of our very eyes.

The Pact resembles Lomas's images more than Hobbes' Leviathan. Its power to augment political capacity is believed to lie in its selectivity, in its capacity to collect and activate a peculiar moral commitment to water without aspiring for its participants to identify holistically with the Pact, much less requiring any form of membership from them. But in order to make that aggregation possible, there is a criterion that needs to be met. A promise needs to be inscribed onto a slip of paper; it is that initial distillation into a declarative statement that allows for the flexible bringing together of promises that share nothing in common content-wise. The Pact's promise of increasing society's capacity to care depends on the possibility of aggregating the form of promises as something that yields collective power to act. It also depends on the exclusion of

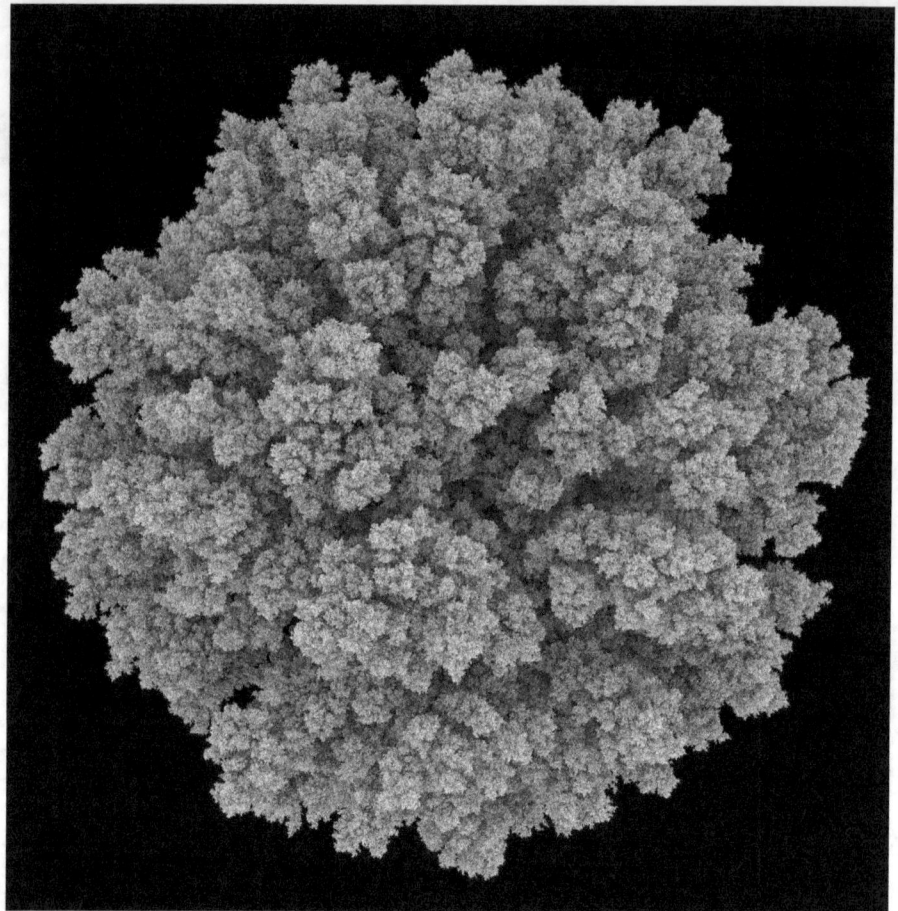

Illustration 3.3. Andy Lomas, Aggregation series. http://www.andylomas.com/.

those commitments that do not abide by that form. That capacity to selectively and temporarily aggregate is its promise.

Conclusion

The designers and organizers of the Pact launched the initiative with the expectation that they could break with history. In a sense, their efforts were designed to breed the untimely (Grosz 2004) or to create a future that could yield a different arrangement of social and material forces to secure access to water. Their innovation, as they understand it, is to ask Pact participants for a type of commitment, a promise to care, that is not totalizing and does not require their full allegiance or membership. The Pact can enrol their promises to care for water without requiring their transformation into subjects subsumed under it.

This peculiar form promises to highlight contradiction as a symbol of the adequacy of the effort. If the promises people make across different scales seem not to fit together and sometimes contradict each other, the purpose of maintaining the specificity of context would have been achieved. Thus, context specificity and the contradictions derived from it at different scales make the Pact a collective that can never be glossed as a unit. The conveners of the Pact see it as a social formation that is open to multiplicity rather than a mechanism for transforming differences into commonalities. This is a political form that promises to yield a type of political affect that is somewhere between intimate and elusive: a gathering predicated upon the possibility of mobilizing 'society', even if that possibility is unenforceable and unverifiable. This is the politicization of care as a bureaucratically decentralized form of human-material ordering. Here, care for water as a form of politics only survives if imagined at different scalar levels and for each social actor in her own particularity.

In Ceará, the launching of this political form required a quantitative aesthetics that privileges aggregation as a method of gathering people's capacity to care. The aggregate is a political form conceived to break with a more conventional political history. It is an intervention built upon the description of its units, a structure of promises for the proliferation of care without a God's eye view from which to verify its fruition. The Pact is a precarious and powerful form of making quantity work for quality, blurring the boundaries between them and creating a form of 'capacity' that cannot be fully domesticated: the capacity to care for the everyday sustenance of life within one's own surroundings or context. This capacity might yield a different water landscape and a more democratic future, but no guarantees are offered.

Acknowledgements

I would like to thank Brit Ross Winthereik, Annelise Riles and Robert Werth for their comments, which helped clarify this chapter. Thanks are due to Rachel Douglas-Jones and Justin Shaffner for inviting me to the join the 'Hope and Insufficiency: Capacity Building in Ethnographic Comparison' workshop and to all participants for their thought-provoking conversations. And lastly, my deep gratitude to all my Brazilian colleagues and friends for sharing their thinking, ambitions and doubts with me as they sought to produce a more democratic water world. Research for this chapter was funded by the National Science Foundation and the Wenner-Gren Foundation.

Andrea Ballestero is Associate Professor of Anthropology at Rice University founder and director of the Ethnography Studio, https://ethnographystudio.org/. Since 2002 she has conducted research in Costa Rica, Brazil, and elsewhere researching how societies define, distribute, and value water. She is currently researching cultural imaginaries of the underground in Costa Rica, particularly of aquifers, to understand how the social world is expanding downwards. Recent publications include *A Future History of Water* (Duke University Press, 2019 and open access) and *Touching with Light* (Science, Technology and Human Values, 2019). Her publications can be found at https://andreaballestero.com/.

Notes

1. Paul Rabinow (2009) defines the contemporary as a moment in which the past is recuperated as a problem space to imagine a new future. The contemporary is characterized by the problematization of concerns that were taken as settled up until recently. That uncertainty makes the contemporary a moment of social emergence rather than of social reproduction.
2. For two different ways of engaging with quantitative forms as qualitatively rich entities, see Verran 2001 and Ballestero 2015.

References

Abram, S. and G. Weszkalnys. 2011. 'Anthropologies of Planning: Temporality, Imagination, and Ethnography'. *Focaal* 61: 3–18.

Aiyer, A. 2007. 'The Allure of the Transnational: Notes on Some Aspects of the Political Economy of Water in India'. *Cultural Anthropology* 22 (4): 640–658. doi:10.1525/can.2007.22.4.640.

Anand, N. 2011. 'Pressure: The PoliTechnics of Water Supply in Mumbai'. *Cultural Anthropology* 26 (4): 542–564. doi:10.1111/j.1548-1360.2011.01111.x.

Anderson, B. 1991. *Imagined Communities: Reflections on the Origins and Spread of Nationalism*. London: Verso.

Anderson, C. W. 2011. 'What Aggregators Do: Rhetoric, Practices and Cultures of Digital and Analog Evidence in Web-Era Journalism'. Paper read at the 12th International Symposium for Online Journalism, Austin.

Arons, N. G. 2004. *Waiting for Rain: The Politics and Poetry of Drought in Northeast Brazil*. Tucson: University of Arizona Press.

Assembleia Legislativa do Estado do Ceará, and Conselho de Altos Estudos e Assuntos Estratégicos. 2009. 'Plano Estratégico dos Recursos Hídricos do Ceará'. Ceará: Fortaleza.

Bakker, K. 2010. 'A Political Ecology of Water Privatization'. *Studies in Political Economy* 70: 35–58.

Ballestero, A. 2012. 'Transparency Short-Circuited: Laughter and Numbers in Costa Rican Water Politics'. *PoLAR: Political and Legal Anthropology Review* 35 (2): 223–241.

Ballestero, A. 2015. 'The Ethics of a Formula: Calculating a Financial-Humanitarian Price for Water'. *American Ethnologist* 42 (1): 262–278.

Barnes, J. 2014. *Cultivating the Nile: The Everyday Politics of Water in Egypt*. Durham, NC: Duke University Press.

Barth, F. 1998. *Ethnic Groups and Boundaries: The Social Organization of Culture Difference*. Boston, MA: Little Press.

Bhabha, H. K. 1994. *The Location of Culture*. London: Routledge.

Borchardt, W. G., J. S. Dailey and P. F. Nunes. 2011. 'New Paths to Growth: The Age of Aggregation'. *Outlook: The Journal of High-Performance Business Issue 3*: 19–27.

Caprara, A., J. Wellington de Oliveira Lima, A. Correia Pequeno Marinho, P. Gondim Calvasina, L. Paes Landim and J. Sommerfeld. 2009. 'Irregular Water Supply, Household Usage and Dengue: A Bio-social Study in the Brazilian Northeast'. *Cadernos de Saúde Pública* 25 (1): S125–S136.

Carse, A. 2012. 'Nature as Infrastructure: Making and Managing the Panama Canal Watershed'. *Social Studies of Science* 42 (4): 539–563.

Coddington, M. A. 2015. 'Telling Secondhand Stories: News Aggregation and the Production of Journalistic Knowledge'. Ph.D. diss., University of Texas at Austin.

Collier, S. J. and A. Ong. 2005. 'Global Assemblages, Anthropological Problems'. In A. Ong and S. J. Collier (eds), *Global Assemblages: Technology, Politics, and Ethics as Anthropological Problems*. Malden: Blackwell, 3–21.
do Amaral Filho, J. 2003. 'Reformas Estruturais e Economia Politica dos Recursos Hidricos no Ceara'. Fortaleza, CE: SEPLAN-IPECE.
Finan, T. J. and D. R. Nelson. 2001. 'Making Rain, Making Roads, Making Do: Public and Private Adaptations to Drought in Ceará, Northeast Brazil'. *Climate Research* 19 (2): 97–108.
Foucault, M. 1975. *Discipline and Punish: The Birth of the Prison*. New York: Vintage Books.
Garcia, A. 2014. 'The Promise: On the Morality of the Marginal and the Illicit'. *Ethos* 42 (1): 51–64.
Gennep, A. van. 1960. *The Rites of Passage. 1909*, trans. M. B. Vizedom and G.L. Caffee. Chicago: University of Chicago Press.
Grosz, E. 2004. *The Nick of Time: Politics, Evolution, and the Untimely*. Durham, NC: Duke University Press.
Guyer, J. I. 1999. 'Anthropology: The Study of Social and Cultural Originality'. *African Sociological Review/Revue Africaine de Sociologie* 3 (2): 30–53.
Haraway, D. 2004. 'Modest_Witness@Second_Millenium'. In D. Haraway (ed.), *The Haraway Reader*. New York: Routledge, 223–250.
Hardt, M. and A. Negri. 2005. *Multitude: War and Democracy in the Age of Empire*. New York: Penguin.
Hayden, C. 2003. *When Nature Goes Public: The Making and Unmaking of Bioprospecting in Mexico*. Princeton: Princeton University Press.
Hobbes, T. [1651] 1991. *Leviathan*. Cambridge: Cambridge University Press.
Juris, J. S. 2012. 'Reflections on #Occupy Everywhere: Social Media, Public Space, and Emerging Logics of Aggregation'. *American Ethnologist* 39 (2): 259–279.
Latour, B. 2005. *Reassembling the Social: An Introduction to Actor-Network Theory, Clarendon Lectures in Management Studies*. Oxford: Oxford University Press.
Lemos, M. C. 2003. 'A Tale of Two Policies: The Politics of Climate Forecasting and Drought Relief in Ceara, Brazil'. *Policy Sciences* 36: 101–123.
Malinowski, B. [1926] 1966. *Crime and Custom in Savage Society*. London: Routledge.
Mauss, M. 1967. *The Gift*. New York: W. W. Norton.
Miyazaki, H. 2004. *The Method of Hope*. Stanford: Stanford University Press.
Morita, A. 2016. 'Infrastructuring Amphibious Space: The Interplay of Aquatic and Terrestrial Infrastructures in the Chao Phraya Delta in Thailand'. *Science as Culture* 25 (1): 117–140.
Mosse, D. 2003. *The Rule of Water: Statecraft, Ecology and Collective Action in South India*. Oxford: Oxford University Press.
Nelson, D. R. and T. J. Finan. 2009. 'Praying for Drought: Persistent Vulnerability and the Politics of Patronage in Ceará, Northeast Brazil'. *American Anthropologist* 111 (3): 302–316.
Philips, A. 2012. 'List'. In C. Lury and N. Wakeford (eds), *Inventive Methods: The Happening of the Social*. London: Routledge, 96–109.
Rabinow, P. 2009. *Marking Time: On the Anthropology of the Contemporary*. Princeton: Princeton University Press.
Ruppert, E. 2012. 'The Governmental Topologies of Database Devices'. *Theory, Culture & Society* 29 (4–5): 116–136. doi:10.1177/0263276412439428.
Simpson, L. D. 2003. 'Integrated Water Resources Management, Ceara, Brazil'. Washington, DC: World Bank.
Strathern, M. 1996. 'Cutting the Network'. *Journal of the Royal Anthropological Institute* N.S. (2): 517–535.

Strathern, M. 2014. 'Anthropological Reasoning: Some Threads of Thought'. *HAU: Journal of Ethnographic Theory* 4 (3): 23–37.
Turner, V. 1995. *The Ritual Process: Structure and Anti-Structure*. New York: Aldine de Gruyter.
Verran, H. 2001. *Science and African Logic*. Chicago: University of Chicago Press.
von Schnitzler, A. 2016. *Democracy's Infrastructure: Techno-Politics and Protest after Apartheid*. Princeton, NJ: Princeton University Press.
West, P. 2006. *Conservation Is Our Government Now: The Politics of Ecology in Papua New Guinea*. Durham, NC: Duke University Press.

Chapter 3

Building Capacity in Ethical Review
Compliance and Transformation in the Asia-Pacific Region

Rachel Douglas-Jones

> Development organizations have begun to realise the difficulty
> of keeping standards for things and those for people apart.
> —Busch, *Standards: Recipes for Reality*

Whether a clinical trial occurs in New York or in Bangkok, it has come to be expected that the people ('human subjects') participating in the testing of drugs or medical devices are protected by standards of research ethics (Petryna 2005). Prompted by the turn-of-the-century increases in multi-sited and 'collaborative' clinical trials, as the 2000s got underway, the term 'capacity building' began to enter research ethics practice and vocabularies. With trial data originating outside the EU flowing towards European drug regulators, the European Group on Ethics declared that 'fundamental ethical rules applied to clinical trials in industrialized countries must be applicable elsewhere', and in order to implement these 'fundamental ethical rules' as well as ensure their observation during the conduct of research, capacity building of 'local committees in host countries' was to be considered a priority (Bosch 2003: 579). Bosch's call, in the British medical journal *The Lancet*, was one of many around that time. In the USA in 2000, the Fogarty International Center of the National Institutes of Health (NIH) began funding programmes that accepted trainees from the Asia-Pacific region 'as part of its wider commitment to strengthen research ethics capacity globally' (Pratt et al. 2014: 68).

Early efforts were captured by Eckstein's 2004 overview of fresh capacity building initiatives, which listed 'new websites, listservs, workshops and diplomas, several Masters courses and research ethics fellowships' (Eckstein 2004) emerging around the world as part of a growing ecology of training programmes, networks and strategic initiatives. At the time, she wrote that the 'top down' approach of providing ethics training could be seen as 'inappropriate': such was the emergent nature of the game that building a 'critical mass' was seen as necessary before 'local' centres could be sustainable (Singer 2004). Five years later, as my doctoral research began in Sri Lanka, the environment had changed (Simpson et al. 2010). More recent documents had asserted the need for 'local' ethics committees in stronger language: 'A clinical trial should not take place in a country in the absence of a review by an Ethics Committee in that country', declared the European Medicines Authority (EMA 2012: 17). If no such committee existed, the EMA recommended that 'it should be established as a pre-requisite before the trial takes place' (2012: 17). This shift has been described as 'two-ended ethical review' (Simpson 2012: 148). Furthermore, international journals had begun to require the 'local' review of all multi-sited research, thus placing a barrier on the publication of unreviewed, or unapproved, research. Formalizing ethical review in this way created what medical sociologist Dingwall called an 'export route for the IRB[1] model': 'Most leading research countries, and many lesser ones ... installed such systems in order to maintain their access to the international scientific community' (Dingwall 2007: 788).

My research, a multi-sited study conducted between 2009 and 2011, focused on the establishment and capacity building of ethical review in the Asia-Pacific region. The organization with whom I worked anticipated and moved with these developments, planning for the need for training that would accompany them. In the early 2000s, the Strategic Initiative for Developing Capacity in Ethical Review (SIDCER) emerged through the support of the World Health Organisation's Tropical Disease Research (WHO-TDR) arm and the Program for Appropriate Technology in Health (PATH). Its primary aim was

> fostering independent in-country decision-making regarding the ethics of health research by establishing an international network for promoting mutual understanding on issues affecting the dignity of research subjects and their communities. (SIDCER 2003)

Its breadth was large, encompassing a 'global network of independently established regional fora for ECs/IRBs [Ethics Committees / Institutional Review Boards]' (Chokevivat 2011: 3) made up of five regional chapters, covering Eastern Europe (FECCIS), Africa (PABIN), South and Central America (FLACEIS), North America

(FOCUS) and the Asia-Pacific (FERCAP).[2] Between 2009 and 2011, I worked with this final chapter, FERCAP, following their operations across the region in Sri Lanka, Thailand, the Philippines, Taiwan and mainland China, meeting delegates from Japan, Bhutan, India and South Korea at events along the way. My role within the organization, with the permission of the coordinators and committees, was primarily one of observation and participation in trainings. As time passed, I was also occasionally asked to assist in facilitating workshops, resulting in doubled fieldnotes – notes on my notes. Of the above-mentioned regional chapters, the Forum for Ethical Review Committees in the Asian and Western Pacific Region (FERCAP hereafter) has been by far the most successful, in part due to the work of a dedicated network coordinator and good SIDCER and WHO-TDR networks in the Asia-Pacific region. Their conferences and trainings are well attended, and they have to date 'recognized' the work of over two hundred ethics review committees in the Asia-Pacific region (FERCAP 2015; see also Douglas-Jones 2015). FERCAP uses initiatives and procedures established by its 'parent' organization, SIDCER, which describes contributing to 'human subjects protections globally by developing capacity building in ethical review and the ethics of health research' as its primary objective. SIDCER's mission is to 'not only help ... build in-country human subjects protection programs, but [also be] a way to measure and provide accountability for the quality and effectiveness of ethical review worldwide' (Karbwang-Laothavorn 2011: 11, see also SIDCER 2005).

This chapter aims to capture some of the tensions in implementing SIDCER's goal to assure 'accountability and effectiveness' of ethical review through 'building capacity'. I explore two distinct forms that the idea of capacity in ethics takes, such that it can be said to be built. The first concerns measurability: to assure accountability and effectiveness, committees need to submit themselves to review. This they have done voluntarily, under the 'Recognition Program' I describe below. Drawing on ethnographic work within teams taking part in the programme, known among participants as 'The Survey', I demonstrate the centrality of compliance, and the way committees position their work in international frames. The second form of capacity building, with a nod to the epigraph, concerns how committee members and trainees are invited to grow their own 'capacity' in ethics. In this second version of capacity building, it is not documents, offices or operating procedures that are the measure of a successful outcome, but committee members and researchers who, it is hoped, will behave differently, and who can give an account of their own transformation. To understand this split between capacity for ethics taking the form of measurable compliance, and it inhering within the newfound attitudes of practitioners, we need to grasp a tension central to the work of the organization. It stems from the non-governmental organization (NGO)'s dual desire to standardize practices in research ethics such that they may be internationally acceptable – demonstrably compliant – and to ensure that their work proceeds with 'respect for cultural, regional and national differences'. The latter phrase comes from the second of SIDCER's three missions, where the objective to 'ensure the quality and effectiveness of ethics review worldwide' is put alongside 'understanding and respect for cultural, regional and national differences' (SIDCER 2003). Through the 'local' of two-ended ethical review – the demand that a 'local' committee review research – there is a recognition that while the bodies of 'elsewhere' may become (or can be imagined as) part of the assemblages of international medical research, the social worlds may not. Indeed, FERCAP exists as a regional organization, building 'local' capacity, precisely because of the principle that such differences in social worlds and ethical norms exist. In the tension that emerges between standardizing practices and localizing ethics, what will count as capacity in ethical review, and by whose measure? How will distinctions be drawn between practices it is both acceptable and desirable to see standardized, and those that embody the kind of 'difference' that must be respected?

These questions are pertinent to a comparative examination of forms of contemporary capacity building, pushing towards questions of the extent to which capacities are defined and measured, and which capacities are seen as transformable. They also prompt us to examine more closely how ethics and capacity become intertwined. I thus attempt to capture one further dimension of capacity building in this chapter, which pertains to its specific intersection with the idea of ethics. In my ethnographic work, ethics and capacity have emerged with certain shared characteristics. Both concepts possess what Miyazaki (2005, 2012) has called 'extensibility': they can be materialized or internalized, pinned and measured or beyond reach, strategically enacted and contemplated as life lessons. Doing ethics in this setting can, at one moment, be the systematic filling of forms, and at another, seem to demand serious deliberation over what it would be right to do when lives may be at risk. Through this extensibility, ethics can move from trainings and workshops into the lives of participants; indeed, some trainings take this to be a marker of high success. Miyazaki, in his work on Japanese high finance, observes that 'extensibility of the gift observed ethnographically has itself afforded the analytical category of the gift distinctive extensibility of its own' (2013: 42). He uses this observed extensibility of the gift-as-category to think about the way high finance concepts, such as arbitrage, have an extensibility of their own, crossing from professional domains into personal, and back. In this chapter, I keep the extensibility of ethics in view as I trace the manifestations of capacity in ethics being built. This is more than saying there is little to which 'ethics' or 'capacity' do not apply. The concrete practices and procedures falling under the heading of capacity building are not self-evident. The interviews, observations and trainings I undertook as fieldwork all follow in the footsteps of Molyneux and Geissler's call that ethnography be enrolled to lend critical depth to these self-justifying developments in what capacity in ethics is taken to be (2008: 693). Just as ethnographic work is therefore required to theorize the manifold workings of 'ethics' at this contemporary juncture, so too can that approach be called upon for understanding the work of 'capacity building'.

What is capacity building in research ethics?

At their first General Assembly at Thammasat University, Thailand on 11–12 January 2000, the Forum for Ethical Review Committees in the Asian and Western Pacific Region (FERCAP) established itself as a network for researchers concerned with improving the protection of human subjects in Asia-Pacific clinical trials. A core founding member who served as network chair for ten years recalled in 2010 that at their first meeting, the group noted that working with government will be very difficult and very slow because of too much red tape. So instead of working with government, we chose to start from scratch and create our own organization starting with the participants of the seminar. (Chokevivat 2011: 7)

To undertake the urgent task of protecting human subjects in clinical trials, the participants of the seminar began building a training and recognition programme, ensuring committees met certain standards. From the participants of the seminar, their rapid growth in membership is documented through archived web pages, as increasing numbers of committees across the Asian region were set up and participated in trainings over the ensuing decade. Drawing together a core of regional expertise and vigorous international networking, their 'grass roots' work also formed a critique of earlier forms of 'capacity building' such as those which Deborah Eade, a longstanding development commentator, called a 'serious-sounding alternative to "training"' (Eade 2010: 205). 'Capacity building', Eade suggested, was rapidly adopted during the 1990s since 'no NGO could admit to funding one-off training workshops whose impact may be short lived, or that risk serving mainly as social events' (2010: 205). This dissatisfaction with 'short termism' was active within the field as I joined it. The American bioethics professor Nancy Kass had stated that 'short workshops cannot effect a sustained impact on their own', and that capacity building initiatives required 'sustained local presence'. In her view, it was both 'impractical and inappropriate for that role to be served by a transient professional from the outside' (Kass, cited in Eckstein 2004). Kass, like others, was arguing that short-term training reinforced existing disparities (Wagner et al. 2001; see also Ulrich 2011; Shrum 2005).

FERCAP therefore took care to differentiate themselves from this burgeoning field of 'one off' or overseas capacity building training courses. Networking within the region ensured continuity year upon year as the organization grew. However, they also differentiated the content of their capacity building from many of the trainings on offer (Eckstein 2004; Pratt et al. 2014). Tomas, a clinical researcher from the Philippines whom I interviewed in 2010, had taken part in trainings by bioethics organizations. As we talked, he commented on the style of reasoning he had observed in encounters with bioethics organizations: 'In the moral dilemma approach, when something is resolved, they introduce another factor so another dilemma emerges. But research ethics needs to be solution oriented'. His example was the preparation of a curriculum that had been drawn up for a collaborative course between the University of the Philippines, Manila, and the Fogarty International Center on Bioethics:

> There was a lot of discussion. [Fogarty] wanted a course on 'moral dilemmas' and they said it was a 'skills' course! Doctors in the course said, 'This is a never-ending discussion!' Suppose someone is run over by a car. Who is responsible? The driver. Suppose the pedestrian is drunk? Well, both. But say the driver … And you keep adding to the issue. It goes on and on. The medical doctors, they said, 'There is no resolution to the issue!' That was the 'skill' they learnt. It is a very different approach.

An approach 'without resolution' did not sit well with committee members,[3] who felt the capacity they needed to be learning was how to decide what research to allow and what to reject. As my interviewees repeatedly remarked, committees must make decisions. Indeed, being able to arrive at a decision – which must also be evidenced (Douglas-Jones 2012; see also Stark 2012) – is as much a part of 'capacity' in research ethics as learning about prior cases and principles. Rather than just taking participants through modes of thinking, in the view of the forum's coordinator, FERCAP's trainings have

> made it possible to operationalize the basic ethics principles of autonomy, beneficence, and justice in the review of health research and translate them into tools, such as checklists and assessment forms to assist the EC/IRB members in reviewing protocols, consent forms, and related documents. (Torres 2011: 49)

This 'operationalizing' today takes place during FERCAP's core activity: implementing the SIDCER Recognition Program. Known colloquially as 'The Survey', the review took place over four days, hosted by the committee under scrutiny. A survey team, made up of a lead surveyor and two or three others – usually two 'international' and two 'local' in total – would work with local trainees to examine the workings of the committee seeking recognition. Surveyors worked through the 'self-assessment form' filled in by the committee prior to inviting the surveyors, and examined a wide range of documentation, from standard operating procedures to approved and rejected protocols, meeting agendas and minutes, membership and staff files. Surveyors also observed a 'full-board' committee meeting, visited the offices of the committee and interviewed key members of the committee. All members of the survey team put in long hours, working to achieve a collective sense of how the committee under review worked, and provide evidence. Recognition was based on five standards: (1) the structure and composition of the committee; (2) adherence to managerial and operational policies 'for optimal and systematic conduct of ethical review'; (3) the completeness of the review process, including timeliness; (4) the after-review process, whereby decisions are communicated to investigators; and (5) documentation and archiving. Assessment was structured around an evaluation of the quality attained by the committee in relation to each of these standards; during the survey, attaining these standards is what 'capacity' looks like. Successful committees receive an engraved crystal trophy and certificate documenting their achievement, specifically their

> compliance with the International Conference on Harmonisation (ICH) Guidelines, Good Clinical Practice (GCP) Standards, Declaration of Helsinki, Council for International Organizations of Medical Sciences (CIOMS) Guidelines, World Health Organisation (WHO) Operational Guidelines for Ethics Committees that Review Biomedical Research, EC/IRB Standard Operating Procedures (SOPs) and Local Regulations and Standards in Ethical Review.[4]

It becomes of interest, then, how the committees are held to these standards, and where they originated. In 2005, during a meeting in Olympia, Washington, USA, a working group that included directors of quality assurance, internal auditors, quality assurance analysts and directors of regulatory affairs convened, in order to arrive at a means of determining whether committees were 'up to standard'. The result was the SIDCER Recognition Program, which took the range of declarations and guidelines listed above and turned them into the five focus areas of the survey: a way of operationalizing and measuring the enactment of these standards.

Committees undertake the intensive recognition process for a range of reasons (Douglas-Jones 2015). In some respects, FERCAP surveys are regarded as a precursor to hosting international research, and it is often hoped that this recognition will attract research to the host institution. During a pitch to a committee considering taking part, the coordinator of the FERCAP network, Cristina, commented:

> [The survey] has an impact on an entire research team. You can put the name on your website. I receive queries from sponsors who ask us if we've visited this EC and if we have recognized them. Sponsors like assurance that [an] EC is doing their job. That's how we do our work. Sponsors would like to have some assurance that the EC is GCP compliant. If it's not, it becomes GCP deviation, a violation, therefore they want to make sure that's adequately addressed. So the Recognition Program becomes important to sponsors as well. So we call it SIDCER Recognition Program. We're part of this global network.

In Cristina's pitch, certification would demonstrate 'compliance' to onlookers at home and abroad. During questions following the pitch above, a committee member asked whether participation in the survey would lead to recognition through the United States Food and Drug Administration (USFDA). Gently differentiating between the USFDA's inspection and FERCAP's recognition, Cristina commented that FERCAP would support the committee in having a 'working system', and contribute towards passing any inspection that might come about. But it also demonstrates, as a delighted Cai Dong-Hu and Chen Yann-Jang of Taipei City Hospital noted in their online announcement of their committee's successful recognition in 2011, 'a strong ambition to participate in the global economy' (Dong-Hu and Yann-Jang 2011). 'International certification', they wrote on the Taipei City Hospital's website, 'will encourage domestic and international clinical trials research institutes to carry out clinical trials in the hospital' (ibid.). Cristina's description, and Taipei City Hospital's declaration, begin to draw out the international arena in which committees experience their work. We have learned that the programme set itself apart from government schemes, to avoid 'red tape'. Here we see the way in which recognition both invites and indicates participation in an increasingly internationalized field of biomedical research.

Capacity, roles and compliance

As drug regulators increasingly include requirements for ethics review committees in the new infrastructures of how biomedical knowledge is made, trainings for committees attempt to ensure that their members understand their role and place in a wider 'ecosystem' of bodies and actors. PowerPoint slides during training workshops invariably included a (usually three circle) Venn diagram of overlapping areas of responsibility. As my time in the field lengthened, I began keeping a collection of these varying Venn diagrams, each of which positioned ethical review slightly differently. Ethics committees might sit alongside legal regimes, or be encompassed by them. They might be the first line of 'national defence', overlapping only with 'the pharmaceutical industry' or with opportunities for international collaboration. They might link up with drug regulators and the behaviour of doctors. Events where these PowerPoint slides were displayed usually took place in liberally air conditioned university and hospital meeting rooms, around tables furnished with bottled water, fruits and snacks. It was during a collaborative FERCAP-WHO training session at Thammasat University that I addressed the idea of capacity building directly with FERCAP's coordinator, Cristina. Trained in philosophy and social science, Cristina had been working with FERCAP for more than five years at the time of my research. Her skill in selecting and encouraging volunteer surveyors and inspiring trainees at workshops meant that under her leadership the network was rapidly growing. When I asked her at lunchtime about what capacity building was, she replied:

> Capacity building? It's getting people to do their thing correctly. Doing what is expected of them. [Learning] what they need to ask, how to review a [biomedical research] protocol. It's being able to fulfil your role. Capacity is always specific to a role. You have to define, like each person has his role in society. You cannot be good for all [things], you do a specific role.

Having set myself the task of exploring capacity building and its specific manifestations within FERCAP, I want to take a moment to unpick what is being said here, since it took me somewhat by surprise at the time. One might imagine that, through exposure to the Venn diagram version of 'doing ethics', I was well prepared to see ethical review as a role – either done correctly or not – within a system of other elements. However, what troubled me was that I had also come to understand FERCAP's work as founded on making space for the idea of 'local difference', as described in SIDCER's mission documents. From the 'role'-based language, and reference to expectation, I wondered how far 'difference' could be stretched. In the quote above, Cristina compares having a capacity in ethical review to having a societal role. The metaphor is made thinkable by a pre-existing model of society that relies on a 'mathematic ... that sees the world as inherently divided into units' (Strathern 1996: 50), transferring to a system of global research divided into units of responsibility. It is how these units translate to roles in which one may demonstrate greater or lesser capacity that interests me in the two vignettes I move to now. A sense of doing one's 'thing correctly' is part of participating in FERCAP's survey programme, oriented at creating accountability for what is 'expected'.

The survey is a means of checking on the checking process of ethical review, something I have elsewhere called 'second order audit' (Douglas-Jones 2015). In a similar way, capacity in ethical review is regarded by some institutions as a means by which other capacities can be built, namely attracting internationally funded research necessitating 'recruitment of personnel ... the formation of ethical review committees: setting up hospital sites; the establishment of monitoring procedures; and the assembly of rooms, computers and other technology' (Simpson and Sariola 2012: 559). As Simpson and Sariola, who have researched the growth of clinical trial activity in Sri Lanka, remark, 'without this capacity, the benefits of future economic, intellectual and social capital will not flow' (2012: 559). Furthering this chapter's interest in the specific intersection of ethics and capacity, then, what can be said of ethics when – once one can demonstrate capacity – it is international guests one hopes to attract?

I attended a training on Good Clinical Practice (GCP) at the University of Manila in 2010, on a hot April day during which a legal scholar from the university was presenting on the theme of conflict of interest (for further discussion, see Douglas-Jones 2012). In order to be compliant with GCP, explained the legal scholar, participants needed to understand what conflicts of interest were so that they could avoid them. After running us through some of the circumstances in clinical and commercial research in which conflicts of interest might occur, the lecturer closed his presentation with a quote from the British philosopher Bertrand Russell: 'Ethics is in origin the art of recommending to others the sacrifices required for cooperation with oneself' (Russell [1917] 1981: 82). Though the lecture had come to an end without explicit discussion of this closing thought, a woman a few rows from me in the hall who had worked as a clinical coordinator pushed him to comment. 'I was thinking', she said, 'how to interpret it?' The lecturer leaned against the lectern, looking down. 'Um, well the way I see it we are all aware of ethical principles', he began. He continued:

> And it really requires a lot of sacrifices. But there is a need for an external body to be able to tell us if what we're doing is ethical or not. Because of the presence of the possibility of conflicts of interest. That's my thought on that. We know that there are sacrifices that we have to undergo when we are involved in ethics but it has to be recommended by others, or to others. I don't know if that's what Bertrand Russell meant, but… [trails off]

'But why would you consider it a sacrifice to comply?' asked another audience member. 'No', he said, 'it's not a sacrifice to comply, it's a sacrifice of removing your interests in whatever study you do'.

The quote the lecturer chose is, in one reading, a Russell quip. It can be read as a laconic reflection on the selfishness of ethics, of teaching to others the sacrifices they must make so they can work with you, given your principles, your 'ethics'. In this interpretation, 'ethics' is the demand of one party upon another. But in the extract from my field notes, the lecturer's explanation carries quite another spin. From his position, one does not make demands on others so they can work with oneself; rather, one is asked to make sacrifices on the request of an external body. This shift of subject position in the reading of the Russell quote is revealing. It neatly reflects the positions of host and sponsor countries in research. As many researchers are very aware, in order to undertake research sponsored by the National Institutes of Health in the USA, the site, investigators and IRB must conform to American specifications. The export of these regulations is exactly – and non-ironically – the requirement of the former interpretation: you must do these things so we can come to your country. A researcher I interviewed in Sri Lanka had been involved with a research project with Duke University in the USA. He made the some perceptive, and revealing, comments on the course he followed in preparation for the project:

> For their IRB, before being researchers we had to follow a course. They sent us the teaching material, [we] read, they asked us questions, we had to mark the correct answers and submit. … What they really want is for us to be educated. They don't want to find out how good I am, they want to educate me on research. I thought that was very good, because before we embarked we knew what is good and [what is] wrong. So we would not

make the same mistakes. [We] would tarnish whatever institution we were collaborating with, if we didn't know.

The researcher's comments above about avoiding 'tarnishing' a collaborating institution by taking training add to the sacrificial spin of the lecturer's interpretation of Russell. Put together, the two comments illustrate how, in collaborating with institutions overseas to do research, ideas about capacity and standards merge: will research bring 'capacity' or should certain capacities be in place already? And where does ethics register – as a 'lack' that might 'tarnish', a form of compliance that needs to be demonstrated (Sariola and Simpson n.d.)? As noted above, FERCAP works in a wide range of settings across Asia, from settings where research provides opportunities for development, to highly technologically motivated 'Medical Cities' where local research is intense and access to publication venues essential. In countries where attracting biomedical collaborations primarily meant the opportunity for research capacity building, committees walked a fine line between facilitating international research and the danger of inviting collaborations that did not present good terms for local participants or researchers (Simpson et al. 2010). Here, the collision of ethics with capacity building gains tension. Growing the capacity in ethics to attract capacity building research – and the 'economic, intellectual and social capital' (Simpson and Sariola 2012: 559) that comes with it – meant ensuring one understood one's given role, one's place in the Venn diagram, the 'correct answers'. This model of capacity potentially puts committees in a position of compliance, where the capacity being built, one could argue, is simply a capacity to comply with pre-defined 'international' standards. Indeed, this is a critique that has been levelled at ethical review in Singapore, a country that, while highly active in international biomedical research, does not and has not participated in FERCAP's activities. Sociologists Holden and Demeritt, who have studied Singapore's high-paced, international research environment (2008), write, for example, of their bafflement at the application of ethical guidelines in the Singaporean setting. 'The mapping of ICH guidelines onto Singaporean society', they write 'defies the very logic of those guidelines', as they found little exploration of the meaning or implication of terms: 'as long as the consent forms are signed and the paper trail is clear, there should be no qualms about what it all means' (2008: 82; for discussion, see Ong 2016).

However, as Deborah Eade, who has worked closely with the idea of capacity building, puts it, 'if capacity building means anything, it is surely about enabling those out on the margins to represent and defend their interests more effectively, not only within their own immediate contexts but also globally' (Eade 2010: 203). Learning to defend the interest of their country and research subjects may be precisely what is intended by involving developing countries in the SIDCER Recognition Program – giving committees the tools with which to assess and decide whether to host research projects originating abroad. But in the 'operationalizing' model of ethics, where committees are assessed by internationally defined standards, do ethics – or decisions – based on values not already defined in the Declaration of Helsinki, or Good Clinical Practice, amount to 'deviation'? Thinking back to Cristina's role-based definition of capacity, how far may one step out of one's 'role', or indeed redefine it?

Capacity and transformation

Where in the previous section capacity in research ethics has had a specific, almost quantifiable character, compatible with measurement and achieved through compliance, I now move to describe the organization's parallel but contrasting reading of building capacity in ethics as transformation. Transformation is often seen as central to building initiatives, presented by the United Nations Development Program (UNDP) as an 'essential ingredient' (2009: 5; see also Hewlett this issue).

In what follows, I analyse parts of capacity building work where ethics capacity is not procedures or protocols, but a form of understanding. The ethnography comes from FERCAP's trainings in ethical review and I have elsewhere used elements of these accounts to illustrate the ways in which professional and audit cultures stand in tension (Douglas-Jones 2015) and where belief in ethics is seen as necessary for the preservation of trust in science (Douglas-Jones 2012). The first example concerns the importance for trainers that participants 'see' ethics, that they come to understand ethics for themselves. In contrast with developing the capacity to perform a role, 'seeing' ethics focuses on a transition in comprehension, a hoped-for interiorization (see also Ellison this issue). The second explores the limit participants themselves perceive in ethics in its standard-like form. Here, I regard these stories through the lens of capacity, to examine how what 'ethics' is shifts from something that one does to an attribute of something one becomes. In this changed emphasis, what it means to demonstrate 'capacity' must also change.

In June 2010, prior to the survey of a local committee in Shanghai, I joined a two-day FERCAP strategic planning session in the meeting rooms of Huashan Hospital, a large teaching hospital affiliated with Fundan University. In addition to discussing upcoming meetings and the work of running an international network, attendees at the planning session were debating the 'attitudes' of trainers and trainees at recent workshops. 'A lot of people can't relate to research ethics', complained one trainer, who observed that a large volume of additional 'trainings' for professionals had led to disengagement with a workshop format. 'Participants need to change their attitude', said another, who had conducted trainings in China for several years, 'so we get better atmosphere at trainings'. Her fellow trainers disagreed: 'We cannot ask them to change their mindset, we let them join us. It's a process. So it's the trainer that has to be convinced'. Ensuring that training participants became 'motivated', the group agreed, was the job of trainers: 'We cannot expect trainees to eagerly want training!'. The desired transformation was discussed as a 'paradigm shift' and 'crossing a line'. A trainer sitting opposite me explained by way of a cycling analogy: 'Do you ride a bicycle?' she asked. I nodded.

> You can ride a bicycle now, but before you could, why [was it] so hard? Do you remember that first time? That moment, the first time you ride the bike, you remember. That's why I try to find examples, what does it mean, when you can't do it, you can't do it, you can't do it, then you suddenly can do [it]. Take that moment.

Some trainings were thought to produce this effect more than others. Cristina, who had been following our conversation, warned the others present not to expect the participants to reach this understanding immediately. 'I've done many trainings', she said. She continued:

> At the beginning, it is true, they don't care. Then they start to listen. It's one of the most transformative. In the beginning, they don't care, then they hear about people being exploited. You see them change, from the baseline with the end. You don't get it with [other trainings] on Standard Operating Procedures, the survey, but this one, I see people really changed. They see different things. This one is not about the knowledge, more about motivating them. That is your duty [as trainers].

FERCAP trainings are thus not merely targeted at making students realize their own ignorance and prompting them to overcome it through learning about the histories and practices which make up research ethics. Rather, the aim is a transformation. Participants at such training events openly discussed the effects that engagement with the organization had on them. At the opening of a surveyor's training, Mark, a Taiwanese surveyor, described how FERCAP had helped him 'see' ethics in these terms:

> Well, before 2005, I [was] just like you, some of you. I sat in the audience for the first time when Cristina came to Taipei to give a symposium on Standard Operating Procedures. I was not an IRB member in that moment, so I had no idea, though I knew what it [ethics] was.

Having set up the 'before' condition, Mark continued:

> Then I had a chance to learn a lot. We had the opportunity to visit Western IRB [in Olympia, Washington] for six months.[5] And after that Cristina gave us a lot of chances to visit other IRBs, a kind of field trip. So we learned from the book then we learned from reality.

The testimonial-style narration of Mark's transition from mere audience member to active participant makes 'ethics' into a condition, quality or state that one can achieve. An anaesthetist by profession, Mark had joined the IRB after some of FERCAP's training sessions, and subsequently became heavily involved as a surveyor, leading one or two surveys outside his home country of Taiwan each year. He is regularly invited to share his experience, his account illustrating the way in which it is hoped 'ethics' will capture those who study it, perhaps even making the standards that are implemented through the surveys secondary to the integrity of the researchers.[6] Returning to Miyazaki's discussions of extensibility, we might say that it is hoped that ethics – like arbitrage in Miyazaki's work – will extend out of the work-based environments in which trainees first discover it, and into their lives. In Mark's case, becoming a professional in research ethics was possible alongside his anaesthesiology practice. If seeing arbitrage requires taking on the double vision that shows it both as an individual action and a market action (Miyazaki 2013: 44), then 'seeing ethics' is the individual action to a much larger, systematized, role-based action.

Interviewing committee members who had undertaken the training and become members of FERCAP's active surveying pool, I found recurring references to the importance of taking ethics as more than a set of procedures, standards or bureaucratic formalities. During a lunch break on a GCP course at Chulalongkorn University, Bangkok, in April 2010, I was talking to Cathy, a committee member from Bangkok, about the presentations we had seen that morning. My head was full of the changes that were taking place institutionally to accommodate international standards for research, and some of the difficulties experienced in implementing rules and regulations. Cathy nodded along as I marvelled at how 'doing ethics' involved so much institutional labour. During a pause, she pointed out something she thought I hadn't quite grasped. 'There is one thing you haven't mentioned', she said:

> The integrity of the researcher. No rule can write it all, to cover every aspect and every speech of the doctor to the patient. Only the integrity of the doctor, and that will control good or bad science and research. Regulators cannot do what integrity and the culture of a faculty can do.

It was this institutional 'culture' that Cathy hoped would be passed between members in her institution by the trainings we were attending that day:

> When you are a young employee, and you haven't come to an ethical issues course, you don't know much. Still, if someone told you 'This is the rule', even if you don't know yet you will not avoid a rule or do something against it or behind the backs of others. So first you recognize that it is a rule. Then someone says there are ethical issues, and if someone has good integrity, to be a good doctor, they will go to the course. And start to understand it. That's when they start to understand 'ethical'; you become ethical not just in your rules but in your life and your mind.

What Cathy makes very clear is that she perceives no rule that could govern the social interaction she sees as constituting that which ethics seeks to govern. The 'rules' she describes are laid out for ethics committees and for the survey; they are also laid out for doctors and patients. More is hoped for in this enculturation than rule following; in my focus on standardization I had – for Cathy – missed the point. 'Regulators cannot do what integrity and the culture of a faculty can do', she said, 'people need to want to be good'. Her reaction to the standardization we were learning about in our GCP sessions was to root action in the staff, not in the 'rules'.

In trainings on GCP, human subject protection and standard operating procedures, then, learning to see ethics – to really understand – is felt to lie beyond the training itself: it requires an extension of these ideas into the lives of those who will serve on ethics review committees. As responses to capacity building in research ethics begin to be published in the countries where FERCAP works, the centrality of education alone is questioned. Sri Lankan bioethics advocate Sumathipala pushes for education, but not just a change in how much is known:

> By creating awareness among the research community, this ignorance [about ethics] can be defeated. This can be done by guiding researchers to do quality research because they believe in the ethical framework: you should promote ethics because ethics produces good research and you should become an ethical researcher because you believe in it and not because somebody has started to police you. (2006: S78)

Moving from how much is known to how it is known, shifting from biomedical ethics as measurable to 'ethical researchers', is one response to the calls for capacity building with which this chapter began. As such, there is a normativity of another kind around ethics, as attractive to FERCAP members as the promise of a 'recognized' committee. Indeed, it sits in an interesting tension with recognition, since as one conference delegate put it, 'Ethics is not definable, not implementable because it is not conscious. It involves not only our thinking but also our feeling'. In this second version, committees and their procedures are secondary to capacity building efforts that focus on the researchers whose research is governed by them.

Conclusions

When capacity building in research ethics is viewed from the vantage point of the European Group on Ethics or the US-NIH, there arise a series of standards with which it is hoped 'local' committees will comply. The sponsors of trials – when selecting sites – have an interest in ensuring the data will be admissible by drug regulators. Researchers they approach also have an interest in ensuring they have an acceptable local committee; without one, they might not be able to attract or carry out international research. When FERCAP inverts this sponsor-oriented view to focus on 'grass roots' capacity across Asia, it attempts to give voice and tools to those who might wish to attract – or deflect – international projects. The means by which they have sought to build capacity has been to merge the audit-like measurement of standard keeping with the close networking culture of the Recognition Program, where, through the meeting of friends and colleagues, a mutual investment grows in documenting and improving the performance, quality and efficiency of one another's committees. With its focus on operationalizing, the Recognition Program does not seek to question either the standards themselves or the decisions made by committees. Instead, it audits, measures, codifies and checks the processes. Providing evidence that an ethics review meets 'international' standards is the focus of the survey; providing evidence for the efficacy of ethics review on conduct in clinical research in general is another concern (McDonald and Cox 2009). We can of course observe that the work required to render a committee visible to an interrogative external system required further kinds of capacities: the survey draws on a rich range of administrative, procedural, operational and documentational skills. In coming to resemble the system in which they are given a 'role', committees became subject to expectations in both form and content. Here, compliance becomes a function of capacity, a measure that capacity has been built.

The second focus made evident in the pitch and tone of FERCAP trainings is the changed practitioners. As the epigraph noted, there is considerable difficulty in 'keeping standards for things and those for people apart' (Busch 2011: 26). FERCAP's objective is not merely to measure, reorder and record; trainers seek to transform participants by developing their capacity to 'see' ethics. In the second section of this chapter, I have shown the eloquence with which many involved in capacity building dispute that their understanding of – or capacity in – ethics could take documented, fixed, auditable form. A particularly memorable rebuke of the idea came from a Sri Lankan interviewee, a neuroscientist who had served on his hospital's ethics review committee for five years. He scoffed at the idea that ethics could be standardized or measured: 'It's like saying someone is beautiful ... How can you prove you are right?' Where in the first sections of this chapter I showed how standards of evidence are applied to capacity in ethics, seeking proof that 'ethics' – the committees and their procedures – are working, the 'ethics' discussed in the latter sections does not lend itself to such methods of evidencing. If ethics is viewed as a set of measurable processes, then it can be proven. Likewise, if capacity is regarded as a set of standards, these can be met.

These two versions of ethics coexist within FERCAP as a capacity building organization, each – with its distinct target – modifying what ethics looks like when it is viewed as a capacity. Capacity in ethics comes to be both an achievement – a self-formation – and the performance of an externally defined role. Instead of taking this 'elusiveness' as a frustration to definitional work, we can see how blurriness at the contours of a concept provides 'the conditions of possibility' for 'extensibility' (Miyazaki 2013: 42). That is, to study capacity building in research ethics is to find two sets of terms that both extend beyond their first domains of use, allowing participants and trainers alike to shift between the capacity to conform and the capacity to transform, and throughout, create a form of capacity building that holds these contrasting modes together.

Acknowledgements

The research from which this chapter draws was funded by the UK's ESRC under grant number RES-062-23-0215 and the International Science and Bioethics Collaboration, where Bob Simpson was the initial impetus behind a critical approach to capacity building. My thanks to Alberto Corsín Jiménez and Sue Wright, whose comments at the 2011 AAA conference inspired the development of these ideas to become the Wenner-Gren workshop in Copenhagen, 2015. I thank the participants of both the panel and the workshop, and the two anonymous reviewers, whose suggestions helped clarify my arguments.

Rachel Douglas-Jones is Associate Professor at the IT University of Copenhagen, where she is Head of the Technologies in Practice research group and co-directs the ETHOS Lab. She conducts research on questions of ethics and the governance of science and technology, and is currently the PI of *Moving Data, Moving People*, a study of emergent social credit systems in China through the lens of trust. Her recent publications include 'Committee as Witness' (The Cambridge Journal of Anthropology, 2021) and 'Bodies of Data' (JRAI 2021). She is the editor (with Antonia Walford and Nick Seaver) of *Towards an Anthropology of Data* (JRAI, 2021).

Notes

1. In the United States, committees that assess the ethics of research proposals are known as Institutional Review Boards (IRBs). In most of the countries where I worked, these committees are known as ethics review committees, or more simply, ethics committees. I retain this last usage, since it most accurately reflects how these bodies are described in Asia, but North American readers should be aware that many of the committees are in institutions such as universities and hospitals, which in the USA would result in them being termed IRBs.
2. The regional fora's full names are: Pan-African Bioethics Initiative (PABIN), Forum for Ethics Committees in the Confederation of Independent States (FECCIS), Foro Latino Americano de Comites de Etica en Investigacion en Salud [Latin American Forum of Ethics Committees in Health Research] (FLACEIS) and the Forum for Institutional Review Boards [IRBs]/Ethics Review Boards [ERBs] in Canada and the United States (FOCUS) and the Forum for Ethical Review Committees in the Asian and Western Pacific Region (FERCAP).
3. It should be noted that this was not, according to Fogarty, what was intended by the training course. For further detail and an evaluation of the programme, see Pratt et al. 2014.
4. Text printed on the crystal trophy and certificate awarded when a committee is recognized.
5. In 2003, SIDCER worked with Western IRB (Olympia, USA) to establish a Fellows programme, the aim of which has been to 'better understand ethics in different settings and to enhance the capacity of individuals from different countries to develop and apply ethical principles and practices when reviewing health research' (Karbwang-Laothavorn 2011: 14).
6. For future-oriented dreams, and a discussion of the resurgence of researcher integrity, see Douglas-Jones 2013.

References

Bosch, X. 2003. 'Improve Trials in Poor Nations, Say EC's Ethics Advisers'. *The Lancet* 361: 579.
Busch, L. 2011. *Standards: Recipes for Reality*. Cambridge, MA: MIT Press.
Chokevivat, V. 2011. 'The FERCAP Story: A Decade of Fruitful Collaboration with Partners in Ethical Health Research'. In C. E. Torres and A. M. Navarro (eds), *FERCAP @ 10: In Commemoration of a Decade of Capacity Building in Ethical Health Research in the Asia-Pacific Region*. Pathumthani: Forum for Ethical Review Committees in the Asian and Western Pacific Region, 6–10.
Dingwall, R. 2007. 'Turn off the Oxygen...' *Law & Society Review* 41 (4): 787–795.
Dong-Hu, C. and C. Yann-Jang. 2011. 'World-Class Medical Assurance Milestone: Taipei City Hospital Certified by FERCAP'. Taipei City Hospital Bulletin. http://english.tch.gov.taipei/ct.asp?xItem=13431960&ctNode=9923&mp=109012.
Douglas-Jones, R. 2012. 'A Single Broken Thread: Integrity, Trust and Accountability in Asian Ethics Review Committees'. *Durham Anthropology Journal* 18 (2): 13–27.
Douglas-Jones, R. 2013. 'Locating Ethics: Capacity Building, Ethics Review and Research Governance across Asia'. Ph.D. diss., Durham University.
Douglas-Jones, R. 2015. 'A "Good" Ethical Review: Audit and Professionalism in Research Ethics'. *Social Anthropology* 23 (1): 53–67.
Eade, D. 2010. 'Capacity Building: Who Builds Whose Capacity?' In A. Cornwall and D. Eade (eds), *Deconstructing Development Discourse: Buzzwords and Fuzzwords*. Rugby, UK: Practical Action Publishing, 203–214.
Eckstein, S. 2004. 'Efforts to Build Capacity in Research Ethics: An Overview'. Science and Development Network Policy Briefs, Middle East and North Africa. http://www.scidev.net/en/middle-east-and-north-africa/policy-briefs/efforts-to-build-capacity-in-research-ethics-an-ov.html.

European Medicines Agency (EMA). 2012. 'Reflection Paper on Ethical and GCP Aspects of Clinical Trials of Medicinal Products for Human Use Conducted outside of the EU/EEA and Submitted in Marketing Authorisation Applications to the EU Regulatory Authorities'. EMA/121340/2011.

FERCAP (Forum for Ethical Review Committees in the Asian and Western Pacific Region. 2015. 'Recognised EC/IRB'. http://www.fercap-sidcer.org/recognized.php.

Holden, K. and D. Demeritt. 2008. 'Democratising Science? The Politics of Promoting Biomedicine in Singapore's Developmental State'. *Environment and Planning D: Society and Space* 26: 68–86.

Karbwang-Laothavorn, J. 2011. 'SIDCER @ 10'. In C. E. Torres and A. M. Navarro (eds), *FERCAP @ 10: In Commemoration of a Decade of Capacity Building in Ethical Health Research in the Asia-Pacific Region*. Pathumthani: Forum for Ethical Review Committees in the Asian and Western Pacific Region, 11–16.

McDonald, M. and S. Cox. 2009. 'Moving Toward Evidence-Based Human Participant Protection'. *Journal of Academic Ethics* 7 (1–2): 1–16.

Miyazaki, H. 2005. 'From Sugar Cane to "Swords": Hope and the Extensibility of the Gift in Fiji'. *Journal of the Royal Anthropological Institute* (N.S.) 11: 277–295.

Miyazaki, H. 2012. *Arbitraging Japan: Dreams of Capitalism at the End of Finance*. Berkeley: University of California Press.

Miyazaki, H. 2013. 'The Gift in Finance'. *Natureculture* 2: 38–49.

Molyneux, S. and W. P. Geissler. 2008. 'Ethics and the Ethnography of Medical Research in Africa'. *Social Science & Medicine* 67 (5): 685–695. http://dx.doi.org/10.1016/j.socscimed.2008.02.023.

Ong, A. 2016. *Fungible Life: Experiment in the Asian City of Life*. Durham, NC: Duke University Press.

Petryna, A. 2005. 'Ethical Variability: Drug Development and Globalising Clinical Trials'. *American Ethnologist* 32 (2): 183–197. doi:10.1525/ae.2005.32.2.183.

Pratt, B., C. Van, E. Trevorrow and B. Loff. 2014. 'Fogarty Research Ethics Training Programs in the Asia-Pacific: The Merging of Cultures'. *Journal of Empirical Research on Human Research Ethics* 9 (2): 68–79.

Russell, B. [1917] 1981. *Mysticism and Logic and Other Essays*. Totowa, NJ: Barnes and Noble.

Sariola, S. and B. Simpson. n.d. 'Research as Development: Biomedical Research, Ethics and Collaboration in Sri Lanka'. Unpublished.

Shrum, W. 2005. 'Reagency of the Internet, or, How I Became a Guest for Science'. *Social Studies of Science* 35 (5): S723–754. http://dx.doi.org/10.1177/0306312705052106.

SIDCER (Strategic Initiative for Developing Capacity in Ethical Review). 2003. 'Policy on Funding and Conflict of Interest v. 2.1'. http://www.who.int/sidcer/about/funding_conflict/en/.

SIDCER (Strategic Initiative for Developing Capacity in Ethical Review). 2005. 'Promoting and Protecting the Health of the People'. Geneva: World Health Organisation Special Programme for Research and Training in Tropical Diseases (WHO-TDR) and SIDCER.

Simpson, B. 2012. 'Building Capacity: A Sri Lankan Perspective on Research, Ethics and Accountability'. In M. Konrad (ed.), *Collaborators Collaborating: Counterparts in Anthropological Knowledge and International Research Relations*. Oxford: Berghahn Books, 147–163.

Simpson, B., R. Douglas-Jones, S. Sariola and V. H. W. Dissanayake. 2010. 'Ethical Review, Remit and Responsibility in Biomedical Research in South Asia'. *Indian Journal of Medical Ethics* 7 (2):113–114.

Simpson, B. and S. Sariola. 2012. 'Blinding Authority: Randomized Clinical Trials and the Production of Global Scientific Knowledge in Contemporary Sri Lanka'. *Science, Technology and Human Values* 37: 555–575. http://dx.doi.org/10.1177/0162243911432648.

Singer, P. 2004. 'University of Toronto MHSc in Bioethics International Stream'. NIH Grant application. Unpublished.

Stark, L. 2012. *Behind Closed Doors: IRBs and the Making of Ethical Research*. Chicago: University of Chicago. Kindle edition.

Strathern, M. 1996. 'For the Motion (1) The Concept of Society is Theoretically Obsolete'. In T. Ingold (ed.), *Key Debates in Anthropology*. London: Routledge, 50–66.

Sumathipala, A. 2006. 'Bioethics in Sri Lanka'. *Eastern Mediterranean Health Journal* 12 (S1): S73–79.

Torres, C. E. 2011. 'Reflections on the FERCAP Experience: Moving Forward with Partnerships and Networks'. In C. E. Torres and A. M. Navarro (eds), *FERCAP@10: In Commemoration of a Decade of Capacity Building in Ethical Health Research in the Asia-Pacific Region*. Pathumthani: Forum for Ethical Review Committees in the Asian and Western Pacific Region, 43–53.

Ulrich, G. 2011. 'Elucidating Ethics in Practice: Focus on Accountability'. In W. P. Geissler and C. Molyneux (eds), *Evidence, Ethos and Experiment: The Anthropology and History of Medical Research*. Oxford: Berghahn Books, 145–170.

UNDP (United Nations Development Programme). 2009. *Capacity Development: A UNDP Primer*. New York: UNDP.

Wagner, C. S., I. Brahmakulam, B. Jackson, A. Wong and T. Yoda. 2001. 'Science and Technology Collaboration: Building Capacity in Developing Countries?' Paper prepared for the World Bank. Santa Monica, CA: RAND Science and Technology. http://www.rand.org/publications/MR/MR1357.0/.

Chapter 4

Corrective Capacities
From Unruly Politics to Democratic *Capacitación*

Susan Ellison

The Bolivian non-governmental organization (NGO) JUNTOS[1] is holding a public *conversatorio* or model dialogue during the annual La Paz, Bolivia book fair. School children race around the stands, laughing and lunging at each other while staff members from JUNTOS instruct others on a puzzle meant to teach cooperation skills and group problem solving. The event is part of JUNTOS's ongoing 'Culture of Peace' campaign, financed by a variety of European aid agencies. The campaign advocates – as many foreign-funded programmes now do – instilling participants with skill-sets, values and communicative practices that encourage tolerance and peaceful conflict resolution.

Invited speakers sit in an inner circle on an elevated platform, while spectators form an outer ring. Over the din of the book fair, organizers play an opening song about the value of cultural pluralism and open-mindedness meant to inspire discussion. The Master of Ceremonies invites us to observe how participants will be modelling a dialogue on diversity, demonstrating the importance of listening and learning to speak one's opinion respectfully while reflecting on the themes from that song. He tells the crowd, 'These skills are useful for addressing both fights in your home, and fights in your neighbourhood as well'. In that brief comment, the Master of Ceremonies summarizes a notion that has guided many recent foreign aid interventions into conflicts in Bolivia: that training individuals in conflict resolution skill-sets will be transferable to larger-scale social conflict. The underlying – and frequently unstated – assumption is that this transfer will help promote greater economic and political stability.

Over the next hour, participants take turns sharing their thoughts about diversity. Most fall back on vague platitudes about the richness of diversity and unity amid difference. They are, almost universally, positive expressions: diversity is good, is beautiful, makes us stronger. That is, all are positive until we reach Julieta Paredes.[2] Paredes is a well-known Indigenous Aymara feminist activist and the only person to explicitly criticize the exercise when given her chance to speak. Julieta sits forward and tells the crowd, 'Look, it's a nice desire, it's well intentioned. But reality isn't like that. We aren't the same, however much we want to be'. She goes on to comment on the hidden economic inequalities that surround everyone observing the model dialogue. 'Some [Aymara women] came here with ten *pesitos* in their pockets to spend on a book', Julieta continues, 'while others can buy as many as they like. If we can't deepen the discussion on these issues, we just end up singing about pretty, superficial things'. As the session ends, I approach Julieta, who smiles wryly. 'How boring was *that*?' she laughs. 'A lot of pretty talk?' I ask. Julieta shakes her head. 'It's like throwing water on something when really we should just burn it all down.'

In this chapter, I argue that *conversatorios* like the one above are representative of a broader shift in donor objectives and platforms operating in Bolivia. It is a shift from a donor concern for 'capacity building' aimed at bolstering state institutions to *capacitación* or skill-set training and values-promotion that aims to transform how Bolivians, and in particular poor, working class and ethnically marked Bolivians, manage conflict in both their interpersonal lives and social organizations. This shift in governance strategies invites a kind of *reason*ablization to accompany the 'responsibilization' often associated with neoliberal reforms.[3] Critiques of neoliberalism have highlighted it as a project that devolves responsibility for citizens' wellbeing from the state to 'empowered' individuals produced through techniques of audit and self-surveillance (Brenner et al. 2010; Shore and Wright 2011). My interest here is in the effort to *moderate* how 'empowered' subjects make political claims. Such conflict resolution programmes explicitly seek to reorient participants towards deliberative democratic means of expressing dissent, and to encourage citizens to adopt negotiation tactics and other habits of conflict resolution into their intimate lives, social organizations and political activism. *Reason*ablization shifts donor priorities from repairing institutions – long the focus of good governance 'capacity building' and even neoliberal reforms – to correcting political cultures, locating inequality's persistence in what critics deem destabilizing and combative political subjectivities and tactics. Yet just as neoliberal logics of 'responsibilization' exist alongside other competing demands for moral personhood and social responsibility (Trnka and Trundle 2014), so, too, projects of 'reasonablization' encounter competing claims of legitimate political 'capacities'.

In Bolivia, foreign-funded conflict resolution programmes have positioned their efforts against the widespread and more confrontational organizing tactics of the country's 'militant' and 'conflictual' trade and neighbourhood associations, social movements and rural peasant unions. These organizations frequently rely on the spatial disruption of urban centres and regional roads to achieve their political goals. Critics characterize these 'unruly' forms of politics as antithetical to the common good and democratic stability, alternately decrying them as self-defeating, overly sectorial or even authoritarian. Anthropologists and historians, too, have pointed to Bolivia's 'culture of rebellion and political turmoil' (McNeish 2008: 92). Yet union members and social movement leaders frequently defend their tactics as necessary to achieve social justice in the context of enduring forms of social and political exclusion, particularly inequalities affecting the country's Indigenous majority (Ellison 2015). John-Andrew McNeish has argued that another way of interpreting these recurring political conflicts is not as a sign of state 'failure', as analysts fear, but rather of Bolivia's 'high-intensity democracy', driven by 'the democratic desires of its largely marginalized populations to put an end to exclusion through various forms of insurgency' (2008: 92).

If Bolivian citizens frequently engage in forms of political 'insurgency', making incursions through disruptive tactics, as McNeish has argued,[4] the *capacitación* programmes I examine here pursue the moderation or 'reasonablization' of political subjects as an antidote to chronic political upheaval. In particular, foreign donors and Bolivian NGOs have held workshops aiming to counteract combative politics through various techniques of conflict analysis, negotiation and transformation cobbled together from Alternative Dispute Resolution (ADR or third party mediation), deliberative democracy and 'culture of peace' paradigms. As Muhlberger (2011) has shown, there are a number of affinities (and rivalries) between theories of ADR and deliberative democracy. However, the distinctive philosophical genealogies of these fields were not neatly drawn in practice, as donor representatives and NGO staff spoke broadly about promoting methods that would enable cooperation towards 'mutually acceptable' solutions to disputes and facilitate conflict transformation – and indeed social transformation – in the country.

Workshops targeting 'micro-level' *interpersonal* and social communication anticipate that such conflict resolution skills will 'scale up' to the level of political disputes. As such, interpersonal practices of conflict 'transformation' become a mechanism for thwarting socio-political conflict frequently expressed in Bolivia through the collective tactics of siege, street protest and strikes. In so doing, programmes offering *capacitación* in conflict resolution identify both a *lack* and a kind of threatening *capacity* within the Bolivian population. That is, aid programmes replace capacity building targeting perceived *weaknesses* within public institutions with trainings aimed at addressing both perceived weaknesses and *pathological strengths* that inhere in Bolivian citizens – and in particular, poor and ethnically marked Indigenous Bolivians. That 'conflictual' capacity is housed in both social organizations and the personhood of Bolivians who have been influenced by their involvement in trade unions, neighbourhood associations and other corporatist organizations that have shaped (and in the eyes of critics, deformed) their political behaviour. The 'lack' these programmes identify is that of effectual conflict management skills – capacities donors characterize as fundamental to building both stable homes and a stable democracy.

Here, I consider two interrelated concepts. The first is *capacitación* as a particular mode of 'capacity building' targeting Bolivians for transformed interpersonal relations and political subjectivity. The second is the *conversatorio*, which I present as the quintessential space of *capacitación* towards those ends.

First, I understand *capacitación*, often translated from the Spanish as 'training', to reflect a practical understanding of instruction that targets individuals and groups for information sharing, guidance and habit formation or skill development around a variety of topics. But here I also use *capacitación* as a conceptual marker of shifting donor priorities. I do not mean to suggest that something called *capacitación* (in the first sense of the term) was not an integral part of previous aid interventions. Indeed, during the 1990s many aid platforms sought to equip judges, legislators and bureaucrats with knowledge and technical skills that, donors believed, would enable them to enact the kinds of institutional reform that many good governance and democracy assistance programmes sought to promote. Additionally, the introduction of Bolivia's Law of Popular Participation (LPP, described below) entailed many NGO projects *capacitando* (training) people in how to make claims on state resources through these new institutional channels. However, in utilizing the term *capacitación* analytically, I want to underscore the ever-greater emphasis on the *person* and the *interpersonal* as the locus of political transformation rather than the agents or institutions of the state – whether national, regional or municipal.

Second, *conversatorios* are ubiquitous in Bolivia and generally refer to forums intended to discuss current events ranging from new anti-discrimination or domestic violence laws to debates over the appropriate use of oil and gas revenues. In my focus on *conversatorios*, I demonstrate how these dialogue sessions emerge as a primary site and technique of *capacitación* targeting the general public (as opposed to technical training targeting bureaucrats or aimed at bolstering institutional performance). Through *conversatorios*, organizers intend for participants to observe and practise listening and communication skills that will de-escalate conflict. Yet, as I show, *conversatorios* also become a space of contestation and frequently evolve into what I playfully dub contest*atorios*. I derive *contestatorio* from the Spanish *contestar*, to respond, but also mouth off, and contrast it against the emic concept of convers*atorio*, which comes from the verb *conversar*, to chat/talk. As one participant quipped when questioning a *conversatorio* facilitator, 'When the Indian is bad, it's because he talks back [*porque es contestón*]'. During such *contestatorios*, participants frequently *refuse* both the content of debate and the ways they are invited to participate within it.[5]

Contestatorios are more like public talk-backs in which participants challenge their conveners, not only on their framing of political issues but also on the very techniques of negotiation, deliberation and political subject formation proposed in these 'capacity building' spaces. By considering these two conceptual axes together, my aim is to analyse shifting governance paradigms and mechanisms, and to show how those governance projects encounter sceptical subjects of reform who assert *alternative* stakes and valorize demonized capacities.

I begin by charting how donors operating in Bolivia, particularly those targeting democratic institutions and the judicial system, framed their work in terms of institutional 'capacity building'. I offer this history not as mere backdrop but rather a central part of my larger argument about how democracy assistance programmes have shifted their conceptualization and application of the notion of 'capacity building' through locally meaningful idioms of training. I then examine how a series of political events set the stage, alongside critical project evaluations, for an adjusted diagnosis of what was ailing Bolivia, invigorating projects aimed at what I call democratic *capacitación*. Finally, I return to the *conversatorio* as one paradigmatic technique of *capacitación* through which donors and their Bolivian implementing partners seek to enable political transformation, even as some target audiences question their motives, assumptions and methods.

'Capacity building' as producing a more responsive state apparatus

In her critique of the buzzword quality of 'capacity building', Eade (2007: 630) shows how its uptake hollows out and obscures its leftist political genealogy. Eade notes that 'capacity building' often circulates as an empty signifier for a variety of 'trainings', endowed with more heft simply by a shift in jargon. Similarly, Kenny and Clarke (2010) describe the ways development agencies have presumed a shared (positive) meaning for the multivalent term. Parallel to leftist consciousness raising activities of the 1970s and 1980s, international development practitioners braided together a preoccupation with 'agency, active citizenship and civil society', suggesting that 'active citizens, participating in the institutions of burgeoning civil societies, have the capacity to steer human endeavour in a direction that can produce self-determining, sustainable societies' (Kenny and Clarke 2010: 6).

By the 1990s and early 2000s, multilateral institutions had adopted the now-ubiquitous phrase 'capacity building' while promoting an array of neoliberal economic reforms and political decentralization campaigns throughout the Americas. In Bolivia, donors[6] framed their democracy assistance and judicial reform efforts as necessary to advance the rule of law, to enable 'good governance' and to extend market liberalization throughout the Americas. Initially, these donor platforms operated with an understanding of 'capacity' as something located within institutions and their personnel, that is, the state agents labouring within them. Programme staff characterized 'capacity building' as a process of introducing institutional reforms and subsequent training programmes seeking to make bureaucracies more responsive to Bolivia's citizenry. 'Capacity building' thus focused on enabling government offices and their technicians to more effectively execute their mandates. These efforts included a range of programmes concerned with justice system reform, including a major, multi-donor effort to help Bolivia transition from an inquisitorial legal system to an adversarial one, as well as the massive overhaul of Bolivia's penal code, among other reforms.

Donors framed their efforts through *stated* goals that foregrounded Bolivia's administrative needs – the *lack*, here, was managerial, technical. Take, for example, the way the World Bank justified its efforts to edge into work once deemed too political and therefore outside the Bank's mandate – including reform programmes targeting Latin American justice systems, among other rule of law and good governance projects (buzzwords also meriting further analysis). Bank officials went to great lengths to frame their rule of law interventions in terms that fit within the Bank's narrow directive of poverty reduction and economic development (Domingo and Sieder 2001; Rowat et al. 1995). Within those confines, Bank documents insisted that 'capacity building – that is, building effective and accountable institutions to address development issues and reduce poverty in borrowing countries – should be at the core of World Bank activity' (Pena et. al. 2000: xii). As such, Bank-sponsored 'capacity building' aimed to produce an institutional environment that would enable democratic governance to succeed *in the service of* economic growth and poverty reduction (the former understood to produce the latter).

By contrast, donors such as the US Agency for International Development (USAID) were at liberty to openly frame their aid as intervening in political institutions while insisting that their interventions were non-partisan. For USAID and its implementing partners, democracy promotion entailed 'capacity building' at the level of drafting new legal codes and institutional arrangements thought to be more amenable to transparency, accountability and efficacy, while also training (*capacitando*) technocrats, jurists and officials in how to administer these new institutional regimes.[7] US donors also focused on improving the credibility of political parties amid widespread disillusionment with political elites.[8]

Donor-sponsored capacity building programmes targeting public institutions accompanied a wide range of neoliberal economic austerity measures and concomitant policies seeking to decentralize the Bolivian state and to transform political practices within the country by creating new channels for democratic participation. Among them was the Law of Popular Participation (LPP), which encouraged new, territorially bounded forms of affiliation through which Bolivian citizens could stake claims on municipal resources[9] (Lazar 2008; Orta 2013; Postero 2007). The stated aims of the LPP and accompanying reforms included further decentralizing decision making as a means to increase local accountability and social control over expenditures. But the LPP's other agenda was to change the ways Bolivians enacted politics by counterbalancing the political power of Bolivia's many 'corporatist' social and labour organizations. As anthropologist Nancy Postero explains, Bolivian modernizers viewed existing models of corporatism as 'anachronistic, costly, and worst of all, inefficient. The LPP was designed in part to redirect political activity to a new public space – the municipality – and to establish new forms of socio-political relations' (2007: 132).

In my own interviews with donor representatives and their Bolivian contractors, 'special interests' often served as a euphemism for these pervasive modes of corporatist[10] politics. Donor projects aimed to support the objectives of the LPP, as well as to further bolster the 'capacity' of political parties and other channels deemed more appropriate for democratic participation. One Bolivian contractor explained:

> The great objective was to bring civil society towards [political] parties ... given that political parties have passed through a period of lost prestige ... but that's because in the 1990s democracy was stable, but the institutions started to deteriorate. [People] expressed their demands through other channels. In some instances, those demands are just, but they [reflect] special interests and not the interests of the people as a whole. We think that political parties should channel demands – and not special interests.

Accordingly, donors coupled institutional reforms with programmes aiming to encourage Bolivian citizens to refocus their energies on claiming resources through *institutional* municipal channels and established political parties.

Yet, by the early 2000s, a number of donors had begun to voice frustration and scepticism about the accomplishments of capacity building projects targeting state institutions and agents, and expressed enormous anxiety about the 'governability' of the country. Creating new institutional arrangements under the LPP, it seemed, had not been enough to quell recurring unrest. Both donors and Bolivian evaluation teams deemed many of those institutional reforms to be, at best, inconsistently successful. Key project evaluations offered scathing appraisals of foreign-funded programmes targeting public institutions, placing much of the blame on 'resistant' bureaucracies and bureaucratic actors. Locating the source of failure in Bolivian institutions and institutional actors, and not, for example, in the relevance or appropriateness of donor agendas for local realities, allowed many project evaluators and donor representatives to insist that institutional reform was destined to fail in Bolivia owing to Bolivia's political culture.

Among programme staff I interviewed, the failure of these programmes was further confirmed by a 2003 uprising in El Alto, a sprawling and largely Indigenous Aymara city that encompasses Bolivia's wealthier seat of government, La Paz. Numerous political analysts attributed the uprising to defective democratic institutions and persistent forms of racial exclusion. Alteños [residents of El Alto], they argued, were exhausted by corruption and backlogs in the courts, and the inability of the state to satisfy their demands for basic social services. Bolivian President Gonzalo Sánchez de Lozada ultimately fled the country after a series of massacres on unarmed protesters. The violence – and his ouster – unsettled the Bolivian political landscape, but it also unsettled donors working in the country. As one Bolivian contractor employed by an American-funded project explained: 'That's why things had to change with foreign aid. After 2003, people I knew were really worried because [democracy promotion] wasn't working ... You made all this effort, and then [the uprising in] October 2003 happens and people said, "we've been working so hard and for what?"'.

Dangerous capacities

Following the uprising, small-scale conflict resolution projects gained new traction, and a heightened sense of urgency. Rather than continue to focus principally on improving state legal services and institutional capabilities, many American and European aid programmes returned their attention to Bolivia's (and especially El Alto's) 'conflictual' civil society. Their *stated* aim was to design programmes that responded to Bolivians' demands for justice while also *capacitando* or training people in skill-sets they considered necessary to generate political stability, instilling deliberative democratic habits. Repeatedly, designers framed this 'culture of conflict' to me as the influence of politically militant neighbourhood associations and trade unions that frequently resort to blockades, street protests and hunger strikes to make demands on the state and to achieve their political aims. In so doing, programme designers relocated the epicentre of much-needed capacity building away from public institutions and into the political subjectivities of Bolivians themselves.

The shift towards what I am calling *capacitación* is threefold. First, it identifies *unwelcome* capacities housed within the 'political culture' of Bolivia's *sindicalista* (union) structures – that is, trade unions, neighbourhood associations and other corporatist forms of politics that the LPP had previously sought to replace (and that critics understand to be destabilizing and 'special interest' rather than oriented towards the common good). Secondly, it prioritizes person-centred capacity building or *capacitación* as a means of instilling individual Bolivians with *alternative* competencies for conflict 'transformation' – not by turning towards state institutions, but rather by turning away from them and inward for the resolution of social and interpersonal conflict. And thirdly, it often locates the need for *capacitación* in the classed and racially marked bodies of Indigenous and union-affiliated Bolivians.

This final point is important in distinguishing *capacitación* as I am analysing it here from training programmes targeting technocrats. Consider, for example, an evaluation of the city of El Alto funded by USAID in the wake of the uprising. As the evaluation stated:

> In this war of El Alto, the official institutionalism of the State and the systems of government are losing battle after battle against a discourse of separation, exclusion and violence, a discourse promoted by a frustrated population that has been put-off and ignored, egged on by the dictatorship of certain neighbourhood and labour leaders, which has meant that official institutionalism has become clandestine, or has been subordinated to those leaders. (Indaburu 2004: 41)

Similarly, Estuardo Molina, the Bolivian Director for one of USAID's civil society programmes, identified what he considered a troubling capacity of *sindicalista* (union) leaders to enforce adherence to blockades and protests. During my interview with his project team, Molina explained that, 'There is a system of cellular clientelism … each block in El Alto is a cell and it has its *dirigentes* [leaders]. And the *dirigente* in every neighbourhood has its higher leader. And all of those from the neighbourhoods gather in the associations, and pretty soon you have a pyramid'.

By contrast, USAID-backed programmes sought to promote an alternative model of participation that countered *sindicalista* organizational workings with a call for informed deliberation among individual citizens. Molina continued:

> We are in the line of the liberal democracy of the eighteenth century, which means [concern for] the balance of powers. Which presupposes a citizenry that is increasingly better informed, more active, more participatory, that has rights and obligations, and that should not only know its rights but also its obligations. These are the primary characteristics [of USAID programming], which we don't claim are original nor exhaustive nor profound … We are selling the idea that truth emerges from the struggle among opinions … this is from the essay by [John Stuart] Mill, right? *On Liberty*.

Molina further contrasted USAID's approach to democratic training with that of *sindicatos* by prioritizing the unencumbered and informed self who is free to dissent. Implicit in such assessments is a critique of Bolivia's first Indigenous president, Evo Morales, and his Movement Toward Socialism party (MAS), which rose to power through – and continues to rely on – *sindicalista* tactics, and that critics accuse of silencing disagreement, including among supporters.

Other American and European-backed programmes operated with similar analyses regarding the need to improve deliberation, communication and negotiation skills among the Bolivian populace in order for deliberative democracy to thrive (Habermas 1984). As one programme manager explained to me, a study by Vanderbilt University raised serious concerns for donors about the *kind* of intolerant participation running rampant in Bolivia. He recalled: 'The Vanderbilt study was interesting, because they said that places with the most intolerance had less participation. But Bolivia broke the rule. We have more participation. Bolivia is intolerant and participatory. We think that if we don't participate, people will play tricks on us'. He continued: 'People talk a lot, but nobody listens. It is necessary to open spaces so that people can speak their positions and come to consensus'.

Following the unrest in 2003, existing civil society projects and nascent conflict resolution programmes intensified their *capacitación* work, now *prioritizing* training aimed at ordinary Bolivians. As Molina's colleague, Raquel, related to me :

> These technical skills develop the capacity [of people] to administer conflict, right? And to transform it in a constructive manner. That is to say … we are educating to not be confrontational. Rather, to seek constructive outcomes that allows us to find the common good. So many of [our collaborating NGOs] work to identify areas we can focus on that cause tension and conflict, to [instead] seek the common good.

Thus, donor-sponsored conflict resolution programmes have sought – through *capacitación* – to cultivate a political culture wherein mobilizing tactics utilized by *sindicatos* are contrasted against the common good, and technical-administrative capacities take root in individual citizens rather than state officials. Among such efforts, *conversatorios* are paradigmatic. Civil society strengthening programmes focus on encouraging Bolivians to interiorize an alternative disposition towards political participation, intersubjective communication and conflict management. It is to those *conversatorios* that I now return.

Conversational politics

Conversatorios are one of the principal training tools of many conflict resolution programmes operating in Bolivia. Alongside butcher paper, icebreakers and certificates of participation, *conversatorios* comprise an important part of the NGO toolkit, whether that NGO works on gender justice, questions of child labour or rural development. But *conversatorios* are particularly reflective of democracy promotion and conflict resolution projects in that the *conversatorio* form mirrors its function: imparting values and skills for political deliberation.

Conversatorio could be translated as discussion group, conversation, forum, public debate or model dialogue. Above, Molina emphasized the democratic value of a 'struggle among opinions', allowing, perhaps, for a more robust notion of debate and dissent. Similarly, some *conversatorio* organizers see their work as engaged in a radical critique of Bolivian society, opening spaces where political issues are explicitly discussed and confrontational forms of activism are welcome. Yet while the notion of holding a public debate places an emphasis on the contentiousness of disagreement and argumentation, the idea of modelling dialogue accentuates harmony seeking (Nader 2004).

In my experience observing such campaigns, organizers frequently intend for the audiences of the *conversatorio* to both witness and begin to interiorize the dispositions that make dialogue and deliberation possible, reorienting themselves towards the negotiation table rather than street protest. Moreover, *conversatorios* seek to reorder how Bolivians relate to each other through often-criticized socio-political organizations such as trade and *campesino* (peasant) unions and neighbourhood associations. These are, organizers insist, skill-sets that know no political party, no political allegiance per se. Instead, they are qualities that people may learn to cultivate across the political spectrum. Thus, organizers present *conversatorios* as *methodological vehicles* for tolerant encounter, deliberation and mutual understanding (Riles 2002).

Some advocates I spoke with argued that these forums could catalyse critical awareness about political and economic issues, arguing that the goal was not depoliticization but rather consciousness raising. Yet in characterizing negotiation skills as non-ideological, advocates frequently submerge the political and normative dimensions of their efforts, offering a kind of post-politics mechanism for resolving political disputes. As one ADR advocate put it to me, blending ideas of responsibility and *reason*ability, 'some think that peace means ... not having the ability to react, or protest, or confront other ideas. But ... you can respond reasonably, with other ideas, without the need to turn to violence. [It] means having the capacity to resolve conflicts maturely and responsibly'. What is normative – and up for debate – however, is what counts as *reasonable*, responsible, mature.

Ethnographic studies of democratization programmes have illuminated how subjectification processes intersect with population-level governance efforts led by state governments and supra-national agencies alike (Paley 2008; Coles 2008). These works examine how an array of institutions promoting democratization, transparency and good governance travel, and may be understood to constitute a transnational apparatus of governmentality (Brown 2006). Kimberly Coles' work on transnational election monitoring is illustrative. Coles shows how transnational election monitoring serves a 'governance strategy aimed at controlling and transforming the conduct of Bosnia-Herzegovina and Bosnians, as well as Bosnian democracy' (2009: 129). Election supervisors enact forms of governance on multiple registers, operating through their 'sheer', 'mere' and 'peer' presence. Though apparently 'passive', foreign election monitors *embody* transnational governance interventions, as well as model the ways Bosnians should perform democracy in their own state. Election watchdogs are symbolic, pedagogic, and they supply a normalizing gaze (Foucault 1995). Similarly, at *conversatorios* like the one described earlier, participants are meant to embody deliberation and dialogue for an audience, while also shoring up within themselves these orientations.

But unlike the kinds of programmes that targeted Bolivians for training in better organizing under the LPP, conflict resolution training programmes do something distinctive. LPP projects emphasized redirecting Bolivians' claims *on* state resources *towards* municipalities, and thus continued to emphasize proper institutional channels for both democratic participation and redressing grievances. What is distinctive in conflict resolution programmes is how they locate hope for generating democratic governability and political and economic stability within the capacity of ordinary citizens to resolve disputes without recourse to public institutions or organizational tactics associated with political strife: 'these skills are useful for addressing both fights in your home, and fights in your neighbourhood as well', the Master of Ceremonies declared. Yet, as I show in the final section, *conversatorio* conveners often encountered audiences that were deeply suspicious of all that talk. Precisely in those spaces of encounter, audience members proclaim their scepticism regarding the means and ends of negotiation, and assert other possible interpretations of conflict, confrontation and 'reasonable' expressions of discord.

A *conversatorio* or a *contestatorio*?

It's a Friday evening and the director of Bolivia's Colectivo Akhulli[11] has invited me to a *conversatorio* with Carlos Hugo Laruta. I've recently heard Laruta, a sociologist who worked for the UN's peace taskforce in Central America, give a talk on his latest book examining Indigenous conflict resolution methods. JUNTOS and other NGOs regularly invite people like Laruta to facilitate trainings and reflective spaces like the one described in the opening vignette.

Laruta's glossy book launch was held in the hip, tree-lined Sopocachi neighbourhood, but this is a very different venue, a working class neighbourhood and an institution known for its critical voice and Indigenous political activism – and I'm particularly keen to hear the exchange at tonight's event. Unlike the kinds of *conversatorios* I was used to seeing run by other NGOs, I suspected this one might be a little different given the audience.

Akhulli, a collective of Indigenous activist-intellectuals based in La Paz, was founded on the premise of critiquing Western epistemologies and historiography of highland Indigenous communities. Tonight's *conversatorio* is intended to discuss a hotly debated anti-racism law that the Morales administration is backing. The new law has sparked strong criticism for its criminalization of any person who expresses – or institution that publishes or promotes – hate speech. I'm hoping the conversation will go a little deeper than the limited discussion at Laruta's press-oriented book launch. But as I wait for the conversation to start, I don't anticipate the degree of outrage the affable Laruta will provoke among Colectivo Akhulli's audience over the next two hours. In this *conversatorio*, Laruta makes an appeal for harmony much as I had seen JUNTOS staff do at the book fair. But the reaction Laruta receives is anything but harmonious. I quickly realize that I am witnessing something better described as a contest*atorio*[12] rather than a convers*atorio*: a heated talk-back rather than easy-going dialogue. In the context of Colectivo Akhulli's long history of political organizing, the NGO idiom of hosting *conversatorio* chafes against its roots in leftist and *Indianista* consciousness raising projects. Laruta finds himself – and the dialogue building project he represents – the subject of enormous scepticism and open critique.

Laruta opens with a story. It's *his* story. Speaking with a pedagogical tone bordering on political stump speech, Laruta recounts how his own parents' marriage crossed regional and racial divides. 'I am telling this story to show you why I made the life decision to work so that Bolivia might live in peace. I do not wager on confrontation because I have decided to opt for life. I prefer to focus on that which unifies us [rather than divides us], and to work in a way that is as harmonious and peaceful as possible'. As the child of a highland Aymara father and mother from Bolivia's lowlands, Laruta describes himself as a child of two worlds, 'the world of *chuño*[13] and the world of citrus and yucca'. As a result, Laruta explains, he seeks reconciliation between the two, and 'pacific and harmonious mechanisms to deal with the problems of our country'.

Laruta shares two stories meant to illustrate his point. The first involves a confrontation in the rural province of Ballivian, where Laruta describes witnessing a clash between two musical bands during an *entrada* or dance parade. One group, Laruta tells us, played *musica autoctona*, or Indigenous music on wind instruments. Their group was suddenly interrupted when a group of *comerciantes* or merchants – a term indexing a wealthier, urbanized strata of Bolivians – came around the corner with a full brass band, their music overpowering the other groups. Their drunken revelry, Laruta tells us, overtook the whole street. The tension almost led to blows. What would have happened, Laruta asks us, if each group had tried to be more accommodating to the 'culture' of the other? How might they have better dealt with the conflict?

Laruta's second story proves to be more provocative. Laruta asks us to think back to the horrifying events of May 2008 in the city of Sucre. On that day, a group of rural *campesinos* (peasants) marching in support of Bolivian president Evo Morales were rounded up into the main plaza, beaten, forced to strip and made to renounce their Indigenous heritage while onlookers jeered them with racial slurs. Their bloodied faces and stripped bodies shocked many Bolivians, provoking outrage at the brutal, unabashed racism. Others suggested that Morales' supporters had strategically provoked the confrontation for political purposes.

The common version of those events, Laruta tells us, was that the event was a racist attack against defenceless *campesinos*, exposing the racism still troubling the country. The event, he tells us, served to justify the new law against 'racism and all forms of discrimination', the very topic of our *conversatorio*. But Laruta suggests that he does not think the 2008 event was driven by racism. Racism was certainly a factor, he acknowledges, but it was secondary; the real root of the conflict was what Laruta terms 'political intolerance'. He tells us, 'We saw that the faces doing the beating looked almost identical to the faces being beaten. What happened in Sucre cannot be understood without contextualizing it: a pugnacious circumstance that dated back months to a conflict between [Sucre's] urban population and the surrounding rural population. It was a politicized context characterized by an ideology of confrontation that already existed'. This wasn't a racist act, Laruta insists, but a political one, complimented by racist ideas. It occurred because 'we haven't constructed a form of citizenship sufficient to address these issues'. Sure, he tells us, there are people who are directly responsible for the attacks, but if we think about it differently, we are all 'co-responsible for creating circumstances that promote political intolerance as a shared feeling'.

Laruta's comments provoke sharp disagreement. In response, a young man I will call Marco, interjects:

> What we have here is the conflict between the Noble Indian and the Savage Indian. When the Indian is bad, it's because he talks back [*porque es contestón*]. He was a submissive

Indian, but when he got into politics, that really hurt. They say Evo is surrounded by white people who control him, but whether you want it or not he's the face [of the government]. So the way I see it is the only way to avoid confrontation is to have the Indian go back to lowering his head. *Cambas*[14] – sorry for the offensive term – will never accept us at their level. It will only be a tranquil country if Indians lower their head once again.

Of course, Marco is not advocating that Indians[15] should adopt such an approach, that they should lower their heads to bring peace to the country. Rather, he is critiquing Laruta's insistence that there might be a harmonious way to achieve social transformation in Bolivia. Peace, Marco argues, is only possible if one group is willing to be submissive. More specifically, peace means asking Indigenous Bolivians to go back to lowering their heads so as to put *Cambas* at ease. If peace is what you want, it's submissive Noble Indians you need. Inverting the racist American idiom of 'uppity' black women and men who step out of their (subordinate) place, Marco claims being *contestón* (mouthy) as an unwillingness to bow before oppression, but argues that it will always be perceived as aggression by people accustomed to power and privilege.

Laruta balks at the suggestion that submissiveness is the only way to avoid confrontation. He holds out one hand and then places the other above it. The problem, he insists, is that 'we were here – with a lot of discrimination against [Indigenous] communities, but instead of levelling things out', he says, flipping the order of his hands and then slapping one down upon the other, 'we are here. We have just reversed the discrimination'. *Indigenas* are now on top, he explains, 'when really, where we should be is here', Laruta says as he intertwines his fingers: 'Integrated'. Laruta repeats these gestures a second time, asserting his point. Bolivia is simply living an inversion of unequal power rather than true integration. I watch the young woman sitting across from me turn crimson as Laruta speaks. She shakes her head vigorously in disgust.

This heated exchange drove several points home to me as I moved back and forth between institutions and activists promoting conflict resolution through *conversatorios*, and as I watched the responses of their target audiences. The exchange highlights just how much incredulity conflict resolution advocates encounter among the people they are trying to convince of the value of peaceful negotiation and its accompanying sensibilities and practices. The context was a debate over a specific law – precisely the kind of topic deliberative democrats might identify as an ideal subject of thoughtful dialogue and negotiation. But the response by Laruta's audience was one of profound scepticism about what was being asked of them.

Marco explicitly interpreted Laruta's call for peaceful dialogue as necessitating Indigenous submission. Anything short of 'bowing his head', he argued, would be interpreted by upper middle class *mestizos* as a form of aggression. Laruta attempted to reframe his point as a call for mutually respectful integration, tolerance and equality, rather than a simple reversal of power relations between historically subjugated Indigenous Bolivians and powerful, European-descendant Bolivian elites. But his activist audience was not convinced. Indeed, this *contestatorio* revealed not only how conflict resolution advocates frame their efforts as adopting a certain disposition of tolerance amid widespread political intolerance, but also how these programmes implicitly – and sometimes quite explicitly – locate *conflictualness* in particular groups of people, namely Indigenous and poor Bolivians' co-production of political intolerance. Laruta's audience interpreted his invitation to deliberation as requiring one side of a larger political struggle to acquiesce by making their demands less threatening to *mestizo* and white Bolivians in the public spaces of encounter and debate. Instead, participants make a *contestatorio* out of a *conversatorio*, talking back against Laruta's appeals to communicative practices that stand in tension with their own analyses of the limits of deliberative ideals.

Conclusion

As I have shown, the shift to what I am calling *capacitación* in conflict resolution skills is revelatory in that it makes visible both the assumptions guiding earlier waves of capacity building aid (centred on institutional weaknesses) and the ways that donors later came to identify what was 'lacking' in Bolivia's citizenry. More telling, however, is what such projects deem dangerously *present*. *Conversatorios* like the ones I have described here were intended to model deliberative democratic behaviour and to serve as a mechanism through which Bolivians might adopt and practise listening and communication skills in contradistinction to confrontational political tactics. In some ways, Bolivia is a unique place to consider what I have called 'reasonablization': the country is notorious for its citizens' willingness to utilize street protest and other disruptive means of dissent, the so-called 'conflictual' and 'rebellious' character of its Indigenous and working class citizenry (McNeish 2008). While some critics naturalize that character as an almost genetic predisposition shared by particular groups of people, it is rooted in historical experiences of domination and struggle. In such a context, activists like the members of Colectivo Akhulli seem to epitomize this critical position vis-à-vis projects they perceive as imperialist or dampening and controlling of tactics utilized especially by working class and Indigenous movements – even as many of their middle class or less activist compatriots long for uninterrupted daily life.

Yet through those *contestatorios*, Marco, Julieta and others lay bare the post-politics of 'capacity building' projects that have proliferated in many parts of the world as aid programmes strive to correct capacities through new competencies in deliberation, negotiation and conflict transformation. Annelise Riles has noted of Alternative Dispute Resolution (ADR) that it often eludes critique as it contributes to the 'hegemonic institutionalization of a heady fantasy of liberal communication, a hope that political conflict can be resolved through new and ever more technological solutions' (2002: 618). Similarly, the broad appeal of 'capacity building' often escapes critical interrogation precisely because of its seemingly apolitical virtues: promising to generate or reinforce strengths that will improve institutional performance or better people's quality of life. Indeed, that is how advocates such as Laruta might characterize their commitments: as good faith efforts to open space for non-aggressive deliberation amid chronic unrest, and to develop new capacities for conflict transformation.

Nevertheless, *conversatorios* frequently raise the hackles of participants who disagree with the assertion that demands for substantive inclusion and social justice can be achieved solely through narrowly defined parameters of what constitutes reasonable communicative practices. Experience tells them that the burden to communicate in non-threatening ways often falls on those who have long relied on protest, on being *contestón*, to make their demands known. In many ways, their critiques echo longstanding debates about alternative dispute resolution and deliberative democracy in the US context (Muhlberger 2011; Sanders 1997). And yet these interrelated approaches remain central to aid programmes seeking to transform countries like Bolivia.

John-Andrew McNeish has argued that, 'in a sense Bolivia's hyper-active civil society is both a curse and a blessing, making long term political stability untenable, but ensuring that democratic commitment, fervour and innovation continue' (2008: 91). For activists like those gathered at Colectivo Akhulli, appeals for the *reasonablization* or moderation of their political voice threaten to demobilize social movements whose power has historically been rooted in an ability to interrupt. In questioning these endeavours, they produce *contestatorios* out of *conversatorios*, disrupting logics of *capacitación* that would tame unruly politics and insisting on the continued need for and, indeed, the virtue of demonized capacities.

Acknowledgements

I would like to thank the residents of El Alto and La Paz, Bolivian NGO staff and donor representatives who generously shared their experiences and perceptions with me. This chapter is the result of a 2011 American Anthropological Association panel and subsequent workshop on 'Hope and Insufficiency: Capacity Building in Ethnographic Comparison' funded by the Wenner-Gren Foundation for Anthropological Research. I am grateful to Rachel Douglas-Jones and Justin Shaffner for organizing both events, as well as all those who participated and offered their generative feedback. The Wenner-Gren Foundation, National Science Foundation, Social Science Research Council and Jacob K. Javits Foundation provided funding for this research.

Susan Ellison holds a PhD in Anthropology from Brown University and is an Assistant Professor at Wellesley College. Ellison worked with Bolivian non-governmental organizations from 2001 to 2005, returning as a researcher in 2008. Her research links debates about democracy, foreign aid, justice, and trust to lived experiences of violence and financial insecurity. Her first book, *Domesticating Democracy: The Politics of Conflict Resolution in Bolivia*, was published by Duke University Press (2018). Her second project examines how widespread accusations of fraud reconfigure the social relations that many Bolivians rely on amid prolonged economic duress. Recent publications appear in *American Anthropologist* and *Geopolitics*.

Notes

1. Or, 'Together'. Because the NGOs described here are well known in Bolivia, they are likely recognizable to a Bolivian audience, and the events described were public. Nevertheless, I have provided pseudonyms to obscure their appearance on search engines.
2. Names changed throughout, except for well-known public intellectuals like Paredes and Laruta, speaking at public events.
3. Recent ethnographic work in Latin America highlights the ways indigenous movements and other social organizations have exploited the political apertures created by neoliberal governance projects. These approaches do not obviate prior critiques but rather suggest there is greater room for social organizations to manoeuvre within and even exploit neoliberal forms of governance towards their own ends and to elude 'efforts at control' (McNeish 2008: 86; see also Gustafson 2009; Orta 2013; Postero 2007).

4. Holston (2008), by contrast, characterized the insurgent citizenship of Paulistas not so much as recourse to disruptive tactics, but rather to the mechanisms of liberal governance (i.e. private property) and human rights discourse to make their claims.
5. Elsewhere I analyse *contestatorios* alongside recent work by Audra Simpson on 'refusal', particularly refusal of the terms of neoliberal multiculturalism described by Glen Coulthard, Nancy Postero, Nicole Fabricant, Charles Hale and Elizabeth Povinelli, among others.
6. A note about my broad use of 'donors': while there are indeed institutional and ideological differences, i.e. between the USAID, the World Bank and European Union, I argue that shared diagnostic patterns emerged across these different donor organizations regarding the 'weaknesses' of the Bolivian state, which in turn shaped patterns of solution making. In so doing, I am in conversation with anthropologists of policy who, drawing on Latour, take an 'assemblage' approach to donor and state policy formation.
7. USAID, *Plan de Acción USAID Bolivia, gestión 1996–1997*. Convenio 511-0634-C-00-601 0-00. Available online at http://pdf.usaid.gov/pdf_docs/pdabp022.pdf.
8. USAID/Bolivia 2 Close Out Report: S0 551-001. Available online at http://pdf.usaid.gov/pdf_docs/pdacd699.pdf; USAID/Bolivia Strategic Objective Close Out Report, for 'Increased Citizen Support for the Bolivian Democratic System', FY 1998–FY2003. See http://pdf.usaid.gov/pdf_docs/pdacd699.pdf.
9. *Construyendo un futuro major: USAID en Bolivia 1961–2013*, published by USAID, September 2013. See http://photos.state.gov/libraries/bolivia/337500/usaidsuccessstories/bolivia%20legacy_spanish_highres.pdf
10. With 'corporatist' often spoken as an epithet.
11. The pseudonym is a reference to the ceremonial act of sharing coca.
12. A dialogue, or talk-back.
13. A blackened freeze-dried potato consumed in the Andes. Here it symbolically stands for highland Indians versus the lowland *cambas*, symbolized by citrus fruits and yucca.
14. Term used for lowland Bolivians in the Santa Cruz region. Generally used to index whiteness and upper middle class status.
15. Here, Marco pointedly uses 'indio' (Indian) rather than 'indigena' (Indigenous), likely to underscore the racism associated with that term, both historically and in the present. Some Indigenous activists also have reclaimed the term in a context where discourses around 'mestizaje' (racial mixture) abound amid persistent structural and interpersonal racism directed toward Indigenous Bolivians.

References

Brenner, N., J. Peck and N. Theodore. 2010. 'Variegated Neoliberalization: Geographies, Modalities, Pathways'. *Global Networks* 10 (2): 182–222.

Brown, K. 2006. *Transacting Transition: The Micropolitics of Democracy Assistance in the Former Yugoslavia*. Bloomfield, CT: Kumarian Press, Inc.

Coles, K. 2008. 'International Presence: The Passive Work of Democracy Promotion'. In J. Paley (ed.), *Democracy: Anthropological Approaches*. Santa Fe, NM: SAR Press, 98–129.

Domingo, P. and R. Sieder (eds). 2001. *Rule of Law in Latin America: The International Promotion of Judicial Reform*. London: Institute of Latin American Studies.

Eade, D. 2007. 'Capacity Building: Who Builds Whose Capacity?' *Development in Practice* 17 (4): 630–639.

Ellison, S. 2015. 'Replicate, Facilitate, Disseminate: The Micropolitics of US Democracy Promotion in Bolivia'. *PoLAR: Political and Legal Anthropology Review* 38 (2): 318–337.

Foucault, M. 1995. *Discipline and Punish: The Birth of the Prison*. New York: Vintage Books.

Gustafson, B. 2009. *New Languages of the State: Indigenous Resurgence and the Politics of Knowledge in Bolivia*. Durham, NC: Duke University Press.

Habermas, J. 1984. *The Theory of Communicative Action I: Reason and the Rationalization of Society*. Trans. Thomas McCarthy. Boston, MA: Beacon Press.

Holston, J. 2008. *Insurgent Citizenship: Disjunctions of Democracy and Modernity in Brazil*. Princeton, NJ: Princeton University Press.

Indaburu Quintana, R. 2004. 'Evaluación de la Ciudad de el Alto'. Contract 511-O-00-04-00047-00, USAID.
Kenny, S. and M. Clarke. 2010. *Challenging Capacity Building: Comparative Perspectives*. New York: Palgrave Macmillan.
Lazar, S. 2008. *El Alto, Rebel City: Self and Citizenship in Andean Bolivia*. Durham, NC: Duke University Press.
McNeish, J.-A. 2008. 'Constitutionalism in an Insurgent State: Rethinking Legal Empowerment of the Poor in a Divided Bolivia'. In D. Banik (ed.), *Rights and Legal Empowerment in Eradicating Poverty*. London: Ashgate, 69–96.
Muhlberger, P. 2011. 'A Deliberative Look at Alternative Dispute Resolution and the Rule of Law'. *Journal of Dispute Resolution* 1: 147–163.
Nader, L. 2004. 'Civilization and its Negotiations'. In S. Falk Moore (ed.), *Law and Anthropology: A Reader*. Oxford: Blackwell Publishing, 330–343.
Orta, A. 2013. 'Forged Communities and Vulgar Citizens: Autonomy and its Limits in Semineoliberal Bolivia'. *The Journal of Latin American and Caribbean Anthropology* 18 (1): 108–133.
Paley, J. 2008. 'Introduction'. In J. Paley (ed.), *Democracy: Anthropological Approaches*. Santa Fe, NM: School for Advanced Research Press, 1–20.
Pena, J, J.L. Guasch, and A. Escribano. 2000. *Reforming Public Institutions and Strengthening Governance: A World Bank Strategy*. The World Bank. Public Sector Group. Poverty Reduction and Economic Management (PREM) Network. [Available online at http://www1.worldbank.org/publicsector/Reforming.pdf.]
Postero, N. 2007. *Now We Are Citizens: Indigenous Politics in Postmulticultural Bolivia*. Stanford, CA: Stanford University Press.
Riles, A. 2002. 'User Friendly: Informality and Expertise: [Commentary]'. *Law & Social Inquiry* 27 (3): 613–619.
Rowat, M., W. Malik and M. Dakolias. 1995. 'Judicial Reform in Latin America and the Caribbean'. World Bank Technical Paper No. 280.
Sanders, L. 1997. 'Against Deliberation'. *Political Theory* 25 (3): 347–376.
Shore, C. and S. Wright. 2011. 'Conceptualising Policy: Technologies of Governance and the Politics of Visibility'. In C. Shore, S. Wright and D. Però (eds), *Policy Worlds: Anthropology and the Analysis of Contemporary Power*. Oxford and New York: Berghahn Books, 1–26.
Trnka, S. and C. Trundle. 2014. 'Competing Responsibilities: Moving beyond Neoliberal Responsibilisation'. *Anthropological Forum* 24 (2): 136–153.

Chapter 5

Capacity Building as Instrument and Empowerment
Training Health Workers for Community-Based Roles in Ghana

Harriet Boulding

This chapter examines the way in which community health officers in Ghana grapple with the project of integrating their mandate of social mobilization with the provision of clinical services. In recent years, a great deal of emphasis has been put on the need to build the capacity of health workers to facilitate positive healthcare relationships within their communities in addition to fulfilling their roles as clinicians. This suggests new forms of knowledge production in the field of developing health systems, in which discourses of capacity building and the social aspects of poverty are being integrated with an ethos of basic, low-cost service provision informed by the economic strategies of the previous decades. Both the recipients and primary providers of healthcare are required to be engaged in capacity building processes in order to create more accessible and culturally sensitive healthcare programmes. This raises questions as to how social mobilization projects can be implemented with clinical service provision in practice, but also how the tools designed to facilitate this integration are constructed and deployed. How do different conceptualizations of capacity building delimit the roles of health workers and how do front-line providers respond to the opportunities and challenges posed by interpretations of capacity building?

The discussion that follows is informed by fieldwork investigating the implementation of the Community-based Health Planning and Services (CHPS) project in Ghana, conducted as part of my doctoral research comparing integrated community health services and their impact on maternal health in Mali and Ghana. During fieldwork conducted between February and April 2013 in the Shai-Osudoku district of Ghana, I observed the day-to-day activities of different cadres of community health workers, and conducted interviews with those providing community health services in addition to district administrators responsible for overseeing the project. Under the guidance of the district health administrator, I selected four project zones that demonstrated the project at various stages of implementation. Three of these had functioning community clinics, and one was a fledgling project site to which community health workers had been posted, but which had no clinic as of yet. Each zone served small, rural populations and accommodated a number of surrounding villages. At the time of my research, two of the clinics were each staffed with a midwife, an enrolled nurse and three community health officers (CHOs). One of these also had a community health nurse (CHN) on staff, while the third clinic was staffed by two CHOs only. The remaining project zone had three CHOs, who lived and kept their medical supplies in their own individual accommodations in the village. Communities were also served by community health volunteers (CHVs), who provided basic services such as oral rehydration, and supported the CHOs in their advocacy work. The majority of my participant observation was conducted in community clinics, or accompanying CHOs on their home visits and community outreach days, which included child welfare clinics.

Drawing on observations from the implementation of the CHPS programme, I suggest that an instrumentalized version of the concept of health worker capacity building has contributed to two particular circumstances that inform health workers' execution of their daily activities in their communities. The first is that the framework in which health workers are expected to perform their social mobilization mandate generates a blueprint for the formation of health worker–community relationships. This blueprint undermines the efficacy of health workers' attempts to effect community mobilization and often produces the same disconnect between communities and the health service that the programme was intended to address. The second circumstance arising from the framework in which health workers are required to operate is that where health workers are unwilling or unable to comply with their social mobilization mandate, they often employ various strategies in order to mediate between their roles as government workers and members of their communities. I view these strategies as brokerages of the kind proposed by Bierschenk et al. (2002), to the extent that intermediaries embedded in a local area play a significant role in determining outcomes for the communities they serve.

I argue that in constructing the capacity building of community health workers as an instrumental endeavour, the rights and empowerment aspects of capacity building exercises are lost, and the role of the health worker is narrowly delineated in terms of the technical services they provide to their communities. A principal question that arises from this perspective is that of whether it is possible for concepts such as capacity building to retain the political elements of empowerment and social justice when deployed in contexts such as health sector bureaucracies, in which the language and architecture repel the very elements that need to be at the heart of effective change. Drawing on Standing (2007), I suggest that it is productive to evaluate the health service's use of concepts such as capacity building using frameworks informed by their own processes, which can be understood on their own terms. I conclude that it is within the scope of the CHPS programme to reformulate the concept of health worker capacity building in ways that empower health workers to deliver interventions in their communities more effectively.

Community-based Health Planning and Services: a dual cadre model

In 1999, the Ghanaian Ministry of Health introduced the Community-based Health Planning and Services initiative (CHPS), a national project designed to offer doorstep healthcare provision with the participation of households and communities. The programme focuses on addressing geographical barriers to access to healthcare, by providing resident nurses in rural districts, rather than relying on remote facilities providing outreach services. Where possible, nurses are assigned to work in communities with which they are already familiar. However, national recruitment procedures can result in CHOs being posted to areas where languages, social customs and organizational structures are unfamiliar (Ghana Health Service [GHS] 2002). The initiative aims to create a dynamic community health system that reduces inequalities in healthcare outcomes related to geographical barriers to health services, and actively engages with community members on matters regarding their health and wellbeing.

The CHPS initiative was pioneered through the Ghana Health Service in order to replicate the results of the Navrongo community health and family planning project. This project was piloted in the districts of Nkwanta, Birim North and Abura-Asebu-Kwamankese, and was designed to address the needs of households and communities in health service provision (School of Public Health [SPH] 2009). The results of the pilot studies suggested that providing resident nurses increased the interactions of community members with health services by eight times that of district health centres (Nyonator et al. 2005; Pence et al. 2001). The CHPS initiative is now considered central to providing healthcare services to those who previously had little or no access, and forms part of the national poverty reduction strategy (Nyonator et al. 2005).

A central component of the initiative involves providing community nurses with additional training designed to help them create partnerships with households, social groups and community leaders, 'addressing the demand side of service provision and recognizing the fact that households are the primary producers of health' (GHS 2005: 7). This feature of the project responds to calls from international agencies for health services to make use of the social resources of communities, including social networks, community organizations, lineages and chieftaincies. In recent years, national and international development institutions have demonstrated a renewed interest in understanding the social causes of health sector inequalities. In particular, addressing the geographical and socio-cultural aspects of inequalities that exist in global health systems has become a primary goal that has informed the administration of community healthcare, leading to healthcare policies designed to create 'synergy' between the social aspects of healthcare and the provision of clinical services (Yazbeck 2009).

The process of scaling up the CHPS system relies on a successful 'community entry' phase, in which dialogue is established between the health service and the community at hand. The project must gain community support, especially from traditional leaders who must offer their support for the project. This is achieved through extensive research on the social systems and leadership structures at work within the community, in addition to gaining greater understanding of the work of traditional healers operating in the area. Talks are established with key figures, which are designed to secure support and resources from the community for moving the project forward. Often, officers from the health service will utilize durbars (community meetings during which music, dancing and discussion take place) as a space in which to foster discussion and feedback on the introduction of CHPS to the area. In order to effectively deliver CHPS services, it is necessary to build a community health compound in an appropriate location, which serves as both clinic and living quarters for CHOs. Building the facility requires significant input from community leaders, who are responsible for mobilizing resources and volunteers for the construction of the compound. The programme seeks to match CHOs to communities with which they are familiar, although this is often not feasible due to the fact that there is little support available in deprived rural areas to sponsor the training of nurses (WHO 2015).

Building health worker capacity

A crucial way in which the delivery of health services differs from that previously offered by district health centres is the training of community health officers to prepare them to live in the community while carrying out both clinical and advocacy work. The focus on redefining the role of CHOs is viewed as one of the greatest strengths of the programme at a national and international level, and much emphasis is put on the need to build the capacity of nurses such that they develop the skills required to fulfil the non-clinical, social element of health service provision in their communities. Therefore, in addition to acquiring enhanced clinical skills, CHOs are now trained in building relationships with community members and given counselling skills.

CHOs provide all aspects of primary healthcare, including family planning, antenatal and postnatal care, immunizations and treatment of minor illnesses. In addition to their clinic work, health workers regularly conduct community outreach programmes, holding child welfare days in villages surrounding the clinics and making home visits. Health workers play an active advisory role, and are the first port of call in their communities for health education and advice. After a successful implementation phase, they are supported by community health volunteers who provide health education services and keep community records in partnership with CHOs.

The CHPS system is built on the premise that CHOs will live and work in their communities in order to build positive healthcare relationships, and receive additional training in order to enhance their social mobilization skills. Yet the interactions between healthcare workers and the communities they serve are highly scheduled, with CHOs required to visit ten households a day, at least four times a week on their outreach schedule. During their visits, CHOs have a checklist of questions they must ask, and are trained to give certain responses to the answers they receive. There is a considerable amount of literature that focuses on the need to train health workers to engage communities with health system directives (Oliveira-Cruz et al. 2003; Haines et al. 2007; WHO 2009), much of which focuses on the instrumental value of integrated services. Emphasis in policy literature in particular is on the capacity of integrated health services to reduce costs, improve project management and as a means to provide coordinated patient care, an approach that is reflected in the health service's understanding of health worker capacity building.

Although there is considerable import attached in health service literature and policy to the notion of building the capacity of community health workers, the term itself has not been well defined by those who employ it with reference to the CHPS programme, and it is used almost exclusively to refer to health worker training. According to the Ghana Health Service, CHOs' capacity must be built through training and skills workshops in order to provide higher quality services and enable them to generate social mobilization and improve partnerships with the communities in which they are posted. Emphasis on the technical aspects of capacity building is demonstrated regularly throughout health service literature, as exemplified by one of the principal health service policy goals:

> Seek and co-ordinate regular technical assistance for capacity building in terms of training for all levels of staff, including the CHWs [Community Health Workers] and development of appropriate community level IEC [Information, Education, Communication] materials for professional and non-professional health providers engaged in community based health care delivery. (MOH 2014: 11)

Similarly, in a review of CHPS programme implementation, the School of Public Health (SPH 2009: 3) cites the need for 'capacity building in midwifery' on the grounds that many programme officers lack basic midwifery skills. With regards to the CHOs' community mobilization mandate, capacity building is also referred to by the health service with reference to the training and skills required for health workers to build the community relationships necessary to effect health-behavioural change. A CHO training workbook (GHS 2009) emphasizes the need to build CHOs' capacity by training them to go through a checklist of health questions when conducting home visits, to record and report their findings in line with programme requirements and to set measurable goals for their community mobilization activities. These requirements serve to instrumentalize their interactions with their communities, and leave little space for CHOs to develop good relationships and respond appropriately to the needs of individuals.

For many health and rights advocates observing community health systems, capacity building in healthcare should be linked to discourses on health as a human right, and employed as part of a broader programme designed to facilitate interventions that promote progressive social change. Awofeso (2013) argues that while the technical aspects of capacity building such as training and equipment are easier to quantify and address, systems, roles and linking these to enhancing people's right to health and wellbeing remain a challenge for developing health systems. In the case of the CHPS programme, health worker capacity building is viewed largely in instrumental terms, with little consideration given to how the role of the health worker is enacted in practice, or the possibility of linking their activities to broader positive changes in health and rights.

In the following sections, I highlight two principal issues to which the health service's instrumental conceptualization of health worker capacity building contributes, and discuss the impact of these on health workers' attempts to perform their community mobilization mandate alongside the provision of clinical services.

The blueprint for social mobilization

The first issue is that health workers' ability to forge positive relationships in their communities is often limited by the very mechanisms that are designed to facilitate this. The health service refers to building the capacity of CHOs through partnerships with donor organizations, particularly United States Agency for International Development (USAID) contracting agencies, which provide technical assistance in developing human resources through training and capacity building activities (GHS 2002). The capacity building activities consistently referred to are initial or enhanced training in clinical skills, community orientation and social mobilization skills (SPH 2009). According to the health service, it is through such training that CHOs can best fulfil their mandate of engaging communities (GHS 2005). On the basis of this, CHOs are required to follow specific guidelines as to the interactions they have with community members, and the topics they cover when making home visitations.

The effect of this is to create a blueprint for forging healthcare relationships in communities that only partially recognizes the needs of communities, and limits CHOs' capacity to respond to individual community requirements. Often, CHOs are only able to respond to healthcare requirements that specifically connect to the community health blueprint. The requirements to collect information from households on child and maternal health and to offer advice on reproductive healthcare are vital, and are hugely significant in providing households in geographically remote areas with healthcare services and information that they would previously not have been able to access (Awoonor-Williams et al. 2013). However, the staffing and scheduling of CHO activities mean that some households miss out on CHO visitations when members are not available, and others receive regular, non-specific visits that are sometimes resented. Lack of sophisticated training in counselling skills and the prescribed nature of points raised during visitations sometimes lead to healthcare issues going unaddressed. The effect of the blueprint for social mobilization is often to limit rather than build the capacity of healthcare workers to formulate effective healthcare relationships in their communities, where only certain kinds of health issues are made visible within the system.

The following account of CHO home visitations in Shai-Osudoku highlights the difficulties encountered by health workers attempting to follow health system guidelines for their community outreach work. In March 2013, I accompanied a CHO for the district of Shai Osudoku conducting home visitations in several villages under the care of her clinic compound. The visits for that day took place in a village some kilometres from the clinic compound, a journey we made on foot due to the fact that the clinic had no available transport. The CHO carried a register with her, in which she recorded the number of children under five years old, noted if women were pregnant and if there had been any deaths for each of the households we visited.

We were approached several times on our way by women who stopped us to ask about family planning, the most common concern being when they were supposed to receive another dose. Not having the records with her, the CHO was unable to answer these queries, but promised to check and make sure that she visited them when it was time for them to take the medication. When we reached the houses she was required to visit that day, we found that some of the occupants were less willing than those we had met on the journey to discuss their health concerns. On several occasions, we arrived at households in the village and were not offered a stool, as is usually the custom. The CHO's questions regarding the number of children and their ages were not directly answered, and her attempts to explain the benefits of contraception and birth spacing were met with silence. At one household, a woman told us that she had become pregnant. After the CHO explained the need to arrange antenatal care, the client informed us that she would not visit the clinic compound because she did not want other community members to see her there. She was afraid of incurring disapproval in the community, and did not want the CHO drawing attention to her. She said that she would visit the hospital for prenatal care, a journey of ten kilometres, which she would have to make on foot. Evaluating these visits, the CHO commented:

> Some people are difficult and never give the right response to us. If we come and we get a case and we can help them, they are happy, but when they have no condition or have no issues for you to tackle it becomes a pest to them. They can get bored or they are busy and will not bring a chair. This is how we know. The hospital think that we need to do this every day … this is a small community so we see the same people every day … they [the hospital] say that this is our job and we should go. There is also the problem with regular visits that people start questioning about the person, are they having a disease. People gossip, it's human nature. (CHO, Shai-Osudoku, 2013)

In order to build the capacity of CHOs to integrate into the community, they are mandated to make regular visits and are provided with sets of questions and issues they must discuss with the occupants of each household, including educating about contraception and birth spacing. Yet what the CHO describes here are instances where in following her health service training she is alienating herself from the community rather than becoming a trusted figure. Eade (1997) argues that effective empowerment of actors in development contexts means enhancing existing and potential relationships, rather than just increasing the number of 'partners' or opportunities for contact. The case study discussed here suggests that the emphasis is indeed on maximizing CHO interaction with community members, without necessarily providing CHOs with the means to enhance such relationships. Here the principle of community–health service relationships is endorsed, but health workers have little capacity to develop the substance and character of healthcare relationships which is necessary in order to maximize the benefits of an integrated health system. In defining health worker capacity building almost exclusively in terms of the training that is or should be made available, the health service neglects the broader elements of CHOs' lives in their communities which influence their efficacy in terms of successfully integrating services.

CHOs in the Shai-Osudoku district often expressed a desire to have more control over the scheduling of home visitations. One CHO noted that she would like to be able to tailor the schedule in a way that reflects the needs of the community:

> Some people do not need the visits in the way that we do them. I would arrange it so that before I see a client for the second time, at least one month should pass. Where there is need, for instance if a woman is pregnant, the visits should be every two weeks … the visits should be targeted where there is need. (CHO, Shai-Osudoku, 2013)

Although CHOs receive additional training intended to build their capacity to engage communities with the health system, the situation described by the CHOs suggests that the prescriptive nature of their training and role prevents them from responding to communities' needs as they perceive them. Allan Kaplan highlights the tendency of organizations involved in development practice to provide training in new techniques in order to fulfil their capacity building requirements, often at the expense of providing practitioners with the opportunities to respond sensitively and appropriately to a given situation:

> … you have to develop effective development practitioners, practitioners who do not work out of books or project manuals, practitioners who do not 'work primarily out of the specifications of the world from which they have been sent' but rather 'out of an accurate and sensitive reading of the particular situation with which they are faced'. And this does not mean training them in new techniques, but fostering their development through guided reflection on action, facilitated self-critique, mentoring, peer reviews, and so on. (Kaplan 1999: 18)

The desire to be sanctioned to make more individual decisions regarding the need, location and nature of home visitations was echoed by the CHOs in all four areas in which I worked in Shai-Osudoku. Here we have evidence that reducing CHO capacity building to providing them with a blueprint for community interaction does not allow for the agency of those responsible for providing health services to the community, and restricts their ability to build positive relationships.

On another occasion, CHOs based in a CHPS zone with no clinic had scheduled home visitations for the morning. We agreed to meet at a central point in the village and walk from there, having first met with a local CHV. One of the CHOs was running late, and her fellow CHO expressed concerns that we might be too late to see the household occupants before they left for work in the fields. At this point, the CHV pointed out that we were too late in any case, and that occupants of the households in the area we were due to visit would have been away at work since 5 AM. When the second CHO arrived, they decided they would not be able to make home visitations to the community in question, commenting that those particular clients had 'never been available at the right time' when they had wanted to visit. They decided that we would visit some of the nearer households instead, choosing the area on the basis that they 'had not been there in a while' and were unable to adhere to the schedule.

CHO home visiting training materials note that visits should be made at times that are suitable for clients, which potentially means that CHOs will have to conduct visits at 'odd hours', including outside normal working hours (GHS 2009). Here, building CHO capacity to interact with communities meant ensuring that they were aware they would have to make visitations at times suitable for clients. However, this requirement is not supported in practice by the health service, which does not supply the staff or resources necessary to allow CHOs to abide by it, or provide a comprehensive feedback system for the CHOs to report issues such as this. Some of the more remote farming communities that are supposed to be covered by the CHOs had in fact never received a visit from them, meaning that people in this area were not receiving any health information or monitoring, despite the fact that the CHPS system is officially designed to target such populations.

This example also highlights the way in which CHOs respond to the limitations of their training and mandates. Not having been provided with the training or resources to cope with the fact that some of the communities they served were difficult to reach, the CHOs in this case adapted their schedule based on what they were able to manage under those conditions. The blueprint, and the informal way in which the CHOs resolved the contradictions they discovered, generates a false impression of successful implementation of the CHPS in this area. As Gasper (2000) points out in his work discussing the impact of logical frameworks, use of such frameworks often precludes the opportunity of learning from issues that arise from project implementation. Here, the blueprint for health service–community relationships supports the 'myth' of social mobilization and integration, while 'concealing divergent and contradictory logics of practice' (Mosse and Lewis 2006: 16).

Health worker strategies: brokering community health

The second circumstance arising from the health service's approach to health worker capacity building is that the restrictions placed on the CHOs contribute to an environment in which new, unplanned healthcare strategies are generated. The strategies employed by CHOs represent their attempts to navigate such restrictions, and are understood here as forms of brokerage in which social actors negotiate their roles as employees of the health service and members of their communities, rather than passively following the logic of the systems in which they operate. As Bierschenk et al. (2002) have observed, the strategies of those who act as intermediaries not only bring social and institutional conditions into view, but actively generate them.

The brokerages that emerge through the implementation of the CHPS system can be viewed as products of a system that views CHO capacity building in purely instrumental terms, leaving no mechanisms in place that empower CHOs to formalize the decisions they make on behalf of themselves and their clients. Goetz (1996) writes of the tendency of empowerment-related objectives to be downplayed in favour of more technical project inputs, a circumstance which in the case of the CHPS programme leaves CHOs with a situation in which the omission of the empowerment aspect of capacity building leaves them with limited means to formally address the issues that arise from the system as it stands.

In practice, the social mobilization aspect of CHO services that relies on home visitations had not been successfully integrated, and CHOs were increasingly defaulting on home visitations and outreach services in favour of providing clinical services within the clinic compound due to an increased client load at these centres. An investigation into the efficacy of Ghana's community health provision notes that the majority of CHOs are now running 'static clinics', without the outreach services that were originally a significant part of their mandate. In particular, home visits take place infrequently, with CHOs remaining in the clinic compound to provide curative services (Ntsua et al. 2012). This is not the result of a policy shift orchestrated by the health service, but rather a product of consensus developing between CHOs as they grapple with the narrow mandates and limited training with which they have been provided. As this trend has progressed, both CHO and community expectations have shifted, resulting in a system in which CHOs are regarded primarily as nurses who provide curative care, rather than community-integrated service providers as was intended. CHVs are increasingly expected to take up the role of connecting with households and feeding back to the clinic compound, but as unpaid volunteers with limited training, they are unable to fill the gap.

CHOs operating at different clinic compounds in Shai-Osudoku have the opportunity to meet when attending supplemental training sessions at the district hospital, or when taking part in 'peer monitoring', an infrequently occurring meeting of district CHOs that allows them the opportunity to discuss with one another their experiences of working in their communities. A key issue for CHOs is the number of home visitations that they are expected to achieve per month, and the difficulties involved in scheduling these visits. The directive to ensure that clients received visits at appropriate times meant that CHOs were essentially required to make visits at night, and to travel long distances on foot where transport is not available. Due to lack of community compound staffing, this meant that CHOs would have to conduct visits alone. Most CHOs in the district would not undertake home visitations alone or at night, after having bad experiences or having heard of problems experienced by other nurses.

One nurse describes an informal meeting of district health workers in which consensus was reached that it was too dangerous to conduct home visits unaccompanied and at night:

> There are risks with it [home visits]. Sometimes when you go to a certain house dogs will be attacking you so we go in twos in case of any problem and sometimes some men … if the person is not normal, will rape you so we have to go in twos. One of the nurses told us that when she went on home visits and some men in the village said they were trying to rape her. They did not but she became scared. When I came here I was going alone, we were given a [visiting] book each. We were four in number and we divided ourselves, one to each village. But we never did this again. Nobody says we can do this but because of the risk, we had to advise ourselves to go in twos. But it's something they [the hospital] want us to do every day. (CHN, Shai-Osudoku, 2013)

The emphasis on capacity building as training rather than empowering health workers to provide feedback to district health officials has led to a practical situation in which they feel they are expected to make visits after dark, which is potentially dangerous. In response, CHOs collaborate, creating new rules and policies whereby they will not make visits alone. The health service capacity building agenda does not focus on providing health workers with a sustained feedback system, therefore some home visits are not carried out, and the problem is not addressed.

A further example of brokerage among health workers emerged from discussions surrounding the low number of births that take place at the CHPS clinic compounds. At one clinic, CHOs reported an average of one or two deliveries taking place in the clinic each month, with many months having passed without any having taken place there at all. One CHN explained that the clinic midwife is afraid that deliveries will be complicated, and concerned that they do not have adequate resources at the clinic. When pregnant women visit, she refers them to the district hospital at Dodowa, about twenty kilometres away. During interviews, the midwife said that 'any little complication I will send them to Dodowa – they have the proper facilities'. This has become a pattern that alarms the CHOs at this clinic, who note that all women are assessed as having potential complications, although these are often not appreciated by the CHOs. It is understood by those in the community that the midwife at this clinic will not perform deliveries at all, and the consensus in the community is that they would not benefit from seeking maternal health services from her. According to the CHOs, community members have taken to referring to the midwife as 'Dodowa', after the hospital to which she sends women to deliver.

The implications of this response to health service limitations for the provision of maternal health services in the area are severe, the hospital being too far away for many women to walk to or pay for transport. Although this issue causes serious concern among CHOs, none have communicated their concerns to the midwife or their supervisors in the district health authority, and instead collaborate in perpetuating the idea that the pregnant women they see are high risk and needed to be referred when asked by district inspectors why the clinic birth rate is low. They have discussed ways to inform the district health authorities, but none have acted on it. One nurse explained their approach to this issue in their clinic compound:

> It is fear. When you hear the stories in town about the midwife, they are saying when they come here the midwife will tell them to go to Dodowa. Meanwhile there is no problem with the person ... The midwife is supposed to deliver the person here, unless there are complications ... but where there is no problem she still tells the person to go to Dodowa. People do not come to this clinic to deliver. They are afraid to come – what they are saying in town is that she will tell you to go away, so they wouldn't even come here now. They are really complaining ... Some will go to Dodowa but others will deliver in the house. We can't tell about this, we will be in trouble. There is a suggestion box at Dodowa, I was suggesting we could write and put it in the box, but I don't know. Maybe I'll write it and ask a client to put it in. That way they will not see it is me. I can't talk. (CHN, Shai-Osudoku, 2013)

This example demonstrates the severity of the consequences that can arise from limiting the definition of health worker capacity building to the basic requirements of training and mandated duties. Although district health workers receive official mandates and training in improving community relationships, they are left to function in a system that occludes mechanisms that would formally empower them, either by recognizing their own expertise gained from their knowledge of their communities, or by providing a comprehensive feedback system for them to communicate problems. Health worker strategies have become a feature of their daily lives, sometimes emerging from attempts to improve the care they provide to their communities, and other times from necessity, either for their own wellbeing or because they were unable to meet the demands of the CHPS programme. As a result of the constraints under which they operated, health workers had become the architects of the version of the CHPS programme that was implemented on a day-to-day basis – they were, as Goetz has put it, 'de-facto policy makers' (1996: 122).

Conclusion: capacity building in health sector bureaucracies

In the case of the CHPS programme, the instrumental conceptualization of capacity building contributed to a situation in which health workers' ability to forge positive community relationships was severely limited, often compelling them to implement their own strategies in order to navigate the demands of the programme and the communities in which they lived. For many who work in development contexts, the concept of capacity building denotes empowering people to determine their own priorities, and providing them with the means with which to effect change (Eade and Williams 1995). Yet translated into the policy language and structure of the existing health service, it has emerged having been stripped of the elements that would serve to empower health workers to effect the social mobilization element of their mandate. In the context of the health service, building health worker capacity means supplying the necessary training, and implementing policies requiring them to expand their roles in prescribed ways. It does not empower health workers to play a formal role in policy development, nor does it explore the possibility of utilizing health workers to further broader social and political processes in their communities.

That concepts designed to empower and facilitate social justice become neutralized buzzwords when exposed to development policy processes has long been a cause for concern as various advocates seek ways to improve lives through policy interventions (Cornwall and Brock 2005). The dilemma with which we are confronted is that of whether concepts such as capacity building might do the transformative work of empowerment and social justice when utilized by anodyne bureaucracies built to deliver exclusively technical services. As Shore and Wright observe, 'policies are most obviously political phenomena, yet it is a feature of policies that their political nature is disguised by the objective, neutral, legal-rational idioms in which they are portrayed' (1997: 8).

It is often assumed in the arena of health and development and beyond that policy is the site at which social change must be performed. However, despite considerable efforts to bring discourses of rights and power to bear on policy through the introduction of concepts such as capacity building, it continues to yield technical solutions that fail to address the structural causes of inequality. Standing provides a useful framework for thinking about the relationship between such transformative concepts and health systems, noting that '[health sector] bureaucracies are not engines of social and political transformation' (2007: 104). She argues that this work must happen elsewhere, through sustained dialogue between advocates of health and rights and the political agencies that generate the structures of governance that informs health policy. When examining state health services, our understanding of the relationship between socially and politically transformative concepts and bureaucracies should be informed by the fact that the two are built on incommensurate logics. Therefore, rather than asking health services to utterly transform the way in which they operate, it is necessary to evaluate their deployment of concepts such as capacity building using frameworks that can be understood on their own terms.

Returning to the case of the CHPS programme discussed here, let us address the conceptualization of health worker capacity building in the programme and ask what it is in their power to do to enhance the role of health workers and improve community–health service relationships. A principal lesson emerging from health service policy and training literature is that it is necessary for the programme to clearly define the term capacity building in the context of health worker management and training. In current health service literature, the term is indirectly defined through repeated references to it in the context of health worker training. It is well within the remit of the health service to offer a clear definition of their use of the term, and to draw clear links between health worker capacity building, improved health worker efficacy and community health outcomes.

A further improvement that could be implemented is to generate health worker capacity building policies on the basis of health worker experiences. Viewed in this way, capacity building would denote not only additional training, but also the development of mechanisms such as feedback opportunities and health worker participation in local policy making. Again, such changes are within the remit of the district health authority to introduce, and could empower health workers to prevent situations in which communities are alienated by frequent, unnecessary visits. Conversely, health worker-oriented capacity building would also help to highlight issues regarding the difficulties in reaching some communities, which could then contribute to improved programme development. There is scope here for community health workers to play a more formal role in determining programme policies, and in this way build the capacity of programme administrators to deliver more effective interventions. Such an approach would also serve to improve the experience of health workers themselves, who often have a substantial burden to bear in their roles as negotiators between an inflexible, underfunded health system and the demands of their communities. As Maes et al. (2014) point out, the importance of improving community health worker labour relations is often overlooked, due in part to the tendency of health programmes to focus on the provision of services rather than the empowerment of stakeholders, including the health workers who deliver the programme.

Examining the relationship between the health service's conceptualization of health worker capacity building and the problems experienced by health workers in adhering to their social mobilization role suggests that there is much that health and rights advocates can do to work with policy architects to improve health worker capacity building. While it may be beyond the scope of a health bureaucracy to take a political stance in driving forward health rights and social justice, it is certainly possible to highlight specific problems experienced by health workers and community members, and reformulate the concept of health worker capacity building such that health workers are empowered to improve the health of the communities for whom they work.

Acknowledgements

This chapter includes case studies drawn from my doctoral research. I would like to thank my supervisor, Professor Naila Kabeer, and the administrative and medical staff of Shai-Osudoku, Ghana, for the permissions and participation that made this research possible. My doctoral research was supported by a grant from the School of Oriental and African Studies. This chapter is the result of a workshop on 'Hope and Insufficiency: Capacity Building in Ethnographic Comparison' funded by the Wenner-Gren Foundation for Anthropological Research. I am grateful to the organizers of the workshop and to the participants for their many insights.

Harriet Boulding is Research Fellow in the Policy Institute, King's College London. Her research focuses on global maternal and child health policy and policy impact from health research. She has authored publications on impact mechanisms in public health research, and has advised the UK Department of Health and Social Care on cross-cutting public health and social policy issues.

References

Awofeso, N. 2013. *Organisational Capacity Building in Health Systems.* New York: Routledge.
Awoonor-Williams, J., E. Sory, F. Nyonator, J. F. Phillips, C. Wang and M. L. Schmitt. 2013. 'Lessons Learned from Scaling up a Community-Based Health Programme in the Upper East Region of Northern Ghana'. *Global Health Science and Practice* 1 (1): 117–133.
Bierschenk, T., J. Chaveau and J. Olivier de Sardan. 2002. 'Local Development Brokers in Africa: The Rise of a New Social Category'. Working paper no. 13, Institut für Ethnologie und Afrikasudien, Johannes Gutenberg Universität, Mainz.
Cornwall, A. and K. Brock. 2005. 'What Do Buzzwords Do for Development Policy? A Critical Look at "Participation", "Empowerment" and "Poverty Reduction"'. *Third World Quarterly* 26 (7): 1043–1060.
Eade, D. 1997. *Capacity-Building: An Approach to People-Centred Development.* Oxford: Oxfam.
Eade, D. and S. Williams. 1995. *The Oxfam Handbook of Development and Relief.* Vol. 1. Oxford: Oxfam.
Gasper, D. 2000. 'Evaluating the "Logical Framework Approach" towards Learning-Oriented Development Evaluation'. *Public Administration and Development* 20: 17–28.
GHS (Ghana Health Service). 2002. *The Community-Based Health Planning and Services (CHPS) Initiative: The Concepts and Plans for Implementation.* Accra, Ghana: Ghana Health Service.
GHS (Ghana Health Service). 2005. *Community-Based Health Planning and Services (CHPS): The Operational Policy.* Accra, Ghana: Ghana Health Service.
GHS (Ghana Health Service). 2009. *Community Health Officer's Training Workbook.* Vol. 1. Accra, Ghana: Ghana Health Service.

Goetz, A. 1996. 'Local Heroes: Patterns of Fieldworker Discretion in Implementing GAD Policy in Bangladesh'. IDS Discussion Paper 358. Brighton: Institute of Development Studies.

Haines, A., D. Sanders, U. Lehmann, A. Rowe, J. E. Lawn, S. Jan, D. G. Walker, Z. Bhutta. 2007. 'Achieving Child Survival Goals: Potential Contribution of Community Health Workers'. *The Lancet* 369 (9579): 2121–2131.

Kaplan, A. 1999. 'The Developing of Capacity'. Development dossier, paper no. 10. New York: United Nations Non-Governmental Liaison Service.

Maes, K., S. Closser and I. Kalofonos. 2014. 'Listening to Community Health Workers: How Ethnographic Research Can Inform Positive Relationships among Community Health Workers, Health Institutions, and Communities'. *American Journal of Public Health* 104 (5): e5–e9.

MOH (Ministry of Health, Ghana). 2014. 'Government of Ghana: National Community Health Worker (CHW) Programme'. Accra, Ghana: Ministry of Health.

Mosse, D. and D. Lewis. 2006. *Development Brokers and Translators: The Ethnography of Aid and Agencies*. Boulder, CO: Kumarian Press.

Ntsua, S., P. Tapsoba, G. Quansah Asare and F. Nyonator. 2012. 'Repositioning Community-Based Family Planning in Ghana: A Case Study of Community-Based Health Planning and Services (CHPS) (Case Study Report)'. Washington, DC: The Population Council.

Nyonator, F., J. Awoonor-Williams, J. F. Phillips, T. C. Jones and R. A. Miller. 2005. 'The Ghana Community-Based Health Planning and Services Initiative for Scaling up Service Delivery Innovation'. *Health Policy and Planning* 20 (1): 25–34.

Oliveira-Cruz, V., C. Kurowski and A. Mills. 2003. 'Delivery of Priority Health Services: Searching for Synergies within the Vertical versus Horizontal Debate'. *Journal of International Development* 15 (1): 67–86.

Pence, B., P. Nyarko, F. Binka, J. F. Phillips and C. Debpuur. 2001. 'The Impact of the Navrongo Community Health and Family Planning Project on Child Mortality, 1993–2000'. Paper presented at the Global Conference of the International Union for the Scientific Study of Population, Salvador, Brazil, 18–24 August.

Shore, C. and S. Wright (eds). 1997. *Anthropology of Policy: Critical Perspectives on Governance and Power*. New York and London: Routledge.

SPH (School of Public Health, University of Ghana). 2009. 'In-Depth Review of the Community-Based Health Planning Services (CHPS) Programme. A Report of the Annual Health Sector Review 2009. Final Report'. Accra, Ghana: Ministry of Health.

Standing, H. 2007. 'Gender, Myth and Fable: The Perils of Mainstreaming in Sector Bureaucracies.' In A. Cornwell, E. Harrison and A. Whitehead (eds), *Feminisms in Development: Contradictions, Contestations, and Challenges*. London and New York: Zed Books, 101–110.

WHO (World Health Organisation). 2009. 'Health-Promoting Health Systems: Imperatives for Action'. Working document for discussion at the 7th Global Conference on Health Promotion, 'Promoting Health and Development: Closing the Implementation Gap', Nairobi, Kenya, 26–30 October.

WHO (World Health Organisation). 2015. *Global Health Workforce Alliance Country Case Study: Ghana: Implementing a National Human Resources for Health Plan*. WHO, 3 July. http://www.who.int/workforcealliance/knowledge/case_studies/CS_Ghana_web_en.pdf.

Yazbeck, A. 2009. *Attacking Inequality in the Health Sector: A Synthesis of Evidence and Tools*. Washington, DC: The World Bank.

Chapter 6

Personal and Professional Encompassment in Organizational Capacity Building
SOS Children's Villages and Supportive Housing

Viktoryia Kalesnikava

What is the purpose of an organization? How does an institution enact or build its perceived capacity? These questions are hardly intriguing or new. Yet once we look past the bureaucratic tiers of regulatory policies and prescriptive practices that govern institutional existence, we face a person who wields the capacity to interpret and enact, even alter, organizational mandates and standards. In the 1970s, many in anthropology claimed that there was no such thing as kinship (e.g. Schneider 1972). Likewise, one could argue today that there is no such thing as an institution, only relational categories and persons 'who are able to mobilise around the power to speak the truth and the capacity to act knowledgeably upon conduct' (Rose 1999: 51). The experts or professionals who comprise and enact organizational cultures of governance across all scales of modern Euro-American sociality are 'new subjects of power and new intermediaries who intervene in the social' (Shore and Wright 1997: 7). These professionals, who are at the centre of this chapter, are not passively configured by forms and structures of power, but act as custodians of organizational values of professional ethics, accountability, 'individualism' and 'freedom of choice', elevated to a cultural logic through expert knowledge practices (Ong 2006).

This chapter is about the conceptual interplay between personal and professional domains mutually constituted through organizational practices. My aims are twofold. Firstly, I explore how organizational capacity to shape the social is achieved through the knowledge practices of professionals and experts. My ethnographic material is drawn from two different Euro-American non-governmental organizations (NGOs), SOS Children's Villages (SOSCV) in Russia and Australia, and Supportive Housing (SH) in the USA. I focus on the everyday activities of employees of these organizations, caretaking and case management respectively, as a way of drawing attention to the way painfully obvious and taken-for-granted organizational practices reveal the not so obvious – but equally taken-for-granted – conceptual divisions and moral incongruences between personal and professional domains. These conceptual divisions directly influence how the capacities of experts are understood.

Secondly, using theoretical foundations supplied by anthropological literature on concepts (Wagner [1975] 1981; Jiménez and Willerslev 2007), kinship (Wagner 1977; Schneider 1980) and organizations (Strathern 2000; Jiménez 2007), I analyse the deployment and function of these conceptual divisions in the context of the two organizational cultures. Through bringing forward ethnographic moments of this 'mundane' work, I show how the professional domain (actualized through the category of expert and employee) continuously encompasses the personal (seen through the category of home or kinship) within a hierarchical relation. When pushed to their limits within the organizational paradigm, I argue, one domain extends out of proportion (Jiménez 2008) towards its limit, and reverses itself, thus encompassing and subsuming the other (Dumont 1980; Barnes 1985). Such dynamic movement differentiates the domains of the personal and the professional, but also threatens the tenuous boundary between them. The consequence is that professional moral conduct is often endangered, proving detrimental to professional employment and even institutional existence.

In examining the interplay between the domains of the personal and the professional, I argue that each concept deploys the other in order to fulfil its organizational function, taking turns in assuming the ground for the other (Wagner [1975] 1981). Arguably, then, a professional is recognized as an expert in a workspace when he or she is able to master the skill of negotiating personal and professional domains and deploy them seamlessly in line with organizational agendas and ethics.

The organizations I have chosen to write about in this chapter are distinct, yet I here draw them under the same framework. Structurally, both perform a similar function in the social, albeit targeting different demographics. SOSCV is a global orphan charity that works with children; SH helps homeless adults and families in the United States. Both organizations are designed to implement social interventions that provide their targeted populations with a 'home', deemed vital to the well-being of a person. Here, the concept of 'home' is used *literally*, as both of the organizations provide physical shelter, and *figuratively*, deployed as a synecdoche, which stands in for the absence of personal functions, relations and roles such as love, family, household, belonging and social support of other persons. Both SOSCV and SH, by allocating their employees to perform certain duties within these homes, attempt to fill personal roles through professional practices and thus position themselves, literally and figuratively, at the edge between personal and professional domains. By virtue of their explicit professional aims, these organizations offer unique case studies through which to illuminate the dynamic binary between the personal and the professional, and an opportunity to magnify their dialectical oscillation.

My ethnographic encounter with SOSCV occurred in 2010 in Russia, where I was conducting summer field research. The encounter with SH happened a few years later, in the United States. Notably, my personal entanglements with these institutions were mediated through the two different roles that I had to assume by the nature of my own professional commitments as anthropologist and social worker, respectively. Formally, I was accepted as an intern at both of these organizations. However, at SOSCV I was seen as a research intern, and at SH, as an intern case-manager. These differences cast a shadow on my understanding of their organizational practices as I draw my comparisons. Although the comparative framework implicitly holds the conceptual space, my purpose here is not to compare the similarities and differences between these institutions, but to explore how 'relations and connections between entities can appear in new configurations as one transfers from one domain of inquiry to another' (Strathern 2004: xv).

SOS Children's Villages: institutional model

The site of my research internship in Russia, in 2010, was SOS Children's Villages (SOSCV), a transnational NGO. SOSCV's goal is to provide long-term care for orphan and abandoned children around the world. SOSCV was founded by an Austrian medical student in 1949, who, by designing the kinship-centred intervention model that SOSCV follows today, aimed to ease the plight of WWII orphans. At the time of writing, SOSCV operates in more than 130 countries. Its unique model of care is explicitly based on kinship, and still embodies the original four tenets of home, mother, siblings and village. Building on these tenets, SOSCV claims to provide every child (orphaned, abandoned or in need) with a 'permanent loving home' and 'family' in a village well integrated with the surrounding community.[1] To be clear, a mother here is not biological, but rather an employee entrusted with the organizational function of mothering admitted orphans. Likewise, children become siblings by virtue of being mothered in a single house by an SOS-mother, although children who are related by blood are intentionally kept under a single roof. Finally, the villages are intentional communities on SOSCV property, although the exact structural configurations vary by country.

I take as my analytical focus the SOSCV's model of care, which is predicated on providing orphan children with a 'home', run by a loving 'mother'. Arguably, it is the category of mother that holds the SOSCV intervention strategy together. By examining the implications of being a professional 'mother', I foreground the seemingly unreconciled division between motherhood as a profession and motherhood as a vocation that is situated at the very heart of what it means to be an SOS-mother. Notably, this conceptual divide that an SOS-mother embodies at once unsettles the categories of 'parent' and 'employee', 'home' and 'workplace' (Peck 1996), and also forces these domains of personal and professional into analogical extensions, and service of one another, thus blurring the ethical boundaries originally drawn and contained within each term. Through the mutual encompassment of the domains of personal and professional, the category of SOS-mother brings forth the following questions: What does it mean to be a good mother versus a good employee? What does it take to fulfil the claim of being at once an 'emotional caregiver' and a 'professional educator'? Who gets to define and redraw the new boundaries between personal and professional domains?

These are but a few of the questions that are always already being negotiated and brought into the institutional fold by the NGO itself. As I will show further, the means of negotiating this split extends beyond institutional walls and discursive facts, forming a way of life for SOS-mothers and a matter of survival for the NGO itself. Here, I will mainly draw on material from SOSCV-Russia and SOSCV-Australia. SOSCV-Australia was closed down in 2005, an event I discuss later, while SOSCV-Russia has been in operation since 1996.[2] In Russia, there are currently six active villages, all clustered around large metropolitan areas such as Moscow, Orlov and St. Petersburg. A total of more than 1,000 children live in these villages. As an intern in Moscow, I was able to move freely between SOSCV administrative offices and actual villages, where mothers and children reside under the leadership and supervision of the village director. This mobility informed my analysis, and allowed me to see the role of SOS-mother from different institutional viewpoints and perspectives.

SOS-mother – an employee or a parent?

What happens when an institution such as SOSCV organizes social practice and intervention on the model of kinship or family, but yet is situated within the context of the social contract and professional ethics? The concept of kinship here is distinct from the anthropological category that stands for a kind of generic relatedness constituted through blood, food, contract or property (c.f. Carsten 2004). Instead, SOS kinship is institutionally sanctioned and aims to be produced and regulated just like any kind of professional service. Importantly, it is less the cultural specificity of the model that matters here – the kind of kinship, or family forged (i.e. patrilineal, matrilineal or single-headed) – but rather the attempt by SOSCV to institute within the space of the organization the idea of love and care that Euro-Americans imagine are inherent in the 'natural' affective bonds of consanguinity (Schneider 1980).

In so far as SOSCV's concept of care is based on the model of the Euro-American family with mechanisms of professional service at its core, one should expect SOSCV to have standard measures and operational procedures designed to 'foster ethical behaviour' and 'good practice' of motherhood. As Strathern points out, these professional measures and procedures are designed to ensure that 'organisations are managing their affairs properly, and this elision of propriety and efficiency requires proof that they are acting as proper organisations' (2008: 465). Indeed, SOSCV has developed a two-year training programme for preparing prospective SOS-mothers. 'International standards for selection, training and support networks for the SOS-mothers are put into practice by each SOS Children's Village and are continually updated', says one of the SOSCV

Newsletters.³ Each woman has to undergo initial training and testing, which is followed up by another year of intermittent training and work. During these preparations, all of the women receive regular pay, other benefits and travel expenses. What, then, is taken as the standard or measure for becoming an SOS-mother and entering the programme? What was being expected and cultivated through SOS trainings? When I asked one of the SOS psychologists, responsible for the selection process of prospective SOS-mothers, how they determine a qualified SOS-mother-to-be in Moscow, Russia, she replied with noticeable delight:

> Here is one of the strategies I employ quite often, which has never failed me as an initial assessment. Every time a new applicant comes in for an interview for an SOS-mother position, I purposefully place a baby doll on the floor several feet away from my table. The woman who picks up the doll is the one who has what it takes. She passes the initial test of character.

This remark, put alongside the 'international standards' of the training programme for SOS-mothers, points to the complex and contradictory nature of the SOS-mother's profession. It reveals that SOSCV is well aware of the highly contested role of a mother upon which their organizational capacity stands – a mother wanting to be trained must also already have 'character'. Once selected for training, the organization attempts to manage the gaps and contradictory distinctions through best practices and professional knowledge. One of the most visible implications of this for SOS-mothers is that their roles and everyday actions within their SOS-families come to be inflected and defined by these illusive measures of quality of professional practices.

In Russia, some SOS-mothers kept foregrounding that they did not feel they could make any important decisions pertaining to children without informing administration. Much of the mothers' daily routine was regulated and subject to inspection (both internal to the NGO, as well as coming from the state government): anything from what pots and pans to use to cook, to house and laundry cleaning and daily schedules. They were obligated to regularly report their actions and ask for permission from the village director, the actual legal guardian of all the children in the village. SOS-mothers were also given weekly allowances, for which they had to be fully accountable by providing relevant receipts. As it turns out, the expense accountability presented some issues, especially at the nearby market, where people sell local produce with no licence or cash registers to issue receipts. At one point, SOS-children shared with me that every time they went to a supermarket, each of them had a duty to pick out as many receipts as possible from the receipt bin. This way, they explained, their mother could submit these receipts for the food they buy at the market, where it was usually fresher and of a much lower cost.⁴

These otherwise mundane details highlight the tangible ambiguity of the role of SOS-mother, which is predicated on the inherent encompassment of incommensurable categories of professional employee and parent that SOS-mothers are asked to assume by the virtue of their employment. Arguably, then, the very nature of SOS-mothers' organizational position throws into question the capacity of SOSCV to measure and control mothering through professional practices and normative regulations.

During one of the interviews with the director at an SOS village in Russia, I was told that 'SOS-mothers are not mothers in a regular sense of the word, but caregivers'. 'Unfortunately', he continued,

> a lot of them think that being an SOS-mother is a real thing, but it is not, it is a work, it is a hard work for which one needs a vocation and determination in order to persevere. We try to make this clear to each and every one of them at the start – during the initial months of education and practice.

During a lunch conversation with one of the SOS-mothers, I asked what brought her to the role. 'Fate and a random newspaper advertisement', she answered with a warm smile, while showing me photos of her married SOS-daughters, sons and grandsons. She has never been married herself, and never had children of her own,[5] and as soon as she welcomed her first SOS-child into her brand new SOSCV two-storied house, she decided to dedicate herself solely to raising 'these' children. 'My children', she instantly corrected herself.

These brief vignettes from interactions with mothers and management within the Russian SOSCV begin to show the subtle and inherently unstable nature of the category of SOS-motherhood as it spans disparate practices and domains. Both mothers and management find themselves in negotiation between the personal and professional domains, revealed as they move between places differentially categorized as the home and the workplace, and between activities that might at one point be quantitative performance measures and at other points personal relations.

The second body of material I draw on to illustrate the tensions inherent in the category of the SOSCV mother comes from SOSCV at Seaford Rise, Australia. This account is based solely on information I obtained from reports[6] issued in relation to the closure of SOSCV-Australia after nearly ten years of operation (1996–2004). In 2005, SOSCV-Australia was forcefully closed down by the Australian Labor Union in coordination with the Department of Human Services (or colloquially 'the Department'). Despite its intervention model explicitly based on kinship, SOSCV is officially considered an orphanage or foster care institution under Australian regulation.[7] Accordingly, an SOS-mother is legally regarded as a professional caregiver and employee of the organization. The Australian Labor Union and the Department, citing an employer code, blamed SOSCV for oppressing and severely underpaying SOS-mothers, arguing that professional 'caregivers' should be paid 'from nine to five', as well as for any overtime and emotional stress.[8] To this, SOSCV responded that an SOS-mother is a 'vocational commitment and that as such they could not be regulated by the provisions of a pay designed for "nine to five" social workers working in an office environment'.[9] In a newsletter, SOSCV-Australia detailed the accusations levelled at them from their opponents:

> The SOS model, based as it is on motherhood, was too simplistic and out of date ... children in care, having suffered separation from their birth families, need more sophisticated care than a mother can give, those of case workers and social workers supported by psychologists, psychiatrists, therapists, mentors, and counsellors.[10]

As such, the Labor Union and the Department representatives insisted on redrawing strict, separating boundaries around the roles of mother and professional employee. In the process, the assignment of expertise fell squarely on the side of the employee, negating any 'expertise' of someone in the role of a mother to raise children. Instead, a social worker, or case worker, was deemed the professional with sufficient capacity to raise and care for a child.

I heard similar criticism of SOSCV in Russia, voiced by some of the state officials and government social workers, who were rather sceptical of the entire model of SOSCV, although their underlying reasons varied. Some officials would not accept that a hired woman could become a 'real parent', and believed that the efforts and funds used on SOSCV were better spent looking for potential adoptive parents, following the legislative mandates to distribute orphans to actual families.[11] From the standpoint of the Russian officials in charge of allocating orphan children, to send children from one institution to another lacked value or incentive, as this would not satisfy, let alone improve their performance measures and statistical outcomes. As a result, in 2010, SOSCV-Russia experienced a chronic lack of children, who, instead, were kept in standard state orphanages or group homes.

As my internship progressed, I was puzzled by a sentiment repeatedly expressed by some SOS-children themselves, who, according to an SOS psychologist, 'think that their SOS-mothers do not have any worthwhile occupation or career. They are paid to stay home and do nothing'.[12] Conceivably, SOS-children, longing for normative divisions and expectations, upheld the structural categories that strictly separate kinship and professional expertise, considering the former as a matter of home and leisure, and the latter as work and career. Whether driven by an implicit desire to assert that their mothers were, in fact, 'real', thus refusing to grant them the status of an employee, or out of refusal to acknowledge mothering as employment, they too insisted on dividing the labour of their mothers along divided lines, despite the fact that it was based on the encompassment of this binary. Thus, in the course of this description, we can see how conceptual divisions between the personal and professional that lie at the heart of the SOSCV model and organizational practices occasionally reach their limit. It is at these points that they assume the ground and subsume the other within their value system, thus influencing the capacity of SOSCV to legitimize and reproduce itself both outwardly and from within.

Supportive Housing: institutional models

Let me now turn to my second case of institutional category work, that of Supportive Housing in the USA, where I carried out an internship as a case manager and social worker. Supportive Housing (SH) has its roots in the economic downturn of the 1970s that followed the Vietnam War, when, during the dismantling of large-scale state psychiatric facilities, homelessness became 'too visible' in major urban centres across the United States. In the 1980s, SH, a US-based federal government-sponsored intervention, emerged as a response to the growing size of the homeless population. Since its inception, SH projects have been spreading, and it is now represented across the US. Supported by the US Department of Housing and Urban Development (HUD) and the US Interagency Council on Homelessness (USICH), SH was designed to address homelessness by providing a combination of permanent housing and professional support for homeless and low-income adults (Erickson 1987).

The institutional model of SH emphasizes a low-barrier approach, where only two entrance requirements exist: the condition of homelessness and/or low-income earnings, and the ability to live without assistance. No requirements for substance use cessation are mandated, although SH residents are actively encouraged to quit. Veterans and people with mild mental or physical disabilities comprise some of the main groups that SH serves. The rent is low or minimal, sponsored through matching grants from local, state and federal governments. SH is based on the premise that by providing stable housing as well as social support, the residents will be inclined to abandon substance use, find gainful employment and become 'functional' members of society. This foundational premise of SH is based on the concept of a 'Housing First' model for chronic homelessness (Erickson 1987). That is, if people are given a home and the stable environment that comes with it, they will transition away from substance abuse towards self-sufficiency and independence.

Just as SOSCV offers a home and parenting to children as an intervention strategy, SH offers a home and social support to single adults and families. The institution is a service and social intervention that works for some, but not for all. Ironically, just as many street children prefer their life on the street to the 'home' and 'safety' of SOSCV (c.f. Hecht 1998), many homeless people choose the streets or woods over the 'home' and 'security' of SH. Repeatedly, I was told by several current and past SH residents, who were formerly homeless, that SH was colloquially dubbed the 'prison' or a 'morgue', mainly due to the punitive regulations and rules that it enforces among its residents.

Indeed, some features of the SH model, manifested through the architectural design and structural regulations enforced in some (although not all) SH apartment buildings and complexes, bear resemblance to a prison. The entrance is usually locked and both the residents and staff have to use assigned passes to gain access. Premises are monitored day and night with countless security cameras. Furthermore, strict policies mandate no overnight visitors, which includes relatives, close friends and partners, and all visitors are required to register at the entrance desk and leave a valid ID. Residents are penalized for violating these rules, sometimes with the direct threat of losing their home.

The physical environment and regulatory practices of SH embody multiple contradictions: a home resembling a prison, independence yet continuous monitoring. These contradictions, however, allow insight both into the role of the institution and its employees, or professionals, who are burdened to keep the institution functional. The explicit goal of SH is fostering 'independence' and 'self-sufficiency' among the residents. Arguably, the punitive nature of SH regulations facilitates the opposite – a sense of powerlessness – while prohibition of overnight visitors discourages the residents from establishing meaningful long-term relationships with people in their lives, who often become instrumental to building a path to 'self-sufficiency'. Additionally, the concept of 'home' is not easily associated with cameras and rules that mandate and enforce a certain external order set up to police and punish. The presence of such restrictions obliges residents to assume the roles of obedient, normalized, 'good' citizens, who are either transformed or tamed through the delivery of 'benevolent services', or forced to leave (Epstein 1999: 10).

Some arguments are cast for upholding the regulations for safety and responsibility. Presumably, the presence of these strict rules and watchful cameras provides a safe and secure environment, thus offering peace of mind to residents, who might fear outsiders not invested in observing the order or in upholding rules of mutual respect. Notably, among at least a dozen of the residents who talked with me about the no overnight visitors rule, only one spoke in its favour.

Several residents brought up the idea of a petition that would convey a collective complaint against the restrictive nature of SH regulations, impinging upon the relations the residents cherished. At their request and in line with (what I thought to be) my role as intern social worker, I drafted a petition to the board of SH directors who had direct oversight of the issue. The process, however, was stalled by my immediate supervisor,[13] who explained that it was fine to write up the residents' concerns, but not in the form of a petition, because 'for the SH staff [to facilitate it] might have unintended consequences'. In my attempt to advocate on behalf of the clients, as an SH staff member I was scolded for potentially stirring up conflict. As a social work student evaluated by the same supervisor, however, I received a mark of distinction for my capacity to advocate on behalf of clients.

This tension points to the irreducible roles of an employee of an organization and a social worker or advocate. These roles – working for the institution versus working for a client – each centre on a value system and enter into a contentious relation, and hence an inevitable moral dilemma. Here, self-preservationist professionalism with organizational values at the forefront takes precedence over the personal values of advocacy, rendering the institutional structures unchallenged and professional hierarchy confirmed.

Social worker – individual or employee?

Employees of service organizations of the kind I have discussed here would attest that their employment is predicated on (at minimum) a dual responsibility, shared between the organization itself and their clients. Likewise, SH employees both promote and maintain organizational values and help the SH residents achieve 'self-sufficiency'. By design, provision of support services, mostly comprised of social workers and counsellors, is one of the central components of the SH institutional model, which is intended to serve as a bridge facilitating transitions towards 'independence' and ensuring that these transitions eventually happen. By design, then, SH social workers are burdened with the difficult task of securing trust among the professional circles with whom SH contracts to provide services for SH residents (often governmental organizations, coupled with bureaucratic demands) as well as with SH residents themselves. The latter are often persons who have lost any sense that society could be just and fair, and are thus reluctant to trust again.

As an SH intern and employee, I would often find myself feeling torn between the roles and power play that social workers have to negotiate throughout their daily routines. As a professional, I would intentionally use my position to tenaciously and shamelessly demand benefits for my clients – anything from disability checks to health insurance and free meals and eyeglasses. Often, my spoken word as an expert was enough to grant or disqualify a client's claim. In my relations with the residents, however, I had to be strategic in negotiating ties. I felt a necessity to be sincere and relate to my clients as individuals with human values and vulnerabilities. This necessity, however, had to be carefully negotiated as I was expected to see the SH residents as only *human enough* so as not to overstep the fine boundaries between 'client' and 'friend'.

Indeed, professional relatedness has to be just *close enough* to preserve the power differential, such that the original categories of employee and client are continuously reproduced and reinstalled again in order to perpetuate the institutional structure and normative hierarchy. Upsetting this fragile balance exposes the inherently relational nature of professional expertise, often resulting in unpleasant repercussions or professional termination. Out of professional obligation to perform their duties well, SH social workers are forced to situate themselves at the edge of the opposing social domains between the personal and professional. But they are under an equally stringent obligation to police these very boundaries or else fall prey to ethical and professional transgressions.

At one point during my internship at SH, I observed an incident that occurred at one of the SH locations. An agency social worker[14] found herself fostering exceedingly dependent relations with her regular clients. Specifically, the social worker would often assume the role of motherly caregiver; she would routinely perform basic chores for the clients, which they were more than capable of completing on their own. She also let them use her name as co-signer on bank accounts, and even helped store their bank information and prescription medications. She would often come to the agency to help facilitate a conflict between clients during late hours or over the weekend, off the clock. In fact, her 'commitment to the cause' meant that the professional and personal gradually became one and the same, and the categories of caregiver and friend began to take precedence over the ones institutionally assigned.

After a period of time, however, she suddenly resigned. She failed to provide the mandated two weeks' notice; neither did she warn any of the agency's staff members of her decision. Everyone, including her former clients, was in genuine shock and disbelief. Her clients mourned her departure; some mourned in rage. They lamented the painful 'loss of a friend'. Several days later, it became clear that she had left with another SH resident. The only follow-up comment from her supervisor was that due to such an abrupt and unethical departure, she would not be able to give a good recommendation to an otherwise excellent employee.

In social work academic programmes, the acknowledgement that employees are bound to occupy more than one category at a time is formally termed an 'ethical dilemma'. The SH employee's eventual departure and the supervisor's comment, however, signal which category of person takes precedence legally, socially and ethically. Personal categories like friend, or kin, cannot be found in training manuals, ethical disclosures or job descriptions. Nevertheless, these other, so-called 'non-professional' categories of person are what a social worker has to make use of as she strives to ensure her job as an expert is not only effective but also possible. The moment these categories become the ground for action, though, everyone – institution and employees alike – is forced to acknowledge what has always been known but otherwise concealed, and the expert suffers immediate consequences. She or he is deemed unprofessional and unqualified. The institution too is forced to dispose of the transgressor – of the one that 'came out' – out of the real danger of losing its own capacity to function, derived from budgets, professional excellence and credibility.

In this regard, the role of a social worker at SH is the inverse of that of an SOS-mother at SOSCV. Although both occupy the position of an expert that spans disparate roles and categories of person and challenges notions of professionalism, ethical behaviour and good practice, a social worker is by default considered to be an expert with theoretical and practical knowledge of policies and personalities, whose professional capacity and practice, nevertheless, come from conscious work towards forging and maintaining intimately personal relationships with clients. In contrast, an SOS-mother obtains her category of a mother through employment, but she has to make a conscious effort at building her capacity as an organizational expert to pass a qualifying test of good mothering practice in the organizational settings.

As such, the positions of organizational employee and expert are inherently relational in their constant negotiation of the disparate roles that make them up. Yet the very phenomenon of an expert is based on the intentional separation and maintenance of clear boundaries between these roles that mutually encompass personal and professional domains. Simultaneously, in the process of intermittent foregrounding and forgetting of the relevant values and practices, a certain occupational and organizational reality is continuously reinstated.

Domain encompassment and differentiation

The demands of delivering social services require clients to fit into an organizational frame and be normalized according to outlined regulations (Howe 1991). What I have attempted to show through my comparative examples above is that this normalization goes both ways. Employees of non-governmental and governmental organizations are shaped by law, professional codes and regulations (Offer 1998). They are moulded into persons who perform the role of professional experts. We saw this in the example of the two institutional cases at hand. Regardless of whether it is SOSCV (and attendant SOS-mother and children) or SH (and attendant social worker and homeless adults), working in an institution means being subject to its regulatory values and professional principles. These shape employees and clients alike, thus establishing and outlining institutional structure and domain hierarchy.

Designed to deliver 'human services', both SOSCV and SH, each in their own way, intervene by fulfilling personal roles for individual clients. The organizations 'step in' for the absence of other persons, whether as parents, friends or other kin. Such person-oriented goals pose inevitable challenges to organizational practices and professional values. Fulfilling personal roles for individuals *structurally and categorically* turns these organizations into 'persons',[15] whereby employees of these very organizations are obliged to serve as both 'persons' and 'organizations'. What is given then is the institution, the public entity, where employees function in the category of 'professionals'. What is not given and has to be negotiated and controlled is how to function as 'persons' with the clients of a particular organization inside of this role. In this chapter, I have illustrated how people at two organizations accomplish these fundamental negotiations through the transitive capacity of concepts that draw upon value systems and normative constructs in line with their respective domains. I have traced how, through the mutual interplay and encompassment between personal and professional domains, these concepts and categories enable or disable organizational capacity.

Through the category of mother and concept of home, SOSCV defines itself in opposition to state-institutional practices, effectively elevating itself above 'impersonal' state-run orphanages. The vignettes I selected illustrate what happens when the work of kinship, as Schneider has it (1980), is deployed by institutions. My intent, however, is not to argue whether what SOSCV does could be construed as kinship, 'real', 'constructed' or otherwise. Instead, I illustrate how the language of kinship that SOSCV uses both facilitates and constrains its organizational practices, placing them at the edges of functionality. Likewise, by decomposing the structural complexities of the daily routine of an SH social worker, I have shown how SH employees learn to balance distinct social categories and domains in order to build the institutional capacity necessary to house self-sufficient adults. Here, I foregrounded two moments of transgression, when one domain reached its limit and took precedence over the other, thus encompassing it in a hierarchical order (Barnes 1985) afforded by personal or professional value systems.

My interest in this chapter has been to draw attention to the capacity of concepts to transgress and mutually encompass each other (Dumont 1980), such that conceptual alterations directly effect organizational social realities in very concrete and tangible ways. On the surface, professional practices and organizational culture clearly differentiate between the professional and personal domains, often excluding the latter altogether. As the ethnographic examples illustrate, however, this exclusion regularly fails in practice. The domains of personal and professional are neither mutually exclusive nor separate, but rather depend on one another, and their proximity, in order to function at all. In other words, their capacity for mutual encompassment necessitates that one deploys the other in order to do its work, so long as one remains the ground for the other (Wagner [1975] 1981). I have suggested that organizational 'incapacity' threatens when the concepts reach their limit and the relation reverses itself temporarily (Jiménez and Willerslev 2007) or collapses entirely, resulting in the termination of relationship or that of organizations themselves. Through careful tracing and articulation of these taken-for-granted conceptual distinctions, I show how the dynamic interplay between opposing domains directly influences and shapes organizational reality – an insight potentially relevant for understanding Euro-American knowledge practices and organizational culture in general.

Acknowledgements

I want to thank first and foremost the people employed or involved within the organizations that I describe here; without their support, this chapter would not have been possible. I also want to make explicit that part of my motivation in critically engaging institutions like SOSCV and SH is to express my appreciation of the important work they do around the world through their daily acts. Secondly, I would like to thank Justin for his constant encouragement and intellectual stimulation; and my son Anton for his patience and nightly meditative readings. Thirdly, I want to thank the Wenner-Gren Foundation that funded the workshop on capacity building in Copenhagen, and the organizers and editors Rachel Douglas-Jones and Justin Shaffner. Finally, this chapter has greatly benefited from comments received from two anonymous reviewers.

Viktoryia Kalesnikava has an MA in Anthropology from the University of Virginia, and a dual degree in Social Work and Public Health from the Virginia Commonwealth University. She is currently pursuing her Doctorate degree in Epidemiology from the University of Michigan. Her dissertation research focuses on the relationship between chronic stress and cardiometabolic health disparities. Recent publications include articles on suicide among older adults, and mechanisms of cardiometabolic disparities.

Notes

1. SOS Children's Villages, 'About Us', *SOS Children's Villages Mission Statement*. http://www.sos-childrensvillages.org/who-we-are/about-sos (accessed 24 February 2014).
2. SOSCV has since resumed operation in Australia in 2012 in a hybrid format and in tight partnership with 'Puddle Jumpers', another NGO.
3. SOSCV UK Newsletter (2011) "In Safe Hands: The role of the SOS mother," *Family Matters*, 2:8. http://goodbye.soschildrensvillages.org.uk/files/familymatters/FamilyMatters_Oct2011_web.pdf (accessed April 2, 2017).
4. These accounts are based on fieldwork conducted in 2010 and thus may not be representative of SOS-children's experiences across different villages. Matters might also be different at the present time.
5. At the time of my internship, SOSCV-Russia restricted the position of an SOS-mother to women who were not married and either had no children or grown-up children. However, this policy was widely criticized, and SOSCV was in the process of softening regulations and allowing SOS-mothers to get married and/or hiring couples for the role of SOS-parents (http://www.sos-childrensvillages.org/who-we-are/contact-us/faqs/working-for-sos-childrens-villages, accessed 15 January 2017).
6. House of Assembly (2004), http://hansardpublic.parliament.sa.gov.au/_layouts/15/Hansard/DownloadHansardFile.ashx?t=historicpdf&d=HANSARD-4-524 (accessed 2 April 2017); Parliament of South Australia (2008) Interim Report of the Select Committee on Families SA, http://www.parliament.sa.gov.au/Committees/Pages/Committees.aspx?CTId=3&PId=51&CId=149&DUId=9061bfb1-e4a8-4c8e-8743-6cd05ecabc78 (accessed 2 April 2017) ; Parliament of South Australia (2008–2009) Final Report of the Select Committee on Families SA, https://www.parliament.sa.gov.au/HouseofAssembly/BusinessoftheAssembly/RecordsandPapers/TabledPapersandPetitions/Pages/TabledPapersandPetitions.aspx?TPLoadDoc=true&TPDocType=1&TPP=53&TPS=2&TPItemID=84&TPDocName=LRC%2B-%2BINTERIM%2BREPORT%2B-%2BPP%2B244%2B-%2B8%2BMARCH%2B2016.pdf (accessed 2 April 2017); and SOS News: Newsletter of SOS Children's Villages Australia (n.d.) 'Government Takeover of Seaford Rise Village', Issue 10 (accessed 4 July 2015).
7. This was the case for SOSCV in both Russia and Australia.
8. SOS News: Newsletter of SOS Children's Villages Australia (n.d.) 'Government Takeover of Seaford Rise Village', 10: 2 (accessed 4 July 2015).
9. SOS News: Newsletter of SOS Children's Villages Australia (n.d.) "Government Takeover of Seaford Rise Village", 10: 2 (accessed 4 July 2015).
10. SOS News: Newsletter of SOS Children's Villages Australia (n.d.) "Government Takeover of Seaford Rise Village", 10: 2 (accessed 4 July 2015).
11. Based on the Family Code of the Russian Federation, the Guardianship authorities were obliged to seek out a family placement as the only long-term option for orphan children ('Статья 123 Семейного кодекса РФ', http://logos-pravo.ru/page.php?id=2242, accessed 15 January 2017).

12. Aware of this concern and in their attempts to build their children's character, SOSCV designed a programme that introduced SOS-children to 'successful' and 'gainfully employed' people, who would often become sponsors or, as SOSCV named them, 'godparents' for the SOS-children.
13. After my internship ended, a different staff member continued to support the issue and was subsequently able to facilitate significant change in the rule.
14. The incident itself and the image of the social worker is a compound character meant to stand in for features of different social workers that I encountered at various organizations and communities, and is not representative of an actual single individual or situation.
15. This language might strike the reader as uncanny in relation to recent debates on the personhood of organizations or corporations, but the very idea that a collectivity, however defined (as an organization or corporation), can act or stand in for a person is actually quite old and could be seen in Roman law or more prototypically in 'house societies' (Bashkow n.d.).

References

Barnes, R.H. 1985. 'Hierarchy Without Caste', in Barnes, D. de Coppet and R.J. Parkin (eds), 8–20. *Contexts and Levels: Anthropological Essay on Hierarchy* (*Journal of the Anthropological Society of Oxford. Occasional papers* 4).

Bashkow, I. n.d. 'House, Temple, State, Corporation: On the Origins of the Corporate Form'. Unpublished.

Carsten, J. 2004. *After Kinship*. Cambridge: Cambridge University Press.

Dumont, L. 1985. *Homo Hierarchicus: The Caste System and Its Implications*. Trans. by Mark Sainsbury, Louis Dumont and Basia Gulati. Chicago: University of Chicago Press.

Epstein, L. 1999. 'The Culture of Social Work'. In A. S. Chambon, A. Irving and L. Epstein (eds), *Reading Foucault for Social Work*. New York: Columbia University Press, 3–26.

Erickson, J. (ed.). 1987. *Housing the Homeless*. Piscataway: Transaction Publishers.

Hecht, T. 1998. *At Home in the Street: Street Children of Northeast Brazil*. Cambridge: Cambridge University Press.

Howe, D. 1991. 'The Family and the Therapist: Towards a Sociology of Social Work Method'. In *The Sociology of Social Work*, M. Davies, ed. London: Routledge, 146–162.

Jiménez, A.C. (ed.). 2007. *The Anthropology of Organisations*. Hampshire, UK: Ashgate Publishing Company.

Jiménez, A.C. 2008. 'Relations and Disproportions: The Labor of Scholarship in the Knowledge Economy'. *American Ethnologist* 35 (2): 229–242. doi:10.1111/j.1548-1425.2008.00035.x.

Jiménez, A.C. and R. Willerslev. 2007. 'An Anthropological Concept of the Concept: Reversibility among the Siberian Yukaghirs'. *Journal of the Royal Anthropological Institute* 13: 527–544. doi:10.1111/j.1467-9655.2007.00441.x.

Offer, J. 1998. 'On Sociological Studies of Interaction between Social Workers and Clients and Why They Matter'. *Social Work & Social Sciences Review* 8 (1): 5–24.

Ong, A. 2006. *Neoliberalism as Exception: Mutations in Citizenship and Sovereignty*. Durham: Duke University Press.

Peck, J. 1996. *Work-place: The Social Regulation of Labor Markets*. New York: Guilford Press.

Rose, N. 1999. *Powers of Freedom: Reframing Political Thought*. Cambridge: Cambridge University Press.

Schneider, D.M. 1972. 'What Is Kinship All About?' In P. Reining (ed.), *Kinship Studies in the Morgan Centennial Year*. Washington, DC: The Anthropological Society of Washington, 32–63.

Schneider, D.M. 1980. *American Kinship: A Cultural Account*. Chicago: University of Chicago Press.

Shore, C. and S. Wright. 1997. 'Policy: A New Field in Anthropology'. In C. Shore and S. Wright (eds), *Anthropology of Policy: Critical Perspectives on Governance and Power.* London and New York: Routledge, 3–34.

Strathern, M. 2000. 'Afterword: Accountability … and Ethnography'. In M. Strathern (ed.), *Audit Cultures: Anthropological Studies in Accountability, Ethics and the Academy.* London and New York: Routledge, 278–304.

Strathern, M. 2004. *Partial Connections*, updated Edition. Walnut Creek, CA and Oxford: AltaMira Press.

Strathern, M. 2008. 'Robust Knowledge and Fragile Future'. In A. Ong and S. J. Collier (eds), *Global Assemblages: Technology, Politics, and Ethics as Anthropological Problems.* Malden, MA: John Wiley & Sons, 464–481.

Wagner, R. [1975] 1981. *The Invention of Culture.* Chicago: University of Chicago Press.

Wagner, R. 1977. 'Analogic Kinship: A Daribi Example'. *American Ethnologist* 4 (4): 623–642. doi:10.1525/ae.1977.4.4.02a00030.

Chapter 7

Community Capacity Building
Transforming Amerindian Sociality in Peruvian Amazonia

Christopher Hewlett

> An essential ingredient in the UNDP capacity development approach is transformation. For an activity to meet the standard of capacity development as practiced and promoted by UNDP, it must bring about transformation that is generated and sustained over time from within. Transformation of this kind goes beyond performing tasks; instead, it is more a matter of changing mindsets and attitudes.
> —United Nations Development Programme,
> *Capacity Development: A UNDP Primer*

In this chapter, I address the centrality of transformation in capacity building projects, and the way a sense of a 'lack' or absence acts as a driving force for them. The notion of transformation within capacity building discourse and its precursors has remained largely unquestioned, embedded in Euro-American ideologies and philosophies regarding personhood, agency, collective organization and outcomes. Although, as in the epigraph above, the transformation of others is often stated as the explicit goal of 'capacity building' (particularly a transformation that gives people the capacities to transform themselves), there remains little space for these 'others' to impact the 'rules of the game', let alone the assumptions upon which the concept of transformation is based. My central argument in this chapter is that understanding capacities through a singular understanding of the term 'transformation' is problematic: if experiences of transformation differ, what capacities are valued and deemed proper for further development? By focusing on enhancing certain capacities, and downplaying, ignoring or even criminalizing others (Ellison this issue; Hale 2004), the overall frame remains that of a 'change' based on a uni-directional movement. What about capacities that are temporary, or that come with new forms of vulnerability?

To draw out contrasting narratives of transformation and to consider how capacities might be otherwise conceptualized, I look back on a programme run by the Evangelical Christian organization the Summer Institute of Linguistics (SIL) which began over fifty years ago in Peruvian Amazonia. As I demonstrate from my historical research into this project, close reading of accounts of former SIL employees and my own fieldwork among a people called the Amahuaca, the SIL's project in Peru was integral to the process of nation building decades before the term 'capacity building' became commonplace. Nonetheless, we can trace some of the same fundamental assumptions and aims from that time into all that the term implies today. While there is a significant amount of literature on the history of 'capacity building' (Eade 1997), 'community capacity building' (Verity 2007) and the development industry more generally (Escobar 1995; Gardner and Lewis 1996), rather than reading my case through this literature, I use the SIL case to examine three different narratives of transformation from a historical perspective. My aim is to bring out both a critique of the assumptions of 'transformation' within capacity building and how projects are evaluated, and to offer a historically and ethnographically informed analysis of early capacity building projects and their contemporary legacies.

My argument unfolds chronologically. I first introduce the Amahuaca project, along with some of the commitments of the SIL organization, locating the SIL's work with Amahuaca historically and framing its intentions in relation to ideas of the self. I go on to show the SIL's growing role in the Peruvian government's aim of building a nation comprised of productive citizens, an ideal dominant in the 1940s when the SIL began their work in the Peruvian Amazon. Having laid out this background, I contextualize the terms capacity and transformation by drawing on my ethnography and published accounts of the SIL's work, showing how Amahuaca people themselves have come to understand their own transformations over the past fifty years. My discussion of Amahuaca notions of transformation in relation to wider Amerindian concerns about encounters with outsiders, and the body as a site of transformation, opens the space to explore some of the complex relations between transformation as understood by the

SIL, Amahuaca people and contemporary capacity building discourse. My interest lies in how we might understand the aims and impacts of these interrelated narratives of transformation with reference to contemporary definitions of 'capacity building' such as that found in the epigraph of this chapter. Let me first introduce the SIL Amahuaca project, and its position in histories of the Peruvian state.

The Amahuaca project

Amahuaca people are classified as part of the Panoan language family, which consists of more than twenty distinct language groups located in northwest Bolivia, western Brazil and eastern Peru. The majority of the Amahuaca are concentrated in six Native Communities, with the largest concentration found in Alto Esperanza, San Juan and San Martin on the Inuya River, an eastern tributary of the lower Urubamba River in the province of Atalaya. In 1953, two members of SIL travelled up the Inuya River to establish the community of Varadero as a mission for Amahuaca people. One of them, Robert Russell, went on to live with the Amahuaca for fifteen years and was the first of three generations of SIL members to live and work among them.[1]

The SIL is a North American evangelical organization that bases its work on the belief that indigenous people should learn about Christianity from the Bible in their own language. Their project in Peru, as elsewhere, is linguistically oriented and a central aim is to use language (e.g. Spanish/indigenous languages) to bring indigenous people, such as the Amahuaca, into the modern Christian world. The ambition in the Amahuaca project was to allow the Amahuaca to participate in Peruvian society while maintaining their cultural identity (Carneiro and Dole n.d.; Hewlett 2014; Huxley and Capa 1964; Russell, pers. comm.). Prior to the 1950s, Amahuaca people tended to live in small hamlets, spread out in the headwaters of the Sepahua, Inuya, Purus and Yurua Rivers, approximately 150 miles west of the Brazil-Peru border. These hamlets, averaging around fifteen people, were dispersed on small tributaries (Dole 1998), but during the initial period of missionization, these kin-based clusters were brought to live together. The Amahuaca came together in Varadero, which, according to historical documents, was part of the work members of SIL viewed as necessary in order to 'save' the Amahuaca from what, at the time, seemed an inevitable fate: debt slavery, loss of culture and language, and eventual extinction. SIL members believed that if they did not intervene and assist Amahuaca people to negotiate relations with outsiders (loggers, governments, colonizers), they would be 'lost to history' (Hewlett 2014; see also Huxley and Capa 1964). In order to prevent this, the SIL 'tried to encourage and reinforce what little tribal solidarity there exists, to knit the group together in a common psychological defense against the "outsiders" while helping them drive a more equitable bargain' (Stoll 1982: 123) when they made exchanges for desired goods such as metal axes, salt and clothing.

SIL members' desire to 'save' Amahuaca people was informed by their faith as Evangelical Christians and the belief that Amahuaca had lacked the opportunity to know the Bible. This could be remedied through members of the SIL learning their language, teaching them Spanish and then translating the Bible into Amahuaca. The SIL thus carried two notions of history simultaneously. Alongside the narrative of progress and civilization so common during the mid to late twentieth century (Escobar 1995; McKinnon 2013) was an equally teleological concept of transformation and temporality (Cova 2014) marked by the return of Christ. Within this transformational framework, an Amahuaca could be 'saved as an individual on the basis of actions they are understood to initiate themselves that bear on their relation to God' (Robbins et al. 2014: 564). Therefore, while the SIL aimed to transform the material relations Amahuaca people had with Peruvians – such as loggers and the government – they also sought to transform something further: the soul. Transformation took on transcendental significance through the potential for Amahuaca people to become good Christians. With the capacity to read and know the Bible, to know scripture, Amahuaca people could transform themselves. This notion of transformation, carried with the SIL's project, is tied to an individual's awareness of their own self, their own soul and their own agency, which will be fully realized as they come to know, accept and live a life of adherence to the scripture; it is central to Christianity (Mauss 1985). It is also a conception of self, formulated within the context of the capitalist modes of production and the construction of modern nation-states. This overlap of Christian and nation-state 'selves' offers some insights into the overlap between the aims of the SIL and that of the Peruvian government for the Amahuaca, as I shall now go on to show.

The SIL's historical role and community development

In the 1940s, the Peruvian government's interest was to bring the Amahuaca and other groups into the folds of state power. A 1945 agreement brought the SIL into this exercise of indigenous integration in ways that would draw on the SIL's linguistic expertise and resources. The government wanted to develop the region, including its inhabitants, and agreed that the SIL could assist in efforts to 'discourage "vice by all means possible" and translate "books of great moral and patriotic value"' (Stoll 1982: 103). The Peruvian government's aims are set out explicitly in the front of bilingual textbooks subsequently published by the SIL:

> … this task of great social and human importance is entrusted to the Summer Institute of Linguistics, whose specialist orientation as mediators through bilingual communication will guide the teaching of literacy and basic knowledge in their own native tongue, then gradually incorporating the Castilian language *with the intention of national integration*. (Instituto Lingüístico de Verano [ILV] 1960, author's translation, emphasis added)

In short, the aim of the Peruvian government's backing of the SIL project was to incorporate indigenous people into the Peruvian national project and make them, and the land they occupied, *productive* in terms corresponding with nation-state consolidation (Barclay and Santos Granero 1998). Peoples like the Amahuaca were understood in terms such as 'primitive', 'non-modern' and 'savage', seen to be 'lacking' the qualities associated with civilization. This problem, it was thought, could be resolved through education focused on literacy, leadership and economic activities (Hewlett 2014). Simply put, the Amahuaca and groups like them were assessed as lacking the 'capacities' to be productive participants in modern Peruvian society, but based on modernist theories of personhood and progress, could be 'transformed'.

As the SIL got to work implementing these changes, successes revealed new challenges. Over the next few decades of the project, Amahuaca people moved downriver, congregating around SIL schools, and at the same time the aims of the programme expanded to include 'community development' projects (Mollhagen 1970). There was a series of interconnected reasons for this shift in programme focus, which occurred at both the local and national levels (Hewlett 2014). I provide an overview here of some key moments in this shift towards 'community development', subsequently developing an analysis of how the new skills were seen as changing the terms of trade and labour engagement with outsiders for the indigenous groups that participated.

The first impetus for the SIL's shifting focus was legislation passed by the Peruvian government in the 1960s that gave indigenous people collective ownership of land under the *ley de Comunidades Nativas* or law of Native Communities. According to the new law, indigenous people could form communities that would be granted land titles. In brief, the process entailed the election of a governing body (president, vice-president, secretary and treasurer) by indigenous people, the demarcation of the land by forest engineers, and certification by the Ministry of Agriculture to formally establish communities (Hvalkof 2005; Yashar 2005). Given the requirement in the land titling law that indigenous people elect community leaders to represent them to outsiders, the SIL's role in leadership training grew. The SIL had been conducting trainings in bilingual education, a role that was consolidated after the 1972 passing of a law making bilingual education an official policy, and the SIL responsible for its implementation. Indigenous leaders had been taking part in these bilingual teacher programmes, and with the *ley de Comunidades Nativas*, the SIL increased the formalization of such training in leadership.[2] By the 1970s, along with bilingual education, 'community development [became] its officially assigned priority' (Stoll 1982: 124). This 'community building' was an idea of its time, based on the idea that individuals, communities and nations that were perceived as lacking certain social, economic or political capacities could be transformed in such a way that they could take control of their own resources whether they be environmental, economic, political, social or personal. As Mollhagen notes, the two most important components of the community development programme were to 'aid in utilising resources already at hand, and the practical application of new skills learned by tribespeople' (1970: 7). Finally, as indigenous people began to live in larger permanent villages, there was a greater need for social, political and economic development. This included bringing indigenous people from their villages to the SIL headquarters and giving them training in specific skills, including agriculture, commerce, carpentry, mechanics, local government, health and domestic arts. As a member of the SIL states, 'the amount of time the linguists were spending on the tribal economic problems was one of the basic reasons for establishing the Occupational Training Course at Yarinacocha in 1964 … In addition to their chosen speciality, they were also required to take a class in Peruvian culture' (Mollhagen 1970: 2).

As the SIL's role shifted beyond that of national integration into community development, an increase in the political and social organization of villages became more important for creating what was known as an 'internal economy'. As Mollhagen's text from the time notes, an internal economy would give opportunities to indigenous people who now had not only the skills to enter the regional economy, but also the 'desire' to improve their position in it (1970: 7). I now turn to how these ideas of training and community creation carried with them assumptions both about what should be and what was 'lacking'.

Producing leaders, building communities

The idea of community aspired to by SIL projects was based on the training of a group of leaders described above – people who would coordinate collective activities through their positions in the political organization. This political organization was considered as an entity separate from and 'above' other kinds of productive activities, as I have discussed elsewhere (Hewlett 2014). In a historical reflection of his own extensive time with Aguaruna people – part of the Jivaroan language group straddling the Peru-Ecuador border – the longstanding SIL worker Dennis Olson makes explicit reference to the bilingual education programme becoming part of the wider process of development known within the SIL as 'Intercultural Community Work' (ICW).[3]

> The bilingual school system provided a model of organisation that modified traditional patterns of organisation. Annual teacher conferences provided a model for inter-community organisation and problem solving. The bilingual school system was a training ground for leadership development. Teachers learned about keeping records and the administrative processes of the dominant culture. (Olson 1995: 31)

This new school system explicitly set out to 'modify' previous forms of social organization, combining a new model with new subjectivities. Leaders were given a key role in mediating and cultivating the 'followership' deemed necessary for 'social and political' organization with many, Amahuaca and others, taken to the SIL base in Pucallpa where they participated in further training. Throughout the 1970s and 1980s, the SIL blended community capacity building, health and hygiene programmes, leadership training and bible studies. Some younger Amahuaca also travelled to Lima to join larger bible study groups. Yet Dyck, who lived and worked with the Amahuaca during the 1980s and 1990s, noted that Amahuaca leadership was still lacking:

> Besides a lack of leadership [Amahuaca] have not learned a followership essential to political and social organisation. They are concerned primarily with their nuclear or extended family. … Literacy and education will contribute toward this goal. (Dyck 1992: 49)

These accounts from Dyck and Olson allow us to see the kinds of capacities that were valued as part of community development initiatives. The SIL's emphasis on 'social and political organization' is based on a series of ideals, from a 'community' comprised of 'individuals' (Macpherson 1962) extending to a group possessing 'culture' or an identity that is shared and valued, thus requiring certain tools for its maintenance (Handler 1988). Also embedded in the SIL's 'ideal community' comprised of 'individuals', however, are the notions of faith, trust and followership. The aim was for the emergence of a new kind of collective based on individuals of faith who work together and help one another on the path to salvation. However, what was perceived as 'lacking' among

Amahuaca was belief: in God, community, society or the state. While Amahuaca people were quick to take on the form of 'civilization' as they moved into communities, voted for their leaders and attended school, they seemed reluctant to put the mechanisms into action to 'develop' their community. The political structure was there, but seemed ineffective. While community came to be highly valued – and was so at the time of my 2009–11 fieldwork – SIL assessments prior to my studies also reflect the perception of transformation as changing how and where Amahuaca lived.

Discourses of assessment I

What kind of effects did these new trainings in leadership, Christianity and community have for Aguaruna social life? Accounts from SIL workers such as Olson offer us an insight into the kinds of skills that were taught in bilingual education programmes, community organization and development initiatives. What, then, was interpreted as the successful building of new capacities? The passage I have selected below is drawn from Olson's 1995 account of teaching and training that took place in the village of Temashnum around 1967. Olson recounts being asked for, and delivering, a platform scale to the village of Temashnum for the weighing of goods, and teaching Aguaruna how to use it. During a later visit, he saw the scale in use:

> I watched with amazement as they brought each sack of rice to the trader from the coast and told him what each one weighed and what it was worth. Without asking any questions, the trader paid each man for his rice based on these calculations. That was quite a different picture from the days of selling rubber when the traders were said to have calibrated muscles. They could tell exactly what a ball of rubber weighed by lifting it up. This new method of doing business put control of weighing and measuring into the hands of the Aguaruna instead of the trader. (Olson 1995: 31)

Olson's description, particularly his historical references to the sale of rubber within the assessment, offers insights into the ways 'empowerment' is understood from the perspective of SIL modes of knowledge and 'transformation'. In particular, it deals with the history of the SIL's engagement with Aguaruna people by marking a disjuncture between a period when bosses cheated them, and a present day when they are able to enter into 'equal' exchange relations based on knowledge of calculation, literacy and their ability to use the scale. During the rubber boom, Olson recalls, exchanges were mediated through the social and bodily capacities of bosses and Aguaruna people – the 'calibrated muscles'. In contrast, analogous relations are today mediated through a 'rational' system of calculation and a machine. This difference draws out both the centrality of certain forms of knowledge for the notion of empowerment and points to the importance of this knowledge for wider structural relationships. We can also see how Olson's account positions the shift – from a 'lack' in mathematical literacy and social organization to the 'possession' of these capacities, within the timeframe of the SIL's programme, following modernization narratives of progress in which rational modes of knowledge correspond to the development of personal autonomy, individualism, free enterprise and empowerment. Perhaps the most powerful image this example conveys is the silence of the trader during the exchange; through this, empowerment is implicitly framed in terms of the Aguaruna having a voice. The power of voice, and its correlation with agency, is a fundamental trope for western notions of individuality, freedom and equality (Mentore 2005). In Olson's recollection of earlier rubber deals, the dominant body of the boss, an individual who seems in total control of knowledge, wealth and the capacity to calculate value, is portrayed as abusive and controlling through his ability to keep indigenous people in debt. According to this logic, his control comes from their desire for wealth and ignorance of rational modes of calculation. The scale itself thus becomes a powerful metaphor for the enhancement of the position of Aguaruna people in relation to traders as a category. It generalizes, or de-personalizes, the trader, framing the exchange as one between autonomous individuals.

I want to suggest, however, that the silence of the traders in this account from Olson, and its apparent significance, may be misleading, for two reasons. To make this argument, let us look more closely at how this relationship is being mediated. First, the metaphor of the scale is powerful exactly because it is based on western notions of balance, equality and justice. The *image* of the scale, the power of rationality as an ideal, silences the trader in the account. While enhancing the parties' ability to relate with one another based on logic, the scale also separates them, shifting the temporal scale of their interaction. Rather than making a relation that binds them through time, the exchange is framed as a totalizing event. Rationality as an ideal is substituted for relationality as interpersonal relations become mediated through the scale. In short, this exchange positions the scale as a symbol of power over and above the persons involved, transforming the relation between them. Second, and related to this transformation, there is evidence that in Peruvian Amazonia relations between workers and bosses are not always understood as asymmetrically negative. According to Walker (2012), for example, many Urarina people, an indigenous group living near the Aguaruna, not only *sought out* bosses in the past, but *intentionally* indebted themselves in order to maintain exchange relations. This is because relations between bosses and workers among many indigenous groups in the region (Bonilla 2007) are not modelled on western logics of individual ownership and autonomy, but on relations between pets and owners, or 'masters' (Fausto 2008). For example, according to Fausto, a 'strategy of submission also contains a lure, since it is a way of eliciting the action corresponding to the owner position, defined as someone who looks after and feeds his children-pets' (Fausto 2008: 347, cited in Fausto 2013). Without glorifying 'debt', then, or downplaying the often violent and abusive means used by bosses in the region, I want to problematize the notion that 'debt' and asymmetrical relations were, or are, automatically and universally negative (High 2012). This valuation not only denies the agencies and capacities of indigenous people, but also frames these exchanges within a western logic of commodities (Fisher 2000). And, indeed, there is evidence that indigenous people do not always perceive relations of indebtedness as ones of submission in ways that are familiar to many readers (Fausto 2013).

By providing an overview of the SIL's expanding role – from early projects designed to convert and integrate indigenous groups into the Peruvian state project to generating 'communities' with leaders who could interact with state authorities – I have shown a number of points where the impetus for transformation, and its outcomes, are based on an idea of a 'lack'. Yet for many Amerindian peoples, personhood and collectivities do not correspond to notions of the possessive individual, or the ways that 'community' is realized in western terms. This has consequences for the entanglement of capacity and transformation, since the entities at which projects aim their efforts (the Christian individual, the independent community) do not always line up with what might already be present, rather than absent in Amerindian settings. Indeed, Amerindian conceptualizations of capacities, agency and community are themselves based on the centrality of transformation to indigenous metaphysics (Viveiros de Castro 2011), a point I go on to explore in the section that follows.

Amerindian corporality and transformation

As I described earlier, the Amahuaca people's initial movement from living in the forest to the mission and later to their own Native Communities was based upon a series of relations they had formed with new people with different capacities – Spanish, clothing, literacy, numeracy – as well as different values and desires. With the move from the forest, Amahuaca began eating different foods, drinking fermented manioc beer, living in communities, holding work parties and sending their children to school. Now that I have reviewed the intentions and commitments of the SIL project, I want to use this move to Native Communities as an entry point for exploring the ways transformation is understood and experienced by Amahuaca people. How were these new relations perceived? Since these understandings and experiences correspond with those found among other groups through lowland South America, I draw on further ethnography from the region to support my argument that to understand transformation in this setting, we need to see both the role played by outsiders and the way bodies are implicated in conceptualizing change.

Like many peoples of lowland South America, Amahuaca sociality is driven by the underlying premise that difference as a general value is potent yet dangerous, while sameness is safe but sterile (Overing 1981). Or, as Lévi-Strauss (1995: xvii) put it when recounting early encounters between Europeans and Amerindians, there is in the region 'an opening to the Other'. Vilaça ([2006] 2010) takes up this theme in her book on the encounter of Wari people and whites, arguing that this openness that defines Amerindian thought is 'physiological'. There is a key relationship between the bodies of persons and the collectivities they generate, which Vilaça refers to as a 'somatic entity, a collective body formed from bodies' ([2006] 2010: 317). According to Vilaça 'the significance of shared substance for the Wari is that it contains not just memory and affect, but above all agency. To become kin, it is necessary to desire to be kin and *to act* as such...' (Vilaça 2002: 352, emphasis added). This notion of personhood, bodily metamorphosis, and particularly the making of bodies of kin out of others, locates capacities in the body. Relations with others entail bodily transformation, as '... the body is not merely the location where social identity is expressed but the substrate where it is fabricated ... the motor of a body process' (Vilaça 2007: 175). This is extended to the wearing of clothing (Ewart and O'Hanlon 2010) as well as the transference of capacities through incorporation of outside knowledge, whether it is from white people, other indigenous groups or spirits.

These associations tying the body and relations with others together shed light on why the notion of 'becoming civilized' is such a common discourse throughout lowland South America. Gow, who worked with the Piro located between the Amahuaca on the Inuya River and the town of Atalaya, has argued that the concept of *gente civilizada*, 'civilized people', is best understood as a position on a continuum between two poles: 'wild Indians' and 'gringos' (Gow 1991, 1993). The quintessential 'wild Indian' for the Piro is the Yaminahua, a closely related group to the Amahuaca, who are considered as such because they 'do not wear clothes, they do not eat salt, and they live off there in the forest' (Gow 1993: 331). While their distance is physically important, based on an upriver/downriver axis, this distinction is also viewed as a 'moral choice'. 'Wild Indians' live in the forest and 'avoid contact with other people, and in particular to avoid exchange relations' (Gow 1993: 332). In short, 'becoming civilized' is a process of seeking to enter into relations with those who are different. In this frame, 'white people' are particularly perceived as having access to desirable kinds of wealth and knowledge.

Transformations that incorporate the capacities and affects of outsiders are not necessarily permanent, nor are they without risk, often resulting in the emergence of new vulnerabilities. These new vulnerabilities have been explicitly discussed by Jose Kelly (2011), whose work with the Yanomami in Venezuela examines new corporealities associated with relations with outsiders. Becoming *nape*, or white, is part of the process of becoming educated, wearing western clothing and eating nape foods. When Yanomami enter into intensive relations with outsiders (missionaries, doctors etc.), this is understood as 'walking the nape's path' (Kelly 2011: 78), an activity that entails bodily transformations. This is expressed clearly when Yanomami speak about 'capacities' and becoming 'capacitados' (Kelly 2011: 81). Kelly describes a comparison drawn by one informant between the way spirit helpers share knowledge with Yanomami shamans, *shapori*, on the one hand, and the ways white people share knowledge with educated Yanomami on the other. According to Kelly's informant, a spirit helper comes 'where the Yanomami are and gives his capacity [to the *shapori*]' (2011: 81). The term 'capacity' is also used in another context, when mission-educated Yanomami describe the process of becoming nape. As Kelly states, '… sharing of knowledge not properly their own makes both *shapori* and educated Yanomami "capacitados". This is but one instance of how the *criollo* technology of reading/writing resembles the shamanic technology of seeing …' (2011: 81).[4]

These transformations in capacities are understood to result in 'interface Yanomami', people who inhabit multiple worlds in much the same way as a *shapori* inhabits multiple worlds. Their ability to mediate between them is what makes them important interlocutors. Therefore, becoming 'civilized' is a bodily transformation, and also implies becoming 'capacitados' in terms of the technologies of the Other. It is a form of becoming, and becoming nape, like becoming civilized, entails the incorporation of 'capacities' as well as making the body open in others ways, particularly to illness. As one Yanomami nurse lamented:

> Our blood is now too blended with the vitamins of nape food and the vitamins of the food we eat in the headwaters. That vitamin doesn't have enough resistance. It has no potency … Nowadays … when a child is still young, it already has hepatitis. They get ill early because they have very low vitamin levels. They are already accustomed. (Kelly 2011: 78)

As I have shown, when transformation is approached from the point of view of Amazonian indigenous groups, it is located in bodily changes, necessarily involving both the incorporation of alternate 'capacities' and the loss of others. If we contrast the Yanomami nurse's account of 'transformation' with the UNDP's understanding of capacity building in the epigraph, what the UNDP definition does not bring into its conceptualization of capacity-as-transformation is that becoming 'capacitados' may also be a process of becoming more 'vulnerable', an experience the Amahuaca share with others in the region (Kelly 2011; McCallum 2014). Transformation in this setting involves building both new capacities and new vulnerabilities.

Discourses of assessment II

How, then, do Amerindian understandings of capacity, community and vulnerability outlined above play out in contemporary accounts of the legacies of the SIL project? Almost sixty years after the SIL's Amahuaca project was initiated, and fifteen years after the project officially ended, my own fieldwork began with this same group of families. Today, most Amahuaca are bilingual, live in established communities and participate in the national economy. Thus, the project I have discussed above seems largely successful – on its own terms – regarding its intention to integrate the Amahuaca into the Peruvian state. However, when I first arrived in the Amahuaca communities where I carried out fieldwork – communities located on the Inuya River – and asked if I could live with them and learn about their history and contemporary life, I was told by the president of the community: 'Yes, come live with us. The government has forgotten us'. A key aspect of my research was examining how these families came to understand their transition from living spread out in the forest to residing in established villages with recognized land titles called Native Communities. There are three, intimately related ideas that I want to use to explore their understanding of this transition. The first concerns what it means to have learned to 'live together'. The second is the axis of 'civilization' and faith that has come with the SIL's activities, and how they relate to place. The third is how Robert Russell, SIL leader and founder of the now established Varadero, was thought to have become 'like them', and came to be referred to in kinship terms. In reviewing Amahuaca assessments of their lives today, and weaving in observations from my fieldwork, I show how transformations intended by the SIL's project appear from the present.

The ability to 'live together' has, among Amahuaca people today, become definitive of what it means to be a good person. There are practical reasons to value living together: doing so opens up avenues for accessing wealth, education and medicines, and the ability to throw large, coordinated parties with an abundance of manioc beer. Beyond the practical, these benefits are seen in terms of resources for making and growing good Amahuaca people. All Amahuaca people consider themselves civilized, almost all of them are either Catholic or Christian, and many of those living in town attend churches. The difference between them is that those who are most civilized are considered less Amahuaca, and those who are more Amahuaca less civilized. This tension carries over to Christianity, and particularly evangelicals. For example, one young woman who primarily lives in town and attends an evangelical church refuses to drink manioc beer for the first few days of her visits home. She cites her faith, and has a cross tattooed on her brow, but after a few days in the community she will begin accepting bowls of manioc beer during parties. This tension is based on a moral tension that opens a conflict between an individual's relation to God and their relation to the 'somatic entities' of their kin (Robbins 2004; Robbins et al. 2014). Knowledge gained through SIL projects has changed how wealth and knowledge are brought in from the outside. While the 'political organization' envisioned by SIL workers is perhaps not valued as was intended, it nonetheless has a central role for Amahuaca, as the following example from my fieldwork demonstrates.

During a community meeting in 2011, outboard motors arrived as payment for the previous year's timber extraction from the community's land. It was the dry season, and the meeting was held at eleven in the morning, in the high strong sun. As I approached the communal building, I saw twelve small 4HP, Chinese-made outboard motors spread out on the ground, one for each family. Almost a year earlier, a community meeting had been held where the contract was negotiated and eventually signed. Despite having other options, such as receiving money or funds for a clinic, there had not been much discussion and each family chose to receive a motor, afterwards signing their name, or marking their fingerprint, to make it official in the community register. As the community members gathered that morning, waiting to receive their share of the wealth, the community president, Manuel Sarasara, began to speak. He specifically emphasized the importance of working together and especially during the *faenas*, or community work parties. Everyone should participate, he said, because if they do not, they will not be able to share in the distribution of wealth, such as the motors. Sarasara also stressed that once the motors were distributed, each family would become responsible and so must take good care of them. He continued by comparing a Native Community with a *caserío*, a village that is not recognized as indigenous, does not share collective ownership of wealth or resources, and where individual families are divided on their own parcels of land. 'In a *caserío*', he said,

> they don't know how to work together. They live apart. Being a *comunidad* means working together. When we have a work party everyone should participate because we live together in a community.[5]

This notion of working together is closely tied to living together, the practical realization of a Native Community among Amahuaca people on the Inuya River. Such a story takes collective work as a specific mode of relating that is valued above, and against, a notion of living apart, whether that is the separations of *caserío* life or living 'spread out in the forest' as they once did. Sarasara's account positions them in a specific moment in their own history, for they both live differently than they did in the past, and also live differently than others such as those in *caserios*.

Let me compare this description of the ways Amahuaca people organize themselves – managing the legal and political framework of the Native Community in order to access wealth – to the example given by Olson of the exchange using the scale described above. What has changed? In the contemporary case, wealth appears through the leader because people are members of a community. The president demonstrates his ability to manage the bureaucratic system of the government, and the motors evidence calculations of what will be given in exchange for the logs removed from the land. It is also now the case that Amahuaca live in a Native Community, so it could be said that rather than working for bosses, bosses work the land for the community. However, while the shift is dramatic, this transformation is not necessarily as empowering as it might at first seem. Despite being a Native Community, Amahuaca do not technically own the trees, which they must gain permission to cut. All contracts drawn up must be certified by the Ministry of Agriculture, meaning that the removal of timber from Native Communities is regulated by government officials and ultimately the decisions are made by the government, not Amahuaca people. Relations between the Amahuaca and loggers remain unequal, and loggers still make significant profits. But Amahuaca people often do not ask for more wealth when signing contracts, but do use their relationship with the logger to make demands throughout the year. In other words, they see the contract as part of an ongoing relation, but not one that delineates a direct exchange of one item for another, trees for motors. Within the frame of capacity building and the equalizing of relations for which Olson's scale strove, we might recall the ideas introduced earlier about relations between bosses and workers among many indigenous groups in the region (Bonilla 2007) and how they take as their model a different logic.

Mechanisms of modernity

My final point develops this theme of Amahuaca relating to the outside world, this time in order to emphasize the centrality of bodies in conceptualizing change for Amerindian groups. Most older Amahuaca today, when recalling the transition to living in communities, say that Robert Russell, founder of Varadero, not only taught them to live together, but also 'became like them'. Over the decades of his work, Russell lived with them, learned their language and consequently became an important figure for the first generation of Amahuaca people to be born and raised in mission communities. Bringing outsiders in to become 'like' Amahuaca is a way of relating to an outside through sharing food, caring for one another and working together (Gow 1991). According to Charitini Karadamou (pers. comm.), a linguist working with Amahuaca people, her process of learning to speak Amahuaca entailed a physical transformation in her throat, which, over time, allowed her to speak 'beautifully'. Similarly, Erik Levin, an anthropologist and linguist who has worked with the Amahuaca for over nine years, has observed Amahuaca painting the bodies of outsiders such as anthropologists and linguists, placing adornments on them and feeding them their foods as a way of making them into people 'like' Amahuaca. He argues that when they speak Spanish, Amahuaca are switching into a different corporality, a different subjectivity, a subjectivity understood as corresponding to the world of mestizos (Levin, pers. comm.). These transformations, expressed at the level of the body, challenge the uni-directional model of transformation implicit in capacity building, in a way I reflect on below in my conclusion.

Conclusion

I opened this chapter with an epigraph from the UNDP, which stated that transformative capacity development 'goes beyond performing tasks; instead, it is more a matter of changing mindsets and attitudes' (UNDP 2009: 5). I have used the SIL's programme, an exercise integrally linked to the process of building the Peruvian nation-state, as a way of tracing ideas of transformation through time, through the decades before the term 'capacity building' became commonplace. By way of concluding, I want to draw out four main points of contribution to a contemporary discussion of capacity building.

First, by taking a historical view, I have been able to show how the early aims and strategies of the SIL in Peruvian Amazonia fit neatly with later models of capacity building. The SIL project, initiated more than a half-century before the UNDP made transformation a central tenet of their development projects, demonstrates quite clearly that the ideologies and conceptualizations contained within capacity building's model of change are not exactly new. Second, I have brought out the problem of assessing the success or failure of a long-term project such as the SIL Amahuaca project; assessment criteria often rely on the same underlying ideologies that made 'capacity building' seem novel when it was introduced contra 'development'. Although capacity building appeared as an 'evolution' in top-down development, focused on bringing about transformation from within, I have shown that the definition of transformation used by many organizations continues to deny indigenous people's understandings of how transformation operates, and towards what ends. Through this denial, I would suggest, the kinds of capacities that are deemed worthy of enhancement continue to be limited, through the definitions within the very systems meant to capacitate people. Third, I have opened the question of reciprocal transformation in projects of capacitation. Empirically, we have seen that becoming 'capacitados' in the technologies of the Other and becoming 'civilized' go hand in hand, the latter clearly read as bodily transformation. When the SIL's project is seen through the experiences of the Amahuaca, it is clear that the success of the SIL's programme entailed both the transformation of Amahuaca as well as the transformation of members of the SIL such as Robert Russell. The changes in capacities demonstrated in dealing with the mechanisms of the legal system do clearly fit into notions of 'transformation' that entail an adoption of the mechanisms of modernity, whether in the form of scales, leadership or government contracts. What it leaves out is why living and working together is such a central theme in this exchange, as well as what it meant for Robert Russell to be transformed from the perspective of Amahuaca people. The transformation of the Amahuaca entailed, or perhaps necessitated, Russell becoming kin to them. When Amahuaca discuss 'becoming civilized', when they differentiate their contemporary lives from who they were, the primary referent is not 'minds' or 'mindsets', but their bodies, and in a sense their 'scale' for measuring transformation. Furthermore, this transformation is reciprocal: those who were integral to Amahuaca processes of transforming were themselves transformed – Robert Russell became 'like them'.

Finally, I have shown how, in this setting, the notion of building certain capacities often entails losing or suspending others. By reading my work with the Amahuaca alongside ethnography of the Yanomami, I have drawn parallels between the way that Yanomami understandings of becoming 'white' can also mean becoming sick and the way that Amahuaca see their 'civilized bodies' as more vulnerable to disease. Even if capacity building activities are driven forward by the identification of a 'lack' in need of remedy, the possibility that 'building' may create new vulnerabilities is rarely part of critical discourse. As a result of these insights, I suggest that capacity building for Amahuaca people should not be understood as uni-directional transformation, or as an individualizing process, as in the terms set out by the UNDP, and the SIL and the Peruvian government before them. It is, instead, a mutual becoming that entails the incorporation of outside wealth, knowledge and capacities, through social and bodily means that have the power to mutually transform. In this, it is perhaps even closer to what was intended by capacity building initiatives of the 1990s, but even as transformation remains central to its forward march, an understanding of the variability of transformation offered by this analysis is, I suggest, rarely seen in practice.

Acknowledgements

I would like to thank Justin Shaffner and Rachel Douglas-Jones for the invitation to participate in the original panel held in 2011 at the AAA, and again in the workshop held in 2015. I would also like to thank all the participants at these events for their insights. The workshop where these ideas were developed was made possible through funding by the Wenner-Gren Foundation, who also funded my fieldwork (2009–11) and a project to construct a cultural heritage centre (2015) in an Amahuaca community. Finally, I would like to thank both anonymous reviewers for their excellent insights and helpful suggestions for improving this chapter.

Christopher Hewlett is currently a Research Fellow at the University of Sussex where he is working on a project: 'Making of an Integrated Landscape of Conservation: Sustainable Development, Environmental Justice and the Politics of Territory in the Amazon'. Christopher is also co-director of the Center for Research and Collaboration in the Indigenous Americas (CRACIA) at the University of Maryland, and serves as President of SHARE International, a nongovernmental organization focusing on cultural exchange and indigenous rights in the Peruvian Amazon. In addition, Chris is an Associate at the American Museum of Natural History.

Notes

1. During the course of my research on Amahuaca history during the twentieth century, I was fortunate to have the cooperation of Robert Russell, as well as anthropologists Robert Carneiro and Joseph Woodside who carried out research in the 1960s and 1970s respectively.
2. The SIL had already been training people as part of the bilingual teacher programmes, a process that doubled as training in community leadership. Thus, the SIL was responsible for producing bilingual material in indigenous languages, training bilingual teachers and overseeing their work in schools located in villages throughout the country.
3. Olson, like other members of the SIL working with indigenous people in Peru, learned the language and lived with Aguaruna people. The Aguaruna are a large indigenous group (approximately 25,000). The missionization of the Aguaruna had begun in the sixteenth century, but they had maintained autonomy from outsiders until the late nineteenth and early twentieth century (Brown 1984). The SIL began

working with them in the 1950s, and Olson's engagement started in 1967, continuing over a number of decades with extensive relationships based on the principle of supporting the needs and desires of the Aguaruna (Olson 1995).
4. In some cases, this relationship between spirit and healer corresponds with, is analogous to (Wagner 1977), relations with other kinds of powerful outsiders. These processes of relating to 'radical otherness' often entail entering into asymmetrical relationships similar to that suggested by Bonilla (2007), Fausto (2008) and Walker (2012).
5. This is a summary and translation of his remarks and is not a transcription.

References

Barclay, F. and F. Santos-Granero. 1998. *Selva Central: History, Economy, and Land Use in Peruvian Amazonia*. Washington, DC and London: Smithsonian Institution Press.
Brown, Michael. 1984. *Una Paz Incierta: Historia y Cultura de las Comunidades Aguarunas Frente al Impacto de la Carretera Marginal.* Lima: Centro Amazónico de Antropología y Aplicación Práctica.
Bonilla, O. 2007. 'Des proies si désirables: soumission et prédation pour les Paumari d'Amazonie brésilienne'. Ph.D. diss., École des Hautes Études en Sciences Sociales, Paris.
Carneiro, R. and G. Dole. n.d. Research Fieldnotes. Personal Archives of R. Carneiro and G. Dole.
Cova, V. 2014. 'Manioc Beer and the Word of God: Faces of the Future in Makuma, Ecuador'. Ph.D. diss., University of St Andrews.
Dole, G. 1998 'Los Amahuaca'. In F. Santos-Granero and F. Barclay (eds), *Guía etnográfica de la alta Amazonía*. Vol. III. Quito: Smithsonian Tropical Research Institute, Instituto Francés de Estudios Andinos y Abya-Yala, 125–273.
Dyck, B. 1992. *The Amahuaca Project: Amahuaca Language Program Research*. Internal unpublished document.
Eade, D. 1997. *Capacity Building: An Approach to People-Centred Development*. Oxford: Oxfam.
Escobar, A. 1995. *Encountering Development: The Making and Unmaking of the Third World*. Princeton, NJ: Princeton University Press.
Ewart, E. and M. O'Hanlon. 2010. *Body Arts and Modernity*. London: Sean Kingston Publishing.
Fausto, C. 2008. 'Donos demais: maestria e dominio na Amazonia'. *Mana: Estudos de Antropologia Social* 14 (2): 329–366.
Fausto, C. 2013. 'Comment: Feeding and Being Fed, Reply to Walker'. *Journal of the Royal Anthropological Institute* 19 (1): 170–178.
Fisher, W. 2000. *Rainforest Exchanges: Industry and Community on an Amazonian Frontier*. Washington, DC: Smithsonian Institution Press.
Gardner, K. and D. Lewis. 1996. *Anthropology, Development and the Postmodern Challenge*. London: Pluto.
Gow, P. 1991. *Of Mixed Blood: Kinship and History in Peruvian Amazonia*. Oxford: Clarendon.
Gow, P. 1993. 'Gringos and Wild Indians: Images of History in Western Amazonian Cultures'. *L'Homme* 33 (126–128): 327–347.
Hale, C. 2004. 'Rethinking Indigenous Politics in the Era of the "Indio Permitido"'. *NACLA Report on the Americas* 38 (2): 16–21.
Handler, R. 1988. *Nationalism and the Politics of Culture in Quebec*. Madison: University of Wisconsin Press.
Hewlett, C. 2014. 'History, Kinship and Comunidad: Learning to Live Together amongst Amahuaca People in the Peruvian Amazon'. Ph.D. diss., University of St Andrews.
High, H. 2012. 'Re-reading the Potlatch in a Time of Crisis: Debt and the Distinctions that Matter'. *Social Anthropology* 20 (4): 363–379.
Huxley, M. and C. Capa. 1964. *Farewell to Eden*. New York: Harper and Row.

Hvalkof, S. (ed.). 2005. *Dreams Coming True: An Indigenous Health Programme in the Peruvian Amazon*. Copenhagen: IWGIA.

Instituto Lingüístico de Verano (ILV). 1960. *Quirica*. Yarinacocha: ILV.

Kelly, J. A. 2011. *State Healthcare and Yanomami Transformations: A Symmetrical Ethnography*. Tucson: University of Arizona Press.

Lévi-Strauss, C. 1995. *The Story of Lynx*, trans. C. Tihanyi. London: University of Chicago Press.

Macpherson, C. B. 1962. *The Political Theory of Possessive Individualism: From Hobbes to Locke*. Oxford: Oxford University Press.

Mauss, M. 1985. 'A Category of the Human Mind: The Notion of the Person; the Notion of the Self'. In M. Carrithers, S. Collins and S. Lukes (eds), *The Category of the Person: Anthropology, Philosophy and History*. Cambridge: Cambridge University Press, 1–25.

McCallum, C. 2014. 'Cashinahua Perspective on Functional Anatomy: Ontology, Ontogenesis, and Biomedical Education in Amazonia'. *American Ethnologist* 41 (3): 504–517.

McKinnon, S. 2013. 'Kinship within and beyond the "Movement of Progressive Societies"'. In S. McKinnon and F. Cannell (eds), *Vital Relations: Modernity and the Persistent Life of Kinship*. Santa Fe, NM: SAR Press, 3–38.

Mentore, G. 2005. *Of Passionate Curves and Desirable Cadences: Themes on Waiwai Social Being*. Lincoln: University of Nebraska Press.

Mollhagen, M. 1970. *Why Community Development*. Dallas: SIL International.

Olson, D. 1995. 'Community Development through Indigenous Leadership'. *Notes on Anthropology and Intercultural Community Work* 18: 30–37.

Overing, J. 1981. 'Review: Amazonian Anthropology'. *Journal of Latin American Studies* 13 (1): 151–165.

Robbins, J. 2004. *Becoming Sinners: Christianity and Moral Torment in Papua New Guinea*. Oakland: University of California Press.

Robbins, J., B. Schieffelin and A. Vilaça. 2014. 'Evangelical Conversion and the Transformation of the Self in Amazonia: Christianity and the Revival of Anthropological Comparison'. *Comparative Studies in Society and History* 56 (3): 559–590.

Stoll, D. 1982. *Fishers of Men or Founders of Empire?* London: Zed.

UNDP (United Nations Development Programme). 2009. *Capacity Development: A UNDP Primer*. New York: UNDP.

Verity, F. 2007. *Community Capacity Building: A Review of the Literature*. Adelaide: South Australian Department of Health.

Vilaça, A. 2002. 'Making Kin out of Others in Amazonia'. *Journal of the Royal Anthropological Institute* 8 (2): 347–365.

Vilaça, A. 2007. 'Cultural Change as Body Metamorphosis'. In C. Fausto and M. Heckenberger (eds), *Time and Memory in Indigenous Amazonia: Anthropological Perspectives*. Gainesville: University Press of Florida, 169–173.

Vilaça. A. [2006] 2010. *Strange Enemies: Indigenous Agency and Scenes of Encounters in Amazonia*, trans. D. Rodgers. Durham, NC: Duke University Press.

Viveiros de Castro, E. 2011. *The Inconstancy of the Indian Soul: The Encounter of Catholics and Cannibals in 16th-Century Brazil*. Chicago: University of Chicago Press and Prickly Paradigm Press.

Wagner, Roy. 1977. 'Analogic Kinship: A Daribi Example'. *American Ethnologist*, 4 (4): 623–642.

Walker, H. 2012. 'Demonic Trade: Debt, Materiality and Agency in Amazonia'. *Journal of the Royal Anthropological Institute* 18 (1): 140–159.

Yashar, D. 2005. *Contesting Citizenship in Latin America: The Rise of Indigenous Movements and the Postliberal Challenge*. Cambridge and New York: Cambridge University Press.

Chapter 8

'Integrating Human to Quality'
Capacity Building across Cambodian Worlds

Casper Bruun Jensen

Walking up Street 63 in Phnom Penh, among beauty parlours and restaurants, one may notice a small sign. It reads 'Integrating Human to Quality'. An internet address at the bottom of the sign directs one to the webpage www.ih2q.com, which presents training solutions for Cambodian professionals. The mission is to 'improve quality of life through innovative training and commitment to encouraging individual taking initiatives and to pursue ever-higher goals in serving and making a difference to their community'.

    The last twenty years have seen an explosion in capacity building, not least in the developing world and among development organizations. Integrating Human to Quality (IHQ) is but a drop in this ocean. A multitude of projects and programmes with a vast set of more or less formalized definitions, goals and aspirations all aim to improve the capacities of a no less diverse set of beneficiaries. The 2008 study report 'Capacity, Change and Performance', written under the auspices of the European Centre for Development Policy Management, captures this heterogeneity well, describing capacity as: 'The ability of individuals, institutions and societies to perform functions,

Illustration 8.1. 'Integrating Human to Quality', Street 63, Phnom Penh.

solve problems and set and achieve objectives in a sustainable manner', as 'the ability of people, organisations and society as a whole to manage their affairs successfully', and as 'the ability of an organisation to function as a resilient, strategic and autonomous entity' (Baser and Morgan 2008: 22).

Awkward phrasing aside, 'integrating human to quality' offers insight into the imaginary of capacity building. Positing a one-way path leading to an abstract and featureless 'quality', capacity is figured at once as universal and vague (Verran 2011).

A similar vagueness cannot be said to characterize the courses offered by IHQ, which, in October 2014, had names and price tags, such as 'High impact workplace communications' (175 USD) and 'Coaching and mentoring: Accelerating capacity building' (185 USD). Bringing together a fuzzy universal sense of quality that shimmers in the distance and quite specific goal-oriented activities that promise to take you there, the slogan 'Integrating Human to Quality' stands metonymically for capacity building as I explore the phenomenon here.

The sense of vague encompassment is no doubt an important component of capacity building's status as a buzzword. For anthropologists skilled in ethnographic contextualization, this opens some easy paths for critique. In the following, however, I engage capacity building neither through detailed ethnographic exposition of the practices where it occurs, nor by critique of its ideological underpinnings. Instead, I find inspiration in Spinoza's (1959: 84) observation that 'the human body can be affected in many ways whereby its power of acting is increased or diminished'. It follows that the capacities of actors have '*as many dimensions* as they have relations' (Latour 1996: 49, my translation and emphasis). Further, such capacities are emergent, growing and transforming in response to the demands of shifting compositions (Bennett 2004: 254).

Beginning with a discussion of how Cambodian bargirls and nannies build capacities in ways that trouble the normative scope of capacity building, I continue by juxtaposing the contexts in which this happens with those of ministry bureaucrats working at the intersection of international development and Cambodian government. Moving capacity building between these contexts makes visible the specificity of its claims to universality. Facilitating identification of some of capacity building's blind spots, this lateral comparison (Gad and Jensen 2015) also holds potential for loosening some of its constraints.

Extending capacities

Paige West (2016: 71) notes that the prominence of capacity building from the 1990s onwards was 'connected to internal and external United Nations assessments of why technical solutions to development problems did not seem to work'. Assuming that development problems were amenable to technical solutions, the visions of technocrats 'set the conditions of possibility for solutions'. This led to the view that the '"underlying human and organizational capabilities" of people in underdeveloped places and in the organisations that managed development needed to be "strengthened"' (West 2016: 71, citing United Nations Development Program [UNDP] 2009).

Such strengthening is often described as taking place at one or more interrelated levels. Thus, 'Capacity Development: A UNDP Primer' presents the reader with a model in which capacities at 'the individual level' are influenced by 'the organizational level', which, in turn, are shaped by the 'enabling environment' (UNDP 2009: 11). Described as comprised of elements as diverse as adaptation and self-renewal, commitment and engagement, the ability to balance diversity and coherence, relating and attracting, and, sitting somewhat oddly with the rest, carrying out technical, service delivery and logistical tasks (Baser and Morgan 2008: 26), the mandate is nothing if not encompassing.

Focusing on Asian medical research governance and ethics, Rachel Douglas-Jones (2013) has analysed how capacity building is materially concretized and conceptually delimited. In contrast, my guiding question is whether capacity building, in spite of its comprehensive mandate, is insufficiently encompassing. In the following, I ask what happens if, rather than aiming for delimitation, one stretches the concept *to the limit*.

I do so by engaging in a lateral comparison (Gad and Jensen 2015) that moves across the seemingly unrelated contexts of Cambodian nannies working for the ex-pat community, bargirls working in Phnom Penh's 'entertainment' area, and government bureaucrats collaborating with international development organizations. Within and across contexts, I survey the '*distribution* of properties among entities, the *relations* they establish, the *circulation* that follows' (Latour 1996: 53, my translation and emphasis), and transformations in people's capacities consequent on these processes.

The aim of this moving juxtaposition is to simultaneously heighten the stakes of capacity building and test its capacities for dealing with foreign contexts. The effect is to trouble the normative scope of capacity building and to make visible a complex set of capacities, which have emerged as creative responses to the divergent demands made upon people by incongruent, intersecting worlds.

Encountering capacities

For several years I have lived and studied in Cambodia. My previous research focused on Phnom Penh infrastructure development, while my present work examines the use of scientific models for imagining and guiding future developments in the Mekong delta. Accordingly, my interlocutors are mainly from bi- and multilateral development organizations, non-governmental organizations (NGOs), research institutions and government. Since I share an 'ex-pat' lifestyle and experiences with many of these people, this is a context where the boundary between research and everyday life is ambiguous.

As I began to think about capacity building, both the term and the practices I knew it through – workshops, training sessions and so on – seemed slippery; at once difficult to get a handle on and difficult to characterize in a way that avoided the kind of generalized banality in which the discourse itself trades.

At a certain point, the possibility of comparison suggested itself. As part of the ex-pat world, my family employs a nanny. One day, as she was listening to English radio lessons while working, it struck me that here was self-induced capacity building happening in front of my eyes. Subsequently, I began to informally talk to nannies about their work, their lives and their hopes for the future, something made easy by the fact that practically all our friends and acquaintances rely on such forms of hired help.

While nannies are not usually part of capacity building activities, it is not beyond the pale to think of their labour in these terms. Having begun to consider how capacity building might be used to re-describe relations and disconnections between officially recognized and valued forms of agency and invisible or undervalued forms, I came to think it might be interesting to put the concept to a more difficult stress test. Thus, I turned to the work of bargirls.

Shortly after arriving in Phnom Penh, new acquaintances in the development world had taken me to play pool at a 'girl-bar' by the riverside.[1] At the time, I had tried to control my embarrassment by engaging in small talk about where they came from, how much they earned and what they thought of working in a bar. Now I returned to several bars, played numerous games of pool and Connect Four, bought many 'lady drinks' and informally interviewed numerous bargirls, some of them several times.[2] This cohort of people included 20-year-old women who had just arrived from the provinces, middle-aged 'mamas' in charge of the bars, and a majority in their mid-twenties to early thirties who had worked in and out of the bar scene for several years. Some desperately wanted to quit, and some did. Many hung in there with mixed feelings, and a few seemed to get by easily.

As the story of the chapter's genesis should make clear, the following discussion cannot, and does not, claim to be based on, or stand in for, thick ethnographies of capacity building. Instead by moving capacity building around, and bringing it into foreign contexts, it develops a lateral comparison that seeks to probe just how (in-)elastic the term is.

Bargirls, nannies...

Chanthy, now in her late thirties, grew up in a province close to Phnom Penh in the years after the devastating civil war. 'You cannot imagine how poor we were', she tells me. Having little formal education, she took assorted low-wage jobs, got married and gave birth to a boy. A subsequent divorce turned her into the breadwinner for the family. With her mother and sister, she moved to Phnom Penh, where she first worked at a market stall, before she managed to get a job as a cook for a Chinese family, then as a nanny for an Australian ex-pat family, then another.

For Chanthy and many other Cambodian women, jobs as nannies for foreigners are in high regard. The monthly salary is in the range of 250–400 USD plus bonuses of the same order for the Pchum Ben holiday and Khmer New Years. That is around the same as a higher administrative position in one of the Cambodian ministries, and about two or three times as much as the monthly wages at one of the Chinese or Malay-run sweatshops that dot the city outskirts. Compared with factory jobs, or running market stalls, it offers additional benefits such as less strenuous working hours and a cleaner and safer environment.

When Chanthy began working for ex-pats, she spoke very little English and was only able to cook Khmer food. However, listening to daily educational radio programmes and taking language classes on the side has improved her English abilities significantly. As for cooking, she is constantly trying to decipher foreign recipes, and experimenting with turning the pictures into her own eclectic dishes.

Chanthy would thus seem to be building her capacities. Indeed, her achievements can be compared directly with the functional definitions 'central to determining the outcome of development endeavours' offered by the UNDP primer (2009: 19). In getting and maintaining her job, she has successfully engaged relevant stakeholders. Her capacities for budgeting, management and implementation are manifest not only in efficiently running ex-pat households, but also in taking care of her own family's economic situation. This situation continues to cause her much worry for her mother is aging and in need of regular hospital visits to Ho Chi Minh City, Vietnam, where the quality of medical service is better.

The capacity to assess a situation and define a vision, that is, thinking about future prospects, is also in clear view. Well aware that, among globally circulating development workers, no job lasts forever, Chanthy constantly works to learn new skills to enhance her future employability. Meanwhile, she is trying to create a better position for her son; she has been able to move him to a private school and she is forcing him to do homework and take additional English lessons rather than play football with his friends. With a bit of persistence, we might even say that her actions elicit her capacity for 'formulating policies and strategies, and evaluating', but here, perhaps, language begins to blur.

As these re-descriptions make clear, it is not very difficult to see Chanthy's experiences in light of the tripartite capacity model: they are structured at once by herself (the individual), an organization (household) and a larger environment (society), which, unfortunately, is far from enabling for most Cambodians. If the language of policies, strategies and evaluation signals the point where Chanthy's story can no longer be easily accommodated within such formal models, this is because these built capacities are not a consequence of *external planning*, being instead emergent responses to practical possibilities (Jensen and Markussen 2007).

That is also the case for 22-year-old Sokhem, whose story poses more difficult questions. When Sokhem's mother died in an accident, she left her siblings, grandmother and her father, with whom she did not get along well, to work in Phnom Penh. Like many other young women, she wanted at all costs to avoid the crunch of sweatshop work. Instead, she found a job at 'Love 'n' Lady', one of the 'girl bars' located in the tourist area behind the riverside. In the evening, red neon signs, advertising entertainment and Angkor beer, flood these narrow streets with light. Tuk tuk drivers and food vendors crowd in front of the bars, waiting for customers. Young women in mini-skirts or skimpy dresses slouch in chairs outside, eating mango dipped in chilli and sugar, waving and calling at passers-by.

Entering 'Love 'n' Lady', one is surrounded by 'bargirls' offering standard greetings: 'Hey, how are you?', 'What's your name?', 'Where do you come from?', 'Come sit here'. Thumping pop and techno music makes conversation more or less impossible. But it doesn't matter much; most of the men come to drink, play pool, flirt, grope, or perhaps go home with one of the women.

This is not strictly prostitution, though sex for money is an important dimension of business. The bars typically pay employees between 60 USD and 90 USD per month. When a customer buys a drink for a girl, she gets a 1 USD provision. Taking a bargirl outside, to go to a club or elsewhere, requires payment of a 'bar fee'. On top of that, any arrangements made between the women and customers are personal matters. Some women have sexual relations with customers on a regular basis, while others don't leave the bar at all. Some form semi-permanent client/girlfriend relationships even as they continue their work (cf. Hoefinger 2010, Zheng 2009).

Sokhem ended up at 'Love 'n' Lady' not least to help fund her brother's education. I ask why that was her problem, rather than her father's, or that of other family members.

'You already know that', she replies, 'in Cambodia, men can't earn money'. The root cause she identifies makes her situation comparable to that of Chanthy, though their practical solutions are different. Both have specific opportunities, directly related to the ex-pat community and the tourist industry, because they are women. Among foreigners and visitors, 'women's services', from household work and babysitting to entertainment and sex work, are in high demand. Men have nothing comparable to offer, with the possible exception of becoming a private chauffeur. While Sokhem's father and brother back in Prey Veng may be able to scrape together 100 USD per month, she can earn upwards of 300 USD, and much more if she chooses to 'go home' with customers.

The situation is fraught with dilemmas. Sokhem would like to support her beloved brother, but she would also like to take an education and plan for the future. Hoping to get an accounting degree in two or three years, she has enrolled in morning classes at a college. Yet her steady income is premised on working late hours, and especially on extracting large amounts of alcoholic 'lady drinks' consumed in the company of customers – an obligation hardly enabling for her morning studies. Meanwhile, her family in Prey Veng continuously asks for money, to the extent, she says, that she can barely save anything. Indeed, Sokhem dreads her trips home for the Pchum Ben festivities because they cost her around 100 USD in gifts and payments, almost a semester's worth of school.

If capacity is 'defined simply as the ability to perform functions, solve problems, and set and achieve objectives', as written in the classic *Capacity for Development* (Fukuda-Parr et al. 2002: 8–9), it is easy to describe Sokhem's life story as a set of growing capacities. And since *Capacity for Development* introduced the canonical three-layer model of capacities (individual–organization–enabling environment), we can recapitulate these capacities by its guidance.

At the individual level, Sokhem's capacities have grown exponentially, especially in the areas of dressing and dancing sexily and in entertaining male tourists in a variety of ways. These capacities are inseparable from the broader 'institutional environment' in which Sokhem finds herself, one characterized by the availability in Phnom Penh of very narrow, well-lit pathways showing young women how to make ends meet. However, Sokhem's capacities for management of money, time and 'strategy and vision' have also grown. These capacities have been gradually extended in response to a set of institutional arrangements that include familial obligations, the inability of uneducated men to find good jobs, and her own educational prospects and future plans.

Though describing the world of 'bargirls' in terms of capacity building may sound more than a little awkward, my point is not ironic. I am convinced that Sokhem *in fact* has 'grown' many capacities as part of her short working life. Moreover, the fact that these capacities are very different from, or even directly at odds with, the ideas usually summoned by capacity building[3] does not speak to the inherent vacuity of that concept. It is, nevertheless, indicative of its *narrowness of conception* and certain attendant *blind spots*.

That narrowness relates to the institutional arrangements within which discourses and practices of capacity building *themselves* normally flow. This is the set of relations that Fukuda-Parr et al. have in mind when they insist that national capacity goes beyond the individual by 'weav[ing] individual strengths into a stronger and more resilient fabric' (2002: 9). What is being woven are specific abilities that allow high-level bureaucrats and governmental elites to partner with bilateral development organizations like the UN or the World Bank. That this resilient national fabric is continuously woven not only by such officials but also by nannies, tuk tuk drivers and bargirls is inconsequential from within that setting.

One can hardly take development professionals to task for not being accountable to the whole set of varied capacities of Cambodia's population. The fact remains, however, that the literature on capacity building continuously conflates society in general with its own far more limited institutional contexts. Thus, we can read, in the midst of discussing capacity building in the *narrow institutional sense*, that 'each *society* has the capacities that correspond to its own functions and objectives' (Fukuda-Parr et al. 2002: 8–9, emphasis added). What comes into view is thus a tension between the universal imagination of capacity building and the particular forms of its own enablement. Yet, if capacity building cannot encompass what has been learnt by Chanthy and Sokhem and provides no insight into why it has been learnt, it is clearly not making any sense of 'functions and objectives' of Cambodian *society* as a whole. After all, it is to just those societal demands they have learned to respond: rather well, as made clear by the regular visits of tourists, businessmen, development professionals and bureaucrats to the bars where Sokhem works.

The report *Capacity for Development* (Fukuda-Parr et al. 2002: 10–11) dedicates a section to what they term 'The Asymmetric Relationship'. Here it is emphasized that one problem with traditional technical cooperation was an assumption of equal collaborative relations, which in practice never held. *Capacity for Development* emphasizes – very relevantly, as we shall see – that the problem of asymmetry should not be ignored or talked out of existence. Laid next to the stories of Chanthy and Sokhem, its acknowledgement of inequality nevertheless appears far too anodyne. Not least, it fails to recognize that there is not simply an asymmetric relationship but several totally incongruent ones.

On the one hand, Chanthy and Sokhem do not live in a world that poses problems for which capacity building, as described in the literature, is the solution. On the other hand, from the point of view of formal capacity building, the kinds of capacities these women have acquired do not appear as capacities at all. Indeed, Sokhem's self-built capacities for surviving and, hopefully, thriving would probably be viewed as de-capacitating, if not perverse.

And bureaucrats…

In contrast to the work of Sokhem and Chanthy, it is unproblematic to relate capacity building to the work lives of ministry officials collaborating with international development organizations. Indeed, they epitomize the kinds of subjects whose capacities are to be built. At the same time, these bureaucrats also inhabit other worlds, as part of which they engage in activities not easily captured by capacity building in its conventional forms. Analogous to the previous stretching of capacity building, I aim here to equip capacity building to take into account these more elusive dimensions of Cambodian bureaucratic work. This is particularly relevant since, situated at the intersection of international development and national bureaucracy, this work happens at the precise point where formal capacity building bumps into 'the broader functions and objectives' of Cambodian society.

In Cambodia, as elsewhere, bi- and multilateral development organizations are involved in a tremendous amount of projects, programmes, policy-making, strategy development and forms of collaboration and negotiation, and they have access to a large amount of funds. Their perceived success is bound up with disbursing those funds effectively while at the same time delivering measurable improvement of things like gender equity, educational quality and environmental sustainability. The efforts to deliver on such goals tie development organizations into tight collaborative loops with line ministries, NGOs and consultants (cf. Jensen and Winthereik 2013: 121–147).

Because these are central contexts for capacity building, the meaning of the term is inflected by the problems that typically circle these loops. In Cambodia, again as elsewhere, these problems include the fact that ministries are rarely able to live up to the demands for speedy delivery, quality, efficiency and transparency made by partners such as the UN, the Food and Agriculture Organization (FAO) or the Asian Development Bank. Due to such misalignments, the disbursement of project money may slow down, or grind to a halt, leading to low-level frustrations and minor conflicts between partners. These types of situations form the context for Deborah Eade's (1997: 34) observation that 'capacity-building is often used simply to mean enabling institutions to be more effective in implementing development projects.'

According to the three-tiered model, such enablement focuses on individuals seen as nested within organizational and societal environments. It is precisely the interrelations between these environments that form the systemic conditions that must be improved. We are thus positioned to consider the systemic conditions and capacities of Sovanny, a medium-ranked bureaucrat working for a ministry that collaborates closely with multilateral donors on environmental issues.

An important dimension of this work is to negotiate agreements about projects, policies and budgets. Thus, Sovanny spends time in meetings, he prepares briefs and presentations and he joins workshops about topics such as deforestation, community-based fisheries and the establishment of ecological corridors. This dimension of Sovanny's work is plainly visible to his development collaborators, and some of it indeed embodies the usual meaning of capacity building. Even so, it covers only part of what he does. For Sovanny is also part of Cambodia's complex political world, the 'objectives and functions' of which are largely incommensurable with those of international development, and cannot easily be registered in terms of conventional capacity building.

Such incommensurability can be exemplified at the level of individual capacities. Whereas international organizations, at least in principle, encourage lower-ranked officers to further their careers by taking initiative and coming up with fresh ideas, decision making in Cambodian bureaucracy is hierarchical and passiveness at the lower levels is the general norm. Moreover, at the level of organizational norms, incommensurability manifests in the contrast between the high value international development places on transparency and accountability and the ranking of Cambodia as 150 out of 167 countries in the 2015 Transparency International corruption perceptions index.[4] Though superficially disconnected, these contrasts are in fact related in a manner that bears directly on capacity building as it is exhibited at the intersection of these worlds.

Cambodia's socio-political system operates through a kind of pyramid system of exchange, where one pays tributes upwards, in return for support and favours transmitted downwards. Because advance in this system is not primarily due to one's professional merit but rather depends on the size of the monetary contributions one pays to build relations, officials have no particular incentive to take individual initiative in the way recognized and valued by international development organizations. In contrast, there is a strong incentive to increase one's income, since it can be converted into social standing and influence.

The problem, however, is that there is no money in the Cambodian bureaucratic system. The tax system is weak, not least because most money is moved through the kinds of informal channels just described. International organizations do, of course, have money. But they are not allowed to make 'compensations' to national ministries or individual employers due to rules about conflicts of interest.

Accordingly, the scene of international development collaboration is one of massive income asymmetries. Monthly salaries for international staff working for the UN or the World Bank begin at 5,000 USD or more, but go much higher. Cambodian nationals working for these organizations earn approximately 1,500 USD. And international consultants, even of dubious quality, can easily gain 500 USD per day for short-term contract work. In comparison, Sovanny, who works for the ministry, has an income of around 250 USD per month, approximately the same as a nanny, and significantly less than a successful bargirl or masseuse.

Sitting across the table from his international collaborators, Sovanny and their colleagues are looking at people with an income somewhere between twenty and fifty times higher than theirs. Disruptive of the ideal of equal partnerships, this disparity also damages concrete collaborations. Having respectable careers and aspirations of upward mobility, Sovanny and his colleagues need additional sources of income. It is their alternative ways of income procurement that generate Cambodia's high score on Transparency International's corruption perceptions index.

International development professionals repeatedly complain about the slow progress of work and their difficulties getting hold of Cambodian counterparts. Typically locating the problem in Cambodian 'culture', they implicitly acknowledge that these problems are only partly due to a lack of capacities that might be solved by offering packaged technical knowledge.

In fact, bureaucrats like Sovanny simply do not stay in their offices very much. To gain additional income, they commonly have multiple side-jobs and dedicate only limited attention to the collaborations. And indeed, this situation can easily be described in the language of capacity building: having learned from the functions and demands of the broader society, Sovanny has gained a more differentiated set of capacities for acquiring the income he needs to improve his standing.

At the broader organizational level, salary asymmetries lead to on-going skirmishes between the ministries and their partners. For example, ministries may request small compensations to incentivize or reward bureaucrats for their involvement.

Such modifications balance at the edge of what is allowable according to the rules of international development organizations, and they are mostly rejected. Yet, since donors can only reach their objectives if the ministries collaborate, smaller or larger deviations from formal rules slip through the cracks. As I have often been told, 'there is nothing to do about it'. If noticed by auditors or journalists, these infringements lead to reprimands and sanctions, and contribute to Cambodia's low ranking on the corruption index. If not, they make practical collaboration easier by slightly levelling asymmetrical partnerships. Doing so, of course, they also heighten the expectation of future repetitions. They help, as it were, to naturalize the grey zone.

Rather than a criticism of Cambodian bureaucracy, the above description is meant to highlight the variance between this world and that of international development. From the point of view of the latter, one might conclude, as is often concluded, that Cambodian bureaucracies are dysfunctional and in serious need of new capacities. Yet it might also be argued that this world and the people who inhabit it have developed capacities very useful for dealing with international development collaboration. Prominent is the capacity to constantly reinvent ways of acquiring funds from international donors *while also* finding ways of not committing too much to the delivery of the promised goods.[5]

Capacity seen twice

In December 2016, I joined a workshop on water accounting, taking place in a second-floor meeting room at the upscale Phnom Penh Hotel. Financed by the Asian Development Bank (ADB), this was the culmination of a one-year collaborative project. A young researcher based at the UNESCO-IHE University in the Netherlands had preliminarily mapped the water flows of the Mekong system. In two previous workshops, she had taught participants from four ministries the basics of how to calculate and account for these flows. Their response, she told me the previous day, had been overwhelmingly positive. This morning, the Dutch grand old man of water accounting speaks from the podium. He emphasizes scientific rigour and policy relevance and thanks the high-ranked Cambodian excellences for the collaboration. The aim for the future, he concludes, is to mainstream water accounting by turning it into a programme component in the ministries.

As he steps down after receiving enthusiastic applause, the floor is taken over by representatives from three ministries. One after another, they make brief PowerPoint presentations that summarize what their ministries have learnt and how it matters for their work. The presentations all end on the same note. Listing kinds of technical knowledge that requires more teaching and future workshops, they all send the message that we are not quite there yet: we would like the project to continue.

From the point of view of the Asian Development Bank, this is a successful case of capacity building. Concrete technical abilities are exhibited on PowerPoint slides, the excitement about water accounting is manifest, and the urge to develop these new capacities further is made explicit. Certainly, there is no reason to doubt that participants find water accounting interesting, or to deny that capacity building has taken place.

Yet, considered from another angle, in the workshop capacity is elicited in a different guise. To see this, we only need to focus on the contrasting ways in which the visiting scientists and the Cambodians envision the ideal future collaboration. From the point of view of the Dutch scientists and the ADB specialist, the purpose of introducing water accounting to Cambodian bureaucrats is to enhance their analytical abilities, making it possible for the ministries to make good decisions. To do so in a lasting manner requires turning water accounting into a standard component of ministerial work. Yet during the workshop not a single bureaucrat mentioned mainstreaming. Instead, each and all promoted the idea of additional projects that would help them learn more.

Contrary to mainstreaming, which entails a commitment of time and money on the side of the ministries, what they sought were forms of short-term collaboration paid for by money from the outside, and demanding little aside from their participation in a manner that testifies convincingly to the power of capacity building. At the point where Cambodian bureaucratic worlds intersect with international development, the distinction between genuine and mimicked capacity building thus blurs. What is clear, however, is that the bureaucrats have developed the capacity to *pass* as adequate subjects for capacity building. From their position, this capacity is tremendously helpful because it facilitates access to the funds and projects of donors.

Whereas Chanthy and Sokhem live outside the realm of formal capacity building, Sovanny and his colleagues are part of that system. And it is *as* part of it that they join workshops in which donors pour funds into building their capacities. Yet, although they are part of the development world, they are part of it only in part. Since their work straddles the worlds of international development and Cambodian politics, they have built the capacities required to navigate these partly incommensurable contexts and demands (Rottenburg 2009).

What happens at this point of intersection is fascinating. In spite of clearly recognized, or more dimly perceived, differences, it is rare to witness any collision of worlds.[6] Indeed, the worlds of Cambodian bureaucracy and international development seem often to run in parallel. This is the case even when, or especially when, their representatives inhabit the same meeting rooms, like the one on the second floor of the Phnom Penh Hotel. In fact, I would suggest that the blind spots of formal capacity building are *instrumental* in generating this odd parallelism.

Although the discourse of capacity building pays lip service to the need for recognizing asymmetries, it is almost impossible for such recognition to have any concrete implication. Capacity building workshops routinely centre on learning particular skills or gaining knowledge about a particular, prescient topic, like water accounting. However, I have yet to encounter a capacity building activity that includes reflexive analysis of the ways in which its own content, form and outcomes are shaped by the divergent demands of 'individual', 'organizational' and 'societal' environments. And in a sense this is understandable, for it is almost impossible to conceive the *practical* point of such an exercise. After all, even if the problematic consequences of economic asymmetries or hierarchical structures were acknowledged and debated, there would be no means of redress. Within the rooms of capacity building there is simply no point in discussing the reasons behind the 'aberrant' behaviour of bureaucrats like Sovanny. Instead, discussions of collaborative troubles, and of their oblique causes, are delegated to informal conversations at private parties, barbecues and weekend outings.

The qualities of people

Moving from a description of the capacities of nannies and bargirls and (backwards) into the world of international collaboration makes evident that the presumed universality of capacity building is only relative. Rather than an encompassing whole, formal capacity building designates a specific domain with its own order *and* others (Berg and Timmermans 2000). Unable to recognize its own specificities, capacity building becomes correspondingly unable to make sense of capacities that fall outside this domain. It presumes forms of commonality that aren't there.

Though the nannies of ex-pats are not normally thought of as building their capacities, they constantly work to improve their skills and employability. Bargirls working in the seedy side streets of Phnom Penh's riverside, too, build capacities that allow them to make a better living than the one afforded by sweatshops. Ironically, this is in part to the benefit of (male) international development workers and government officials, not a few of whom frequent bars and karaoke parlours after working hours. As for the officials, they engage in genuine or dissimulated forms of capacity building within international development while simultaneously building capacities for extracting benefits from that system.

Since I have characterized capacity building as a vague whole, the specificities of which are hidden under its mantle of universality, it is reflexively relevant to query the extent to which this argument is generalizable. In one sense, relating only to a small sub-set of people in Phnom Penh, the situation I have described is obviously utterly specific. Yet there is reason to think that the dynamics of incommensurable capacities are quite general, likely to play out, with variations, more or less everywhere capacity building is promoted.

'Integrating Human to Quality', the slogan with which I began, provides a good example of this simultaneous specificity and generality. On the one hand, it tells us that the generic human can be integrated to generic quality. Promising to 'accelerate capacity building' in order to achieve such integration, it makes explicit the universal pretensions that the discourse of capacity building covers over by paying superficial respects to diversity. To this extent, we are in a realm of complete generality. Yet, this consultancy firm of course makes its business in a Cambodian context where, for reasons touched upon previously, promises to accelerate capacity building and create high-impact workplace communications gain very specific inflections that bear little resemblance to what these practices would entail in Europe or Japan.

I end with a brief remark on the relation between capacity building, hope and insufficiency. Conceivably, the capacities built by bargirls and nannies in the course of their uncertain lives could be mapped, point for point, onto Baser and Morgan's (2008: 26) list: 'adaptation, self-renewal, commitment, engagement, balancing diversity and coherence, relating and attracting…'. Building such capacities might well be seen as an important part of what makes it possible for these women to sustain hopes for a better, less insecure future. Certainly, also, these capacities are often insufficient to realize such hopes. Yet more insufficient, however, is the blinkered, relative universalism of capacity building, which makes it constitutively unable to recognize the actual capacities that sustain the lives, and hopes, of these women.

Acknowledgements

I would like to thank Rachel Douglas-Jones and Justin Shaffner for their comments and advice, and for organizing the Wenner-Gren workshop that led to the writing of this chapter. Also thanks to the workshop attendants and reviewers for their suggestions. This work was supported by the Japanese Society for the Promotion of Science KAKENHI Grant Number 24251017.

Casper Bruun Jensen is an anthropologist of science and technology currently residing in Phnom Penh, Cambodia. He is the author of *Ontologies for Developing Things* (Sense, 2010) and *Monitoring Movements in Development Aid* (with Brit Ross Winthereik) (2013, MIT) and the editor of *Deleuzian Intersections: Science, Technology, Anthropology* with Kjetil Rödje (Berghahn, 2009) and *Infrastructures and Social Complexity* with Penny Harvey and Atsuro Morita (Routledge, 2016). His work focuses on climate, environments, infrastructures, and speculative and practical ontologies.

Notes

1. For a detailed discussion of this scene, see Hoefinger (2010).
2. The anonymized depiction of development worlds and their challenges is based on numerous formal and informal conversations with people from a broad range of organizations. The stories of Sokhem and Chanthy are condensed from a set of interviews with bargirls and nannies.
3. The Cambodian Women's Network for Unity (WNU) discussed by Melinda Cooper (2013) can be described as aiming to extend capacity building into the informal realm of sex workers. Among other things, WNU offers training in legal and human rights, and provides informal education to prepare children of sex workers for enrolment in school. Cooper argues that WNU's critical responses to the use of Cambodian sex workers as subjects for the trial of the HIV/AIDS drug Tenofovir in the early 2000s constituted 'both a novel form of labor politics and a compelling instance of radical public health activism'. Despite its important accomplishments, however, most Cambodian sex workers are not affiliated with WNU, nor have even heard of it. Further, the WNU has so far not succeeded in its worthwhile goals to remove the stigma of sex work, improve health access and ensure the social inclusion of sex workers. Its interventions, up to this point, fall outside the scope of what international development and national policy recognizes and supports as capacity building.
4. The index is available at http://www.transparency.org/cpi2015#results-table (accessed 13 March 2017).
5. *Cambodia's Curse*, written by the journalist Joel Brinkley, describes the unending, never successful efforts of international donors to hold Hun Sen's government accountable for the use of funds. Over the last decades, an international push for the government to introduce anti-corruption legislation has been central to this endeavour. Yet this push itself has continued to fail. By March 2008, Brinkley (2011: 287) wrote, using a curiously mixed metaphor, 'the anti-corruption law had become a uniquely Cambodian chimera lost in a shell game'. Nor are such pressures and evasions a new phenomenon. As the historian David Chandler (2008: 174) noted: 'Under French pressure ... [King] Norodom agreed in 1877 to promulgate a series of reforms'. Due to various tactical ploys, however, 'these were never carried out'.
6. It is not that there are *no* conflicts but simply that they rarely escalate (outbursts and threats by Prime Minister Hun Sen aside), operating mainly as a constant minor irritant to collaboration. Commonly, for example, bureaucrats create hurdles or minor obstructions, the removal of which can be used as bargaining chips with which to negotiate various grey zone benefits with donors.

References

Baser, H. and P. Morgan. 2008. 'Capacity, Change and Performance: Study Report'. Discussion paper no. 59b. European Centre for Development Policy Management.
Bennett, Jane. 2004. 'The Force of Things: Steps toward an Ecology of Matter'. *Political Theory* 32 (3): 347–72.
Berg, M. and S. Timmermans. 2000. 'Order and Their Others: On the Constitution of Universalities in Medical Work'. *Configurations* 8 (1): 31–61.
Brinkley, J. 2011. *Cambodia's Curse: The Modern History of a Troubled Land*. Collingwood, Australia: Black, Inc.
Chandler, D. 2008. *A History of Cambodia*. Boulder, CO: Westview Press.
Cooper, M. 2013. 'Double Exposure: Sex Workers, Medical Prevention Trials and the Dual Logic of Global Public Health'. *Scholar and Feminist Online* 11 (3). http://sfonline.barnard.edu/life-un-ltd-feminism-bioscience-race/double-exposure-sex-workers-biomedical-prevention-trials-and-the-dual-logic-of-global-public-health/.
Douglas-Jones, R. 2013. 'Locating Ethics: Capacity Building, Ethics Review and Research Governance across Asia'. Ph.D. diss., Durham University.
Eade, D. 1997. *Capacity-Building: An Approach to People-Centered Development*. Oxford: Oxfam.
Fukuda-Parr, S., C. Lopes and M. Khaled. 2002. *Capacity for Development: New Solutions to Old Problems*. London: Earthscan.
Gad, C. and C. B. Jensen. 2015. 'Lateral Comparisons'. In J. Deville et al. (eds), *Practicing Comparison: Logics, Relations, Collaborations*. Mattering Press, pp. 189–220.
Hoefinger, H. 2010. 'Negotiating Intimacy: Transactional Sex and Relationships among Cambodian Professional Girlfriends'. Ph.D. diss., Goldsmiths, University of London.
Jensen, C. B. and R. Markussen. 2007. 'The Unbearable Lightness of Organizational Learning Theory: Organizations, Information Technologies and Complexities of Learning in Theory and Practice'. *Learning Inquiry* 1 (3): 203–218.
Jensen, C. B. and B. R. Winthereik. 2013. *Monitoring Movements in Development Aid: Recursive Partnerships and Infrastructures*. Cambridge, MA and London: MIT Press.
Latour, B. 1996. 'Om aktør-netværksteori: Nogle få afklaringer og mere end nogle få forviklinger'. *Philosophia* 25 (3–4): 47–65.
Rottenburg, R. 2009. *Far-Fetched Facts: A Parable of Development Aid*. Cambridge, MA and London: MIT Press.
Spinoza, B. de. 1959. *Ethics*. London: J. M. Dent.
UNDP (United Nations Development Programme). 2009. 'Capacity Development: A UNDP Primer'. New York: UNDP.
Verran, H. 2011. 'Imagining Nature Politics in the Era of Australia's Emerging Markets in Environmental Services Interventions'. *Sociological Review* 59 (3): 411–431.
West, P. 2016. *Dispossession and the Environment: Rhetoric and Inequality in Papua New Guinea*. New York: Columbia University Press.
Zheng, T. 2009. *Red Lights: The Lives of Sex Workers in Postsocialist China*. Minneapolis, MN and London: University of Minnesota Press.

Afterword

Measurable Subjectivities and Discoverable Worlds

George Mentore

In his contribution to this collection, Chris Hewlett recounts a measuring scale deployed in rice deals in the Peruvian Amazon in the 1960s. The scale is a technology doing its work of weighing in the place of the boss's 'calibrated muscles' (Hewlett, this volume, citing Olson 1995:31). As he observes, the transformation described by Olson is one of the coming-to-capacity of the Aguaruna, now capable of participating in a time-bound rice trade, in contrast with ongoing trade relations of the past. For the observer of the time, Olson, a new capacity had been built.

When referring to "capacity," we are often drawn to do so in terms of some measurable mass, some quantifiable amount of matter, or some calculable physical body. If not directly, then certainly indirectly, we tend to imagine capacity in measurable terms. This insistence appears ubiquitously in the development literature (Liberato et al., 2011). It appears in the chapters of this collection as monitoring and evaluation exercises, accountability regimes, and – more implicitly – as a quantified underpinning of transformation accounts. In conversation with Macintyre's preface, the linguistic 'verbal sophistry' (Macintyre, this volume) of capacity building, I use this afterword to comment on what "measurability" does within and for capacity. I reflect not only on its place in capacity-building projects but also, drawing on my work in Amazonian anthropology, the critical ways it shapes and limits anthropological analysis.

Throughout the collection, from the 'professionalizing' studied by Kalesnikava and LaHatte (this volume) to the presumed capacities for 'democracy' Ellison describes (this volume), or the 'blueprints' quantifying regular health visits Ghanaian health services (Boulding, this volume), capacity is tied to markers of 'modernity.' I want to draw out upon what these depend. Even before capacity-building projects are subjected to monitoring and evaluation measures, the capacity building itself already incorporates a sense of measure, a tacit calculation.

First, let us consider ideas about life-lived in linear irreversible time. This idea is about time that counts down (and out) the perishable body, which goes only in one direction. Indeed, the development narrative (LaHatte, this volume) contains this linearity and becomes visible when resistance to change becomes a transgression against the normative movement of time. Capacity has its directionality.

Second, we see ideas about *numbers*, regularly used in making-measurable.[1] Ethnographies show numbers as concealed, hidden, or disguised not simply *in* the world but rather as the world (Verran 2001). The cultural placement of modernist numeracy into western rationalist logic satisfies the rigor of truth-claims made about capacity – what our Introduction terms capacity building's 'persuasive power' (Douglas-Jones and Shaffner, this collection). Therefore, the work of investigation amounts to a kind of, if not precisely, that of mathematics, whereby finding and revealing the truths of the world amount to "discovering" their hidden arithmetic.

Then, insisting on the "measurability" of capacity additionally implicates beliefs about "having a subjectivity." Put otherwise, capacities, large or small, begin to be thought in terms of privately owned property, something possessed. The editors observe in their Introduction that this idea of an internal human capacity – something one could 'hold' of oneself – shapes how capacity building is thought. In her fieldwork in Mount Hagen, Strathern observed that the unit equivalence of transacted items operated as metaphors for their substitutability; there is a computed equivalence (1992). The measure of an object becomes, by metaphor, the object itself. The object itself becomes its measure—the measure and the object substitute for each other. I return to this point below, extending it to how we think about capacity and capacity building itself.

So finally, to capacity building's transformational character, its mode of "becoming." This mode works because we give *form to emptiness*. Here is the 'insufficiency' pointed to in the title of this collection. From a Heideggerian perspective (1971), the "object" of capacity produces its own "thing" of an emptiness, which must be filled or forever gesture the promise of completion. In this way, capacity is a thing "discovered" both in people (Moore et al. 2006) and things (Bester 2015).

Viewing capacity building as a set of moves dependent on specific logics and making those logics visible allows us to mobilize them in Western development discourses. Capacities become things discovered following the philosopher Rorty's requirements for effective "metaphors of discovery" (1989:40). Moreover, "discovered" objects of knowledge become the private property of an individual's conscious intent. By this strategy, the object "discovered" serves to confirm the individualized subjectivity of its discoverer and provide how claims of ownership over the object are made. On how, then, can it be acted? To return to Strathern's point, then, the capacity for change or movement that capacity building so desires can only be possessed and calculated in terms of an interaction between "computed equivalences."

Force

Returning to Hewlett's vignette, there are numerous examples where Amerindian peoples are exposed to modernity and its logic in missionaries, rubber barons, and cocaine bosses to NGOs, tourists, and national governments. Capacity building is the latest instantiation. Achieving measurable capacity or sustaining a quantitatively total capacity occurs, I suggest only within a context of force. Force is required for movement and depends on the interaction between one measure and another. To make capacities move and accelerate, one needs to exert force between one measurable capacity and another, a relation of pushing and pulling. Alternatively, in the proper context of our western paradigms of conflict analysis, they can be achieved only through dualist thinking, opposition, and reconciliation, in other words, war and victory over the other as the enemy.

Take the description below concerning the Amazonian Barasana, drawn from an analysis of business and barter, trade goods, and motivations for consumer goods. In his essay, Hugh-Jones describes 'very real forces which push Indians to accept and demand an ever-increasing range of consumer goods, from the creation of debt to the introduction of new technologies or even the cultivation of ridicule' (Hugh-Jones 1992: 54). Nevertheless, the narrative is not just about the pressures; he says:

> alongside the 'push' to consume provided by the forces of acculturation in the name of 'civilization' and the market, there is also a significant and important 'pull'. This 'pull' is not simply a blind and mechanical response [by Barasana] to alien social manipulation, nor is it simply the reciprocal of the advances which unscrupulous traders force onto unwilling Indians to guarantee their future indebtedness. It is also a demand which has its own internal reasons and which shapes supply (Hugh-Jones 1992: 54).

This statement is an intriguing way of explaining indigenous desires for western-produced goods, one promising to give serious consideration to Amerindian "regimes of value" (a la Appadurai 1986). It introduces an anthropologically pleasing element of cultural relativity, arguing for "cultural redefinition" of those goods passing from the Western to the indigenous regime. It goes directly for meaning: the cultural ways in which western consumer goods (and even the wage labor which produces them) possess *different signification* and importance when desired and used by traditional Amazonian peoples. Nevertheless, despite this promise, I suggest that what it does not do is to take seriously the contribution to meaning made by indigenous thought *all the way* to its possible conclusion.

To have pursued this argument further, the critique and analysis would have first established the grounds upon which the similar measurements we use to determine capacity existed in the alternative Barasana regime, that is, under its modes of calculations. This conclusion seems counterintuitive since to be recognized as "different," that difference must have resulted from cultural forces dissimilar to those producing the measures we use in our regimes of thought. As it stands, the *premise* by which western goods acquire their value for western consumers *appears to remain the same* for indigenous consumers, even after the goods have passed into the latter's regime and have presumably acquired their different priorities of signification. In other words, while Hugh-Jones's argument above provides the indigenous context with causal force to transform the meaning given to western goods, this same force is not additionally attributed with the power to transform the "true" hidden meaning of value itself.

Anthropological Moves

Where does this leave analyses of capacity building as a widespread practice, especially as concerns its intent to transform? Let me draw my arguments together. I have established that capacity building depends on a knot of logic that *creates* both those attributing capacity and those in possession of it. I have also presented a narration of a transformational encounter, commenting on the mode of ethnographic analysis deployed. My suggestion is this: when anthropology reserves the power of 'discovery' just for itself, we end up considering two different regimes of value. Their differences then have no consequence on our dominant, singular understanding of value itself. The quoted "pushing" and "pulling" end with the same result – in this case, a one-way movement by Amerindian receivers of Western commodities in the direction of "acculturation," "civilization and the market." This presumption is disappointing: anthropological analysis seems to offer us little more than the continuing saga of having to consider indigenous thought from on-top-down, without the benefit of following the promised alternative to its ultimate conclusion. What challenges, what alterities to modern rationalist thought might we encounter if we do so?

In this example, the measurable capacity of value stays the same even as deployed to help state that indigenous regimes produce different signification. Here the implicit carryover of hidden measurable quantities waiting to be discovered appears obvious: it often aids anthropology in making its untested claims about universality. So frequently do we insist on possessing the hidden measurable capacity, presumptively asserted, the seamless making of its truth often goes unreferenced and undetected. We hardly notice our classic Newtonian laws of motion at work, surreptitiously allowing indigenous inertia (cast as capacity unfilled, the potential for development) forced into movement by the exertion of or contact with modernity. Measurable gravitational pushes and pulls apply equally to modern markets as they do to indigenous desire. However, without some alternative "measure," that is, some indigenous means of quantifying Amerindian capacity, it seems rash to judge their calculations to be the same as ours. Without some inclusion of (or, if you prefer, capitulation to) indigenous interpretations and their range of substitutability, testing for the different meanings capacity might hold will remain limited. Once thoughtfully included, however, how different, or similar to ours would their understanding of capacity be? Could we even continue to speak in terms of "capacity" after such a comparison has been made?

George Mentore is an Associate Professor in the Department of Anthropology at the University of Virginia, and author of *Of Passionate Curves and Desirable Cadences: Themes on Waiwai Social Being* (2005). He has worked for many years in Guyana and Brazil with the Wai Wai, Wapisiana and Macushi. His work has appeared in *Anthropology and Humanism,* and *Tipití: Journal of the Society for the Anthropology of Lowland South America.* Currently he is working on completing a manuscript entitled "Remaking the Self, Reliving the World: the Poetics of Severance in Modern Anthropology and its Alternative of Folded Thought for Indigenous Amazonia". And he continues his research on the topic of cruelty and its double.

Notes

1. I am here reminded of the famous quote by the German logician, David Hilbert (1862–1943): "Mathematics knows no races or geographic boundaries; for mathematics, the cultural world is one country."

References

Appadurai, Arjun (ed). 1986. *The Social Life of Things: Commodities in Cultural Perspective*. Cambridge: University of Cambridge Press.

Bester, A. 2015. 'Capacity Development: A Report Prepared for the United Nations Department of Economic and Social Affairs for the 2016 Quadrennial Comprehensive Policy Review'. Geneva: United Nations

Heidegger, Martin. 1971. *Poetry, Language, Thought* (translated by Albert Hofstadter). New York: Harper Collins Publishers.

Hugh-Jones, Stephen. 1992. "Yesterday's Luxuries, Tomorrow's Necessities: Business and Barter in Northwest Amazonia" in *Barter, Exchange and Value: an Anthropological Approach* by Caroline Humphrey and Stephen Hugh-Jones editors. Cambridge: University Press.

Liberato, S. C., J. Brimblecombe, J. Ritchie, M. Ferguson and J. Coveney. 2011.' Measuring Capacity Building in Communities: A Review of the Literature. *BMC Public Health* 11: 850.

Moore, S., R. Severn, R. P. Millar. 2006. 'A Conceptual Model of Community Capacity for Biodiversity Conservation Outcomes', *Geographical Research* 44 (4): 361–371.

Rorty, Richard. 1989. *Contingency, Irony, and Solidarity*. Cambridge: Cambridge University Press.

Strathern, Marilyn. 1992. "Qualified Value: the Perspective of Gift Exchange" in *Barter, Exchange and Value: an Anthropological Approach* by Caroline Humphrey and Stephen Hugh-Jones editors. Cambridge: University Press.

Verran, Helen. 2001. *Science and African Logic*. Chicago: University of Chicago Press.

Verran, Helen. 2010. Number as an inventive frontier and in knowing and working Australia's water resources. *Anthropological Theory* 10 (1-2): 171–178.

Index

absence, xi, 2, 6, 8, 11, 52, 102, 111, 117
accountability, x, 17, 22, 28, 30, 32, 53, 58, 66–68, 74, 102, 105, 115, 141, 148
aggregates, 35–37
aid, x–xii, 3–4, 14–15, 20–25, 27–32, 69–72, 74–75, 82–83, 100, 120, 146–147, 151
    development aid, 14–15, 20–22, 25, 28, 30, 146–147
Amahuaca, 10, 117–122, 124–131
Amazon, 10, 117, 130–132, 148
audit, 2, 6, 11, 15–17, 22, 31–32, 58, 61, 64, 66, 70, 115
Australia, x, xii, 10, 16, 102, 104, 106, 113, 147, 152
Aymara, 70, 75, 80

bank, ix, xii, 21, 30–32, 37, 49, 68, 73–74, 84–85, 100, 110, 140–143
    Asian Development Bank, 141, 143
    World Bank, ix, xii, 21, 30–32, 37, 49, 68, 73–74, 84–85, 100, 140, 142
belief, 5–6, 30, 61, 118, 122, 149
body, 11, 13, 41, 44, 54, 57, 59, 65–66, 76, 80, 106, 117, 120, 123–125, 128–132, 135, 148–149
Bolivia, 2, 69–77, 79–85, 118
Brazil, v, 2, 8, 33, 35–37, 39, 41, 43, 45, 47–49, 84, 100, 114, 118, 132
Bueger, Christian, 2, 5, 7, 14
bureaucracy, 9, 12, 25, 43, 73, 75, 88, 97–98, 100, 141, 143–144
buzzword, xi, 15, 20, 66, 73, 97, 99, 135

Cambodia, 1–2, 136, 139–143, 146–147

capacity, iii, v–vi, ix–xii, 1–25, 27–31, 33–36, 38, 40, 43–47, 51–61, 63–79, 81–103, 105, 107, 109, 111–113, 115–152
    capacitación, v, 69–73, 75–77, 79, 81–83, 85
    capacité, 5
care, v, 8, 10, 21, 23–27, 29, 33–41, 43–47, 49, 55, 62, 89–92, 95, 97, 99, 103–104, 106–107, 127, 137
China, 1, 13, 15, 53, 61, 65, 147
Christianity, 2, 14, 16, 118–119, 122, 126, 132
collaboration, 2, 11, 15, 17, 57, 60, 65–68, 130, 141–147
collective, v, 9–10, 13, 33–37, 39, 41, 43, 45, 47, 49, 56, 71, 79, 109, 117, 120–121, 124, 127
colonialism, 6
commodities, 23, 123, 151–152
community, v–vi, x–xii, 2–3, 5, 8–9, 11, 13–14, 22, 32, 35, 39, 42, 48, 52, 63, 79, 81, 85–100, 103, 114, 116–133, 136, 139, 152
    comunidad, 127, 131
    health officers, 11, 86–87, 89
    Native Community, 118, 120, 124, 126–128
    policing, xi, 15
comparison, iii, v, 1, 10–11, 14–15, 30, 47, 83, 99, 103, 125, 132, 135–137, 142, 147, 151
concepts, 7, 10–13, 15, 35, 54, 71, 88, 97–99, 102, 112
conceptual borrowing, 2
conflict resolution, 69–71, 75, 77–79, 81–83
contestatorios, 11, 72, 82–84
conversation, 1, 3, 11, 15, 27, 30, 39, 47, 61, 77, 79, 84, 106, 138, 144, 146, 148

conversatorio, 9, 11, 69–70, 72–73, 77–83
criminalization, 79

democracy, 9, 31, 43, 49–50, 71–78, 82–85, 149
dependence, 21–24, 26, 43
description, 3, 10–12, 37, 43, 47, 57, 107, 110, 122, 127, 138, 143, 145, 150
development, x, xii, 2–7, 12, 14–18, 20–25, 27–32, 51–52, 54–55, 60–61, 65–68, 72–74, 77, 84, 88, 90–93, 97–100, 107, 116–117, 119–122, 129–133, 135–149, 151–152
discourse, xi–xii, 3, 6, 14–15, 17, 66, 76, 84, 86, 90, 97, 117–118, 122, 125–126, 130, 136, 139, 144–145, 149
documentation, 25, 42–43, 56
documents, x, 8–10, 17, 32, 35, 38–40, 42–44, 52–53, 56, 58, 73, 118
donor, x–xii, 4, 15, 22, 24, 28, 70–75, 77, 82–84, 91, 141, 143–144, 146
    donor agency, x

Eade, Deborah, 3–4, 7, 15–16, 20–21, 30, 55, 60, 66, 73, 84, 92, 97, 99, 117, 131, 141, 147
employee, 9, 27, 63, 94, 102–112, 117, 138
empowerment, v, 20, 32, 85–89, 91–95, 97–99, 122–123
ethics, 9, 11, 13, 15, 17, 22, 32, 48–49, 51–68, 102, 104, 115, 136, 147
Euro-American, 5, 101–102, 104, 112, 117
evaluation, x, 4–5, 16, 31, 43, 56, 66, 73, 75–76, 99, 138, 148–149. *See also* monitoring *and* evaluation.
evidence, x, 9, 12, 22, 32, 42, 48, 56, 64–65, 67–68, 93, 100, 123, 127
expert knowledge, 102
expertise, 15, 55, 85, 97, 107, 110, 119
experts, 12, 37, 101–102, 110–111

failure, 20, 22, 24, 28, 31, 37, 71, 75, 129
family, 10, 23, 26, 31, 88–89, 92, 100, 102–108, 113–114, 118, 121, 126–127, 136–139
Fiji, 1, 67
futures, v, 2, 5–9, 11, 13, 19–21, 25, 27–31, 36–41, 43, 46–48, 58, 66, 115, 131, 136, 138–139, 143–145, 150

Ghana, v, 2, 9, 86–88, 90, 95, 99–100

governance, 5, 13–14, 16–17, 20, 22, 27, 31, 33, 37, 65–66, 70, 72–74, 78, 83–85, 98, 100–101, 115, 136, 147

Haiti, v, 2, 8, 19–21, 23–25, 27–32
health, 4, 9, 11, 14–16, 21, 30, 39, 42, 52–53, 56, 59, 66–68, 86–100, 110, 113, 120–121, 132, 146–147, 149, 152
history, 2, 5–6, 10, 15, 34, 38, 41, 43, 46–47, 62, 68, 72, 79, 117–118, 122, 126–127, 130–132, 147
Hobbes, Thomas, 37, 44–45, 49, 132
home, 8–9, 25, 32, 57, 62, 69, 71, 79, 81, 87, 89–91, 93–96, 102–104, 106–108, 112, 114, 127, 138–139
hope, i, iii, 1–2, 4, 6–8, 10, 12–14, 16–18, 20–22, 24, 26, 28, 30, 32, 34, 36, 38, 40, 42, 44, 46–50, 52, 54, 56, 58, 60, 62, 64, 66–68, 70, 72, 74, 76, 78–80, 82–84, 88, 90, 92, 94, 96, 98–100, 102, 104, 106, 108, 110, 112, 114, 118, 120, 122, 124, 126, 128, 130, 132, 134, 136, 138, 140, 142, 144–146, 150, 152
housing, vi, xii, 10, 24, 101–102, 107–108, 114

incommensurability, 141
Indigeneity, 16
inequality, 70, 97, 100, 140, 147
infrastructure, 1, 5, 8, 15, 33–34, 36–37, 48–50, 57, 136, 146–147
institutions, xi, 4, 6, 9–10, 20, 22, 34, 37–40, 42, 58, 60, 66, 70–76, 78–79, 81, 85, 88, 100, 103, 112, 133, 136, 141
insufficiency, i, iii, xii, 1–2, 4, 6–8, 10–14, 16, 18, 20, 22, 24, 26, 28, 30, 32, 34, 36, 38, 40, 42, 44, 46–48, 50, 52, 54, 56, 58, 60, 62, 64, 66, 68, 70, 72, 74, 76, 78, 80, 82–84, 88, 90, 92, 94, 96, 98–100, 102, 104, 106, 108, 110, 112, 114, 118, 120, 122, 124, 126, 128, 130, 132, 134, 136, 138, 140, 142, 144–146, 149–150, 152
international development, 3, 14, 16, 21, 27, 30, 73–74, 88, 91, 100, 135–136, 140–146
intervention, x, 6–10, 16, 21, 27, 29, 31, 38, 43, 47, 70, 72–74, 78, 88, 90, 97–98, 102–104, 106–108, 146–147

kinship, 6, 31, 101–104, 106–107, 112, 114–115, 126, 131–132

Index

knowledge, ix, xi, 3, 7, 11, 15–17, 22, 34, 38, 48, 57, 62, 67–68, 72, 84, 86, 97, 100, 102, 105, 111–112, 114–115, 119, 122–125, 127, 130, 142–144, 149

labor, 106–107, 114, 146, 150
lack, xi, 6–8, 36, 60, 71, 73, 90–91, 95, 107, 117, 121–122, 124, 130, 142
language, ix, xii, 3, 42–43, 52, 58, 84, 88, 97, 112, 114, 118–119, 121, 128, 130–131, 137–138, 142, 152
lateral, 10–11, 15, 19, 23, 135–137, 147
law, xi, 6, 15–16, 34, 37, 66, 72–74, 79–81, 84–85, 111, 114, 120, 146, 151
Lea, Tess, 12, 16
leadership, 14, 18, 58, 89, 104, 119–122, 129–130, 132
Leviathan, vii, 37, 44–45, 49
logics, 15–16, 44, 49, 70, 83, 94, 98, 123, 147, 149
Lomas, Andy, vii, 37, 44–46

Mali, 87
management, ix, xi, 1, 4, 15–16, 18, 39, 42, 49, 71, 77, 85, 90, 98, 102, 106, 133, 137, 139, 147
market, x–xi, 36, 62, 73, 105, 114, 137, 147, 150–151
McNeish, John-Andrew, 71, 82–83, 85
meetings, 8, 17, 35, 39–42, 44, 61, 89, 141
Mentore, Laura, 12–13, 16
Miyazaki, Hiro, 7, 16, 39, 49, 54, 62, 65, 67
modernity, 31, 84, 128–129, 131–132, 149–151
Morocco, 1
motherhood, 103–104, 106

neoliberalism, xi, 70, 114
network, 13, 15, 17, 22–23, 29, 33, 35–36, 49, 52–54, 57–58, 61, 66, 68, 84–85, 88, 104, 146
NGOs, 4, 13, 16, 20–21, 24, 28, 30, 32–33, 38, 41, 71, 77, 79, 83, 102, 136, 141, 150

obligation, 20–21, 23–27, 33–34, 44, 76, 110, 139
Olson, Dennis, 121–123, 127, 130–132, 148
organization, x, 5, 16, 19–22, 24–30, 32–34, 36, 42, 48, 51–56, 61–62, 65, 69–71, 74, 78, 83–84, 88, 91, 93, 101–106, 109, 111–112, 114, 117–118, 120–122, 127, 129–130, 133, 136, 138–143, 146–147

Papua New Guinea, xi–xii, 13, 18, 50, 132, 147
participation, x, 11, 14, 20, 30, 32, 40, 53, 57, 72, 74, 76–78, 88, 98–99, 144
partnerships, 14–15, 17, 68, 88, 90–91, 142–143, 147
performance, x, 16, 36, 48, 64–65, 72, 82, 106–107, 133, 147
personal relationships, 22–23, 111
personhood, 23, 70–71, 114, 117, 119, 124
Peru, 2, 117–118, 121, 130
Peruvian, vi, 10, 116–120, 123, 126, 129–132, 148
Philippines, 2, 53, 55
policy, ix–x, xii, 4, 7, 9, 11–14, 16, 21, 31–32, 41–43, 49, 56, 66–67, 74, 84–85, 89–90, 95–101, 108, 111, 113, 115, 120, 133, 138, 141, 143, 146–147, 152
    policy documents, x
    policy interventions, 97
    policy language, 42, 97
    policy makers, 12, 97
    policy process, 97
potentiality, 6–7, 17
practices, x, 2, 7, 9, 13, 22, 24, 27, 30, 34, 48, 53–54, 62, 66, 69, 71, 74, 81–82, 101–103, 105–108, 111–112, 135–136, 139, 145
profession, 62, 103, 105
    professionalization, v, 19, 149
progress, ix–x, 5, 12, 20, 28–29, 119, 122, 142
project, x–xii, 2–5, 8–13, 16–17, 20, 22, 24–25, 28–29, 37, 59–60, 64, 70, 72–79, 82–83, 86–90, 93–94, 100, 107, 117–121, 123–124, 126–127, 129–131, 133, 141, 143–144, 149
promises, v, vii, xii, 2, 5–8, 20–21, 27–30, 33, 35–47, 49, 145
property, 45, 84, 103–104, 136, 149

rationality, 123
re-description, 11, 138
reciprocity, 21, 23–27, 31
reporting, x, 4
research, xii, 13, 15–17, 24, 30, 39, 47, 49, 51–68, 83, 85, 87, 89, 99–100, 103, 113, 117, 126, 130–131, 136, 147, 152

rhetoric, x, 4, 18, 48, 147
rights, iv, 33–34, 76, 84–85, 87, 90–91, 97–98, 130, 146
Riles, Annelise, 47, 78, 82, 85
roles, v, 10, 57–58, 86–87, 90, 94, 97–98, 102–103, 105, 107–109, 111
Russia, 2, 10, 102–107, 113

Sariola, Salla, 11, 17, 58, 60, 67–68
scale, 1–2, 5, 34, 37, 39–44, 47, 71, 75, 101, 107, 122–123, 127–129, 148
sector, 2, 5, 30, 34, 37–38, 85, 88, 97, 100
Shore, Cris, 2, 11, 16–17, 70, 85, 97, 100–101, 115
short termism, 55
Simpson, Bob, 2, 11, 13, 17, 60, 65, 67–68
skills, xi, 1, 3, 7, 9, 22, 55, 64, 69, 71–72, 77–79, 82, 89–91, 120, 122, 138, 144–145
social work, 109–110, 113–114
Sri Lanka, 17, 52–53, 58–59, 67–68
standards, 4, 8–9, 51, 55–57, 60, 62–66, 101, 104–105
    international standards, 63, 104–105
standardization, 22, 63
state, x–xii, 2, 4, 12–13, 15–16, 21–22, 26, 29–44, 57, 62, 66–67, 70–78, 84–85, 91, 98, 102–103, 105, 107–108, 112, 114, 118–120, 122–123, 125–126, 129, 132, 151
    Nation-state, 35, 119, 129
strategy, ix–xi, 2–3, 11, 17, 28, 34, 36, 70, 78, 85–88, 94, 97, 103, 105, 108, 123, 129, 138–139, 141, 150
Strathern, Marilyn, 152
Suriname, 1, 15
sustainability, 32, 141
systems, 6, 13, 18, 24, 39, 52, 65, 73, 76, 86, 89–91, 94, 97, 99–100, 112, 129

Taussig, Karen-Sue, 6–7, 17
technocrat, 34, 74, 76, 135
technocratic, 36

technology, 2–3, 13–14, 17, 34, 37, 42, 47, 49, 52, 58, 65, 68, 85, 115, 125, 129, 146–148, 150
    technical cooperation, 16, 140
    technical resources, 34
    technical services, 88, 97
    technical solutions, 6, 97, 135
Thailand, 30, 49, 53–54
training, v, xi–xii, 1–2, 6, 9, 11, 20, 24, 28–29, 42, 52–64, 66–67, 70–79, 86, 88–99, 104–105, 110, 120–122, 130, 133, 136, 146
transformations, xii, 7, 9–10, 15, 17, 22, 29, 117, 125–126, 128, 132, 136
transparency, 22, 48, 74, 78, 141–142, 146

unions, 71, 75–76, 78
United States, 2, 30, 57, 66, 91, 102–103, 107

Venkatesen, Souhmya, 5, 18
Vietnam, 107, 138
vocation, 103, 106

Watanabe, Chika, 5, 7, 18
water, v, 1, 5, 8, 12, 15, 33–49, 58, 70, 143–144, 152
West, Paige, 5–6, 13, 18, 33, 50, 135, 147
work, x–xi, 2–3, 5–13, 15, 17–18, 21–24, 26–29, 34–35, 38, 41, 43–45, 47, 53–65, 72–73, 77–78, 80, 83–84, 87–89, 91, 93–94, 97–99, 102, 105–114, 117–118, 120–121, 124–125, 127–130, 132, 135–136, 138–149, 151
workers, xii, 5, 9–10, 23, 28, 31, 41–42, 86–92, 95–100, 106–107, 109–110, 114, 122–123, 127–128, 138, 145–147
workshop, vii, xi–xii, 1, 12–13, 15–16, 28, 30, 40, 42, 47, 52–55, 57–58, 61, 65, 71, 83, 90, 99, 113, 130, 136, 141, 143–144, 146
Wright, Susan, 2, 11, 13, 16–17, 70, 75, 85, 97, 100–101, 115

Yarrow, Tom, 5, 14, 18

www.ingramcontent.com/pod-product-compliance
Lightning Source LLC
Chambersburg PA
CBHW072158100526
44589CB00015B/2278